D

045666

THE HENLEY COLLEGE LIBRARY

106297

Produced for the Politics Association

*Studio 16, 1-Mex Business Park,
Hamilton Road, Manchester M13 0PD*

Series Editor Duncan Watts

Other titles in this series;

Introducing Comparative Government and Politics
   Alan Davies

Introducing Concepts and Doctrines in British Politics
   Ian Adams and Bill Jones

Introducing International Politics
   Peter Jones

NB   The views expressed by the writers in this series are personal ones.
They do not necessarily represent those of the Politics Association.

Designed and typeset by Design Studio, Learning Centre,
Sheffield Hallam University
Printed By Print Unit, Sheffield Hallam University

Sheffield Hallam University Press
Learning Centre
Howard Street
Sheffield S1 1WB
www.shu.ac.uk/shupress/

© Sheffield Hallam University 1996
ISBN 0 086339 6569

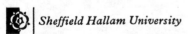 *Sheffield Hallam University*

INTRODUCING THE EUROPEAN UNION

Duncan Watts

About the Author

Duncan Watts is the Editor of the Politics Association Resource Centre. He was an 'A' Level teacher for many years in both a Grammar and a Comprehensive School. He now tutors part-time in Politics and in Modern History, and is also an examiner and writer. He has written widely on issues in modern British and International politics, and among his works is a study of Britain and the EU, Reluctant Europeans.

Foreword to Introducing the European Union

With all the mass of claims and counterclaims which are made about the European Union by friend and foe alike it is extremely important to have fair and thorough account of exactly what the European Union is and what its impact on the citizens of Europe has been in the past and will be in the future. Yet as Chief Examiner for ULEAC Paper Four, Politics of the European Union, I have become increasingly aware of the lack of good text books on this option. Too many texts dealing with Europe are written in a way almost designed to put students off. They are inaccessible and obscure. This is why I felt there was a need for a lively, well written and accessible text which would be 'user friendly' and yet at the same time authoritative. Duncan Watts has supplied exactly such a book. It is written in such a way that the student and teacher are able to use it as a workbook with very helpful sections including examination questions and teach yourself exercises and the text is enlivened by use of cartoons, maps and tables. The language is clear and direct and the analysis is well illustrated with examples. The recommended reading list is sensible and designed to allow students and teachers to follow up points raised in the text.

This book has been designed with the ULEAC syllabus in mind, I am sure that it is not just students doing the ULEAC paper who will find it helpful; it is going to be equally useful for anyone studying the politics of the European Union at advanced or undergraduate level. It is up to date, balanced and stimulating and I am sure a lot of students and their teachers are going to be very grateful for its existence.

Alan Davies

This book has been compiled in close consultation with the Chief Examiner and Subject Officer of the University of London Examinations and Assessment Council.

The Hansard Society welcomes this publication as an extremely valuable contribution to the field of political education.

Contents

NB A Teach Yourself study guide is to be found at the
    end of each of the six chapters.

Introduction

Europe Matters

Since Britain joined the European Community in 1973, many millions of pounds have been channelled into projects in the United Kingdom, some large, some small. Much of this money has come from the Regional and Social Funds operated by what is now called the European Union.

Without realising it you probably use or pass by a number of ventures supported by the EU. They may affect your quality of life. They come about not least because of that EU support. But, you might ask, from where does the Union get its money? Ultimately, from the member states, for countries such as Britain contribute substantially to the budget. Critics would point out that we pay too much, that Britain along with Germany and some other countries effectively subsidise the Union.

But does it give us value? Although some of the money spent by the Union goes on development in Britain (see overleaf) the bulk of it still goes on agriculture, a sector which employs far fewer people in Britain than abroad. Critics might say that the Common Agricultural Policy (CAP) is a fiasco. We end up paying higher prices for our food than we could purchase food for on the world market, all to help 'inefficient French farmers'. These are very political issues involving a choice of priorities. All parties would in varying degrees like to reform the CAP, although opinions vary on how best to do it.

The European Union

The European Centre in Llangollen for encouraging traditional Welsh culture. Grant £143500

The famous three spires of Lichfield Cathedral. Essential restoration work to two spires, the stone work and the vaulting attracted an EU grant of £1045000 - half of the costs.

The City Council established a European Unit in 1984, the year in which Birmingham was granted UK Assisted Area status. It aspires to be a 'great European city' of the 21st century and has made extensive use of EU funding to improve airport facilities and its inner road network. Amongst other developments the canal network has been renovated, the Jewellery Quarter restored and the International Convention Centre and the surrounding complex (pictured above) constructed. In all, the city attracted £256.6m of 'European money' in the first ten years of the development programme.

You may be concerned about the export of live animals to the continent for slaughter, or about the plight of British fishermen who find that their opportunties to fish have been much reduced in recent years and who face increasing rivalry from Spanish trawlermen. What can be done about it? As with agriculture, many of the decisions are taken in Brussels and Britain has one voice out of fifteen when such issues are discussed.

Then have we not surrendered too much control to Brussels if we cannot control our own destiny? Are we committed to ever-increasing Brussels control? Do the bureaucrats of the EU really wish to regulate or interfere with the British diet, as an episode in a once-popular television series suggests?

> *The Europeans have gone too far. They are now threatening the British sausage. They want to standardise it - by which they mean they'll force the British people to eat salami and bratwurst and other garlic-ridden greasy foods that are totally alien to the British way of life. They've turned our pints into litres and our yards into metres, we gave up the tanner and the threepenny bit. But they cannot and will not destroy the British sausage! (Jim Hacker, Yes Prime Minister).*

But isn't regulation a good thing if some of the standards of the European Union are better than our own? Brussels regulates the quality of our drinking water and grades our beaches. Isn't that a case where European standards are higher than ours?

Areas of Debate

Many of these are highly contentious matters. Some impinge on our ideas of national sovereignty. For many people it is a painful process to accept that Britain, victorious in war between 1939-45, should now meekly accept a situation in which representatives of countries which Britain defeated or which were overrun, now have the collective power to make and implement decisions which can change the way of life of British citizens.

For many enthusiasts for British membership, haggling over the the details of agricultural policy or Brussels interference is not what the Union is all about. It was Harold Macmillan, the Prime Minister who tried (unsuccessfully) to take Britain into the Community, who made the point that there was more to the European venture than haggling over the price of butter! We may have lost the right to make many decisions ourselves and the trend of recent years has been towards more power being taken by Brussels. But haven't we also gained in influence? On our own, would the British voice in the world have any significant impact at all?

This is a key point in the political debate. We may have lost nominal power, but perhaps as a member of the Union we have an influence which would otherwise not be there. Does sovereignty really matter in the present day world? Is not the whole trend of the postwar era one in which countries have recognised their increased interdependence, and is not membership of the Union a recognition of the fact that Britain no longer has the resources to 'go it alone'?

Those who support the European cause and British participation in the evolution of the European Union often point to the success of the member countries in achieving what was their real aim, ending war on the continent between two old historic rivals, France and Germany, and bringing about closer political cooperation between them. Those two countries had been at war three times in the years between 1870 and 1945, and that they have now succeeded in working together in peaceful friendship for fifty years is surely a success for those who dreamed of a new Europe in which past enmities should be cast aside?

The idea of a united Europe has a long history. Attempts have been made to unite the continent by force, first under Napoleon and then under Hitler. But they were unsuccessful. The failure of the Fuehrer's bid was to prove the inspiration for a different type of initiative. That process of uniting the continent by peaceful means and bringing about a degree of political and economic cooperation has not been achieved without setbacks and crises, for each member state is inevitably watchful of it own interests and anxious to preserve its own traditions. Each step forward has had to be painstakingly and sometimes painfully negotiated. Yet however slow the progress has been at times, the direction in which The Six (and now The Fifteen) are moving, has never been in doubt.

4

A People's Europe? What does it mean to be European?

Some of the issues we have raised so far are economic, some social and some political. They are all matters which affect people British citizens. But the very term 'British citizens' gives insufficient weight to another label which we possess in common with more than 310m people living in fourteen other countries. Since the signing and ratification of the Maastricht Treaty in 1993 the peoples of the UK, along with those of all member states of what is now the European Union, have become 'European citizens'. Even the Queen shares this status with you and me.

The Union has tried to promote a common European identity and awareness, hence the European flag and the European anthem (Beethoven's 'Ode to Joy'). Other innovations such as the European passport and driving licence are both of practical value to travellers and reminders of a common citizenship. Yet as an island race, many British people do not feel European.

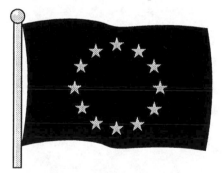

They have reservations about our European commitment, and many surveys indicate that a large % still think of Europeans as being those who live across the Channel. Perhaps not surprisingly, the younger generation tends to view our continental partners more sympathetically.

The EU does not aim to stifle national awareness. The French are very conscious of their traditions and independence, and are no less French for also being European. There is much diversity in the Union, and national

5

and regional cultures persist and flourish; there are eleven official languages in use within the organisation.

Yet many people in Britain, Denmark and elsewhere, feel a lack of identity with the Union, and its institutions are often seen as remote and irrelevant. Because of this, many EU spokesmen are increasingly talking about a Citizen's Europe. They speak of making it less of an organisation for governments and bureaucrats. Instead, they want to create a Union for the future which is based more on people, their rights, duties and aspirations.

Britain and Europe

The EU is a distinctive creation. There have been several examples of countries which have joined up with one another in ventures of mutual benefit, but in aim, method and achievement this one has gone much further than the others. The Union has always been more than just a customs union. From the beginning, it aimed for an ever-closer-union of its peoples. It developed supranational institutions with powers binding upon its members. It has been more successful than its rivals. The steady enlargement of the Community into the Union, with several other nations queueing up to join, points to its health and vitality.

Since 1973, Britain has been part of that Union, but the relationship has been an uneasy one. For many years before we joined, we stood by and watched from the outside. Our attitude was expressed by Winston Churchill whose often pro-European rhetoric has been an inspiration to many Europhiles today; 'We are linked, but not comprised...we are with Europe, but not of it'.

Now we are part of it, but journalists, politicians and others still agonise over our precise commitment. Attitudes in Britain range from the fervently pro-European (Eurofanatics) who believe that Britain must become more European in outlook and work enthusiastically to make a success of British involvement, to the outright hostile. Opponents of closer ties either feel that Britain should never have joined, or that we gone as far as we need to, for 'enough is enough'. These Europhobes or Eurosceptics stress Britain's need to cling to its sovereign power. In between are many who accept Britain's membership, who feel that it may on balance benefit us and who

6

believe that Britain would be isolated and exposed outside the Union, but who nonetheless have doubts about surrendering further powers to Brussels (Euroagnostics).

Coming to terms with a reduced status in the world has not been easy for Britain, and discussion of Britain's position has aroused passionate dispute at Westminster and been the cause of sharp division within both main political parties. Pro-Europeans have been encouraged by many of the steps which The Fifteen have taken recently, whereas others see these moves as a serious erosion of national sovereignty.

In Britain, there is much discussion of independence and sovereignty, although in the last fifty years much of this has been whittled away. There is still some reluctance to accept that when we embarked upon closer involvement with Europe in 1972 by signing the Treaty of Accession we took a far-reaching constitutional step whose implications were not fully explained at the time. The Union does not just offer advice, it can and does produce and enforce obligations upon its member countries. The only ultimate expression of Parliamentary Sovereignty left untouched is the right that Britain has to withdraw from the Union.

The implications of membership are now becoming ever more apparent. It has an effect not just upon our constitutional arrangements but upon the attitudes of political parties and the fortunes of politicians, and on the activities of pressure groups who have seen the need to gear their lobbying to Brussels where so many decisions are now taken. As we have seen, life in the Union affects our daily lives. Britain has a voice, one of fifteen, in drawing up Union proposals, but as their impact is felt at home, many people have been confirmed in their doubts.

Other countries are often impatient with what they see as the essential negativism of British attitudes, and see Britain as the country which always says 'No, No, No'. At home, there is a lack of enthusiasm and commitment to the European cause. But Europe will not go away. Whether you are a convert to the European enterprise or a doubter who believes that Britain can still enjoy a 'splendid isolation', the issues involved in British membership are important ones which are likely to shape our lives for the foreseeable future.

The Need for Knowledge

Surveys by Eurobarometer usually show that around four out of ten citizens claim to be 'highly' or 'to some extent' interested in matters relating to the European Union. The Danes are revealed to be the most interested peoples, the Portuguese the least concerned. Even many of those who express little interest feel that they should 'know more' and 75% of the British interviewed in December 1994 wanted more information. 85% were 'not well informed', and only 15% 'well informed'.

Interest in politics in general and in Europe in particular is not very extensive other than when an election looms. The level of information available on the European Union often

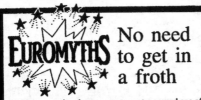

No need to get in a froth

THE best stories always seem to centre around one of Britain's favourite pastimes — enjoying a drink at the local. Last month, the EC inspectors were rumoured to be making a beeline to evict man's best friend, this month nothing less than the sacred brew itself is reported to be the target.

An authoritative source reckons that 36,000 beer drinkers from CAMRA are worried that an EC directive on hygiene for the food and drinks industry would lay down such strict standards on washing and cleaning that the use of wooden barrels for the fermentation of beer would, in effect, be ruled out.

This, the story continues, would mean the end of some very fine speciality beers, such as Theakston's Old Peculiar and Marstons Pedigree, and what is more Belgian brews such as the renowned Belle Vue Lambic.

Needless to say, we are happy to assure our real ale drinkers that once again this is nothing more than a figment of the imagination — perhaps reached after several pints.

The directive in question is concerned with establishing good hygiene practice and allows the member states to impose national standards. Now if national civil servants want to use it to try and set tougher regulations that would affect the beer trade, well that is another matter!

EP News, 14-18 December, 1992

Euro-baffled!

THE British people were confused about Europe rather than sceptical, said European Movement chairman, Giles Radice, after sifting through the results of an opinion poll for the organisation carried out by Gallup.

After questioning 805 people in December, the poll found that 56% described their knowledge of Europe as poor or very poor as against just 8% who consider their knowledge as good.

The survey also revealed marked divisions over whether or not Britain should join a single currency. Some 24% were in favour of rejecting the single currency now, while 13% supported the UK participating from the start. A much larger 48% was in favour of keeping the options of joining open until a later date.

EP News, 15-19 January, 1996

does little to promote worthwhile national debate. The tabloid press and some members of national parliaments, especially in Britain, are apt to peddle stories about foolish EU intervention. Similarly, some government spokesmen, having difficulty in selling policies to their voters, are apt to blame 'Brussels bureaucrats' for things likely to be unpopular.

All sorts of Euro-myths, Euro-scares and Euro-lunacies have been put forward. The EU is not banning round cheeses, forcing fishermen to wear hairnets nor insisting that York ham can only be produced in York. 'Carrots are fruit sprouts Brussels', 'Sauce; EC set to ban naughty seaside postcards', 'Eurocoffin rises from the dead' are just some of the headlines of recent years. Almost every piece of bureaucratic stupidity is attributed to Brussels which never did launch an initiative to outlaw bent cucumbers or do many of the other things suggested by imaginative journalists. Enough confusion exists already without such distortions, and many stories written are downright misleading.

It is time to generate light out of darkness. As a writer on pressure groups once pleaded, 'Light, more light'.

A Note on Terminology

This book is about the **European Union**, although for much of its history the organisation has been known by other names. In the early days, it was usual to speak of the Common Market to cover the area of the six nations which made up the European Coal and Steel Community, the European Economic Community and Euratom. When the three communities were merged, the term European Community (EC) was more often used. The EC officially became the European Union when the Maastricht Treaty was ratified in November 1993.

When writing of early events, the title appropriate for the time has been adopted. In any references to more recent events and future prospects, the European Union is the term employed.

The book is primarily concerned with the EU as an entity, rather than the relationship of Britain and Europe. Examples are drawn from several member states, but in some cases the discussion stresses the impact of institutions and policies on the United Kingdom. Such references help to make the material more intelligible and relevant. They also cater for the requirements of ULEAC and other examination Boards.

A Profile of the Union
Key Dates

1950 Schuman Declaration
1951 Treaty of Paris, setting up ECSC
1952 ECSC in operation
1955 Messina talks on further economic integration
1957 Treaties of Rome, setting up EEC and Euratom
1958 EEC and Euratom in operation
1962 Common Agricultural Policy agreed and in operation
1967 Merger Treaty; ECSC, EEC and Euratom combine to from EC
1973 Accession of Denmark, Ireland and United Kingdom
1975 Lome Convention agreed and in operation
1979 EMS in operation
Direct elections to European Parliament
1981 Accession of Greece
1985 Withdrawal of Greenland
1986 Accession of Portugal and Spain
1990 Accession of East Germany
1991 Maastricht Treaty (TEU)
1993 Ratification of Maastricht, establishing European Union
1995 Accession of Austria, Finland and Sweden
1996 Intergovernmental Conference

The Member States

Country	Accession Date	Population	GDP per head*
Austria	1995	8.0m	112
Belgium	1958	10.1	112
Denmark	1973	5.2	114
Finland	1995	5.0	92
France	1958	58.0	110
Germany	1958**	81.5	108
Greece	1981	10.4	62
Ireland	1973	3.5	83

Italy	1958	57.2	102
Luxembourg	1958	0.4	158
Netherlands	1958	15.4	102
Portugal	1986	9.9	68
Spain	1986	39.1	77
Sweden	1995	8.8	98
United Kingdom	1973	58.2	101

Total Population =   370.7m (October 1995)

NB   *   *Expressed as purchasing power parities; EU average = 100*

   **   *German unification occurred on October 3, 1990; before that references to Germany allude to West Germany*

Glossary of Key Initials and Terms
Initials

APC	African, Pacific and Caribbean countries
CAP	Common Agricultural Policy
CFSP	Common Foreign amd Security Policy (formerly known as European Political Cooperation)
COR	Committee of the Regions
COREPER	Committee of Permanent Representatives
CSCE	Conference on Security and Cooperation in Europe
EAGGF	European Agricultural Guarantee and Guidance Fund
EC	European Community
ECSC	European Coal and Steel Community
ECU	European Currency Unit
EDC	European Defence Community
EEA	European Economic Area (19 nations, EU + remaining EFTA) countries
EEC	European Economic Community

EFTA	European Free Trade Area
EIB	European Investment Bank
EMS	European Monetary System
EMU	European Monetary Union
EP	European Parliament
EPC	European Political Community ; same initials later used for European Political Cooperation
ERDF	European Regional Development Fund
ERM	Exchange Rate Mechanism
ESC	Economic and Social Committee
ESF	European Social Fund
EURATOM	European Atomic Energy Community
EU	European Union
GATT	General Agreement on Tariffs and Trade (now known as WTO)
G7	Seven advanced industrial countries
IGC	Intergovernmental Conference
NATO	North Atlantic Treaty Organisation, sometimes known as the Atlantic Alliance
OECC	Organisation for European Economic Cooperation
OECD	Organisation for Economic Cooperation and Development
QMV	Qualified Majority Voting
SEA	Single European Act
TEU	Treaty on European Union
WEU	Western European Union
WTO	World Trade Organisation

Terms

Additionality
The principle that EU aid should be additional to spending by national governments, and not a substitute for it

Benelux
Belgium, Holland and Luxembourg

Bilateral aid
Direct aid to other countries, eg, from Britain to Bangladesh

Cohesion
Action to reduce regional differences within the EC, brought about by structural funds to boost living conditions

Common Market
Original name for tariff-free area of The Six

Communautaire
Sympathetic to the EU

Convergence
The idea that the economic performance of EC nations must be brought more closely into line before full economic and monetary union can be achieved

Democratic Deficit
The lack of democracy and accountability in the decision-making processes of the EU

Euro
The new name for the proposed single currency

Eurocorps
A mainly Franco-German brigade (plus Benelux and Spain) established in 1993 as a fighting force; operational from 1995

Federal
Strictly speaking, a division of responsibility in which power is divided between one central authority which tackles major issues such as foreign policy and defence, and several states or provinces which deal with other matters. It is often used as a description for policies

leading in the direction of closer European integration

Intergovernmental Conference A conference summoned by member states with the intention of amending EU treaties

Multilateral aid Aid given to other countries indirectly, eg, channelled through special agencies such as the UN

Schengen Accords Agreements to abolish frontier controls between several EU countries

Subsidiarity Refers to the limits of Community action; the idea that functions should be carried out at the lowest appropriate level

Supranationalism This implies the transfer of some national sovereignty to a multi-national organisation which acts on behalf of all the countries involved - eg, from Britain to the EU

Third World The poorer countries of the world, sometimes known as the developing countries. The capitalist countries are the First World, the communist ones (not many now) are the Second. Third World is a misleading term, for it groups together once-backward countries which are now thriving, developing and undeveloped ones

Transparency EU jargon for opening-up the institutions of the EU to the public gaze; more openness in decision-making

Treaty of Rome In March, 1957, six nations signed this Treaty establishing the European Economic Community

14

The European Union Today

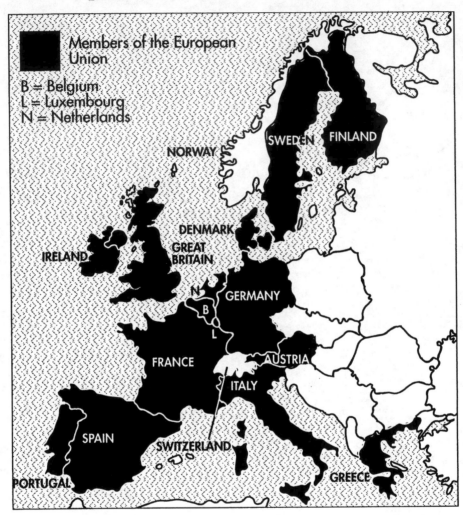

Members of the European Union

B = Belgium
L = Luxembourg
N = Netherlands

NORWAY

SWEDEN   FINLAND

DENMARK

GREAT BRITAIN

IRELAND

N

B

L

GERMANY

FRANCE

AUSTRIA

ITALY

SPAIN

SWITZERLAND

PORTUGAL

GREECE

HISTORY

Europe in 1945;
The Drive for Unity

> *[A] major transformation...has occurred in the political consciousness of Europeans, something which is completely new in their history. For centuries, neighbouring countries were seen as potential enemies against whom it was necessary to be on one's guard and ready to fight. Now, after the end of the most terrible of wars in Europe, these neighbours are perceived as friendly nations sharing a common destiny.*
> *Altiero Spinelli, a long-time Italian federalist, 1985.*

Over many centuries, the nations of Europe have warred continuously, but the present one has witnessed death and destruction on a scale unknown ever before. Two major civil wars within the continent have pointed to the danger of unrestrained nationalism. In 1914, Europe was the centre of world affairs. Thirty years later, it was in ruins, and world leadership was passing into the hands of two Superpowers, the Soviet Union and the United States of America.

World War Two had resulted in millions of deaths and physical and economic destruction across the continent. It was the culmination of a long and bitter enmity between France and Germany. In that struggle, Hitler had almost succeeded in uniting Europe by conquest, and the common experience of defeat and occupation was one that no-one wished to repeat. What then emerged from the war was a series of sovereign states, many of whom were disillusioned with the nationalism which had so tarnished the century. It was time to forge a new unity, designed to preserve an era of peace.

The nations of Europe were virtually bankrupt, and faced the prospect of a long struggle to regain the position they had attained before hostilities. Britain, which had been the world's greatest trading nation in 1914, was now a debtor, and had little chance of returning to its former glory without assistance. To get back to earlier levels of production and standards of living would need outside help from the United States which alone had the money and resources which Europe lacked. It would also depend upon the willingness and ability of the European nations to put their own house in order, and work together in a new spirit of cooperation.

Why Was Unity Desirable After 1945?

In the postwar era, there has been economic, political and military cooperation between the countries of Western Europe as never before in peacetime. It has been encouraged by the United States and stimulated by fear of the Soviet Union, for soon after World War Two it became apparent that the main threat to Western Europe came from the USSR, rather than from Germany. At first not everyone recognised the danger posed by the Soviet Union which over the next few years was to split the continent in half and dominate the Eastern sector via its puppet governments. However, as the Cold War developed, so too did the feeling that unity might give more security.

Beyond this tactical consideration, however, there were other factors. Above all, there was a desire to bring about a lasting peace in Europe. At the time, there was a feeling that fighting could break out all over again, and the Frenchman, Jean Monnet (one of the inspirational figures in those early postwar days), later described the atmosphere as one in which there was an acceptance 'of a war that is thought to be inevitable'. **Martin Holland** makes the point very clearly;

> *Hindsight should not make us undervalue this preoccupation; East-West*
> *relations were confrontational; the status of Berlin remained precarious,*
> *Germany was formally divided; French economic recovery was*
> *stagnating; and the proliferation of atomic weapons had begun.*

After many wars, there tends to be a mood of idealism, a feeling that the horrors of war must never be allowed to haunt the world again. This happened after World War Two, and especially it was felt that there was a need to bind France and Germany in an alliance of friendship, support and mutual interest. For Monnet, such an axis was the key to stability in Europe.

To him and others, the developments we are about to survey were not just a series of useful steps along the road towards recovery. To them, Europe was more than an economic or a political concept. It was, in Monnet's words, 'a moral idea'. It was all about a new venture in international relations whose main objective would be peace and reconciliation. This would end the anxiety in France which continued even when the war was over. For Frenchmen, the question on many lips was 'What's to be done about Germany?'. Monnet's instinct was to end national rivalries in Western Europe once and for all. In so doing, he believed that Western nations would be taking a step towards securing a larger peace which would prevent the continent from experiencing the century's third civil war.

A 'European Idea' developed, the idea of a strong, independent, prosperous and above-all peaceful Europe. There was certainly a need for cooperation to bring about renewed economic strength, for following the appalling destruction the continent was devastated, France, Germany and Italy reduced to chaos, their peoples often out of work, sometimes starving or homeless, always poor. Common action, it was believed, might help industry and agriculture to recover.

There were, then, good reasons for Europe to come together. Many countries were based in a relatively small continent. They had a great deal in common, for they all faced the same task of rebuilding. Yet as they approached the task, there was still a legacy of distrust between France and Germany. It was a brave vision of Monnet and Schuman to seek to bring Germany back into the community of nations, and in so doing to cast aside the dark days of recent years.

Along with other statesmen such as Adenauer in West Germany and De Gasperi in Italy, they recognised that economic reconstruction was an immediate and necessary practical goal, but it had to be underpinned by political reconciliation. Without this, economic recovery would merely serve to fuel the engines of future war, and so the 'founding fathers' of Europe wanted to make war not only morally and practically inconceivable, but materially impossible.

Robert Schuman (F), De Gasperi (I), Stikker (H), van Zeeland (B), Adenauer (G) and Bech (L)

The Position of Britain

These and other European statesmen looked to Britain for a lead, for its commitment to the cause of freedom and parliamentary government was implicit in the way it had fought against the German dictatorship in World War Two. During the hostilities, exiled leaders from several nations had based their operations in London. They noted the pronouncements of the

Prime Minister, Winston Churchill. Just before the fall of France in 1940, at Monnet's instigation, he had proposed a union of Britain and France into a single state.

Churchill's interest in the future of Europe had already been made clear to his Foreign Secretary in 1942, when he wrote a minute containing the following words;

> *My thoughts rest primarily in Europe - the revival of the glory of Europe, the parent continent of the modern nations and of civilisation. It would be a measureless disaster if Russian barbarianism overlaid the culture and independence of the ancient States of Europe. Hard as it s to say now, I trust that the European family may act unitedly as one under a Council of Europe. I look forward to a United States of Europe in which the barriers between the nations will be greatly miminised and unrestricted travel will be possible...Of course we shall have to work with the Americans in many ways and in the greatest ways, but Europe is our prime care...*

His vision survived the war, and by then out of office he outlined his thoughts in a major speech in Zurich, in 1946;

> *If Europe is to be saved from infinite misery, and indeed from final doom, there must be an act of faith in the European family...What is the sovereign remedy? It is to recreate the European family, or as much of it as we can, and provide it with a structure under which it can dwell in peace, safety and freedom. We must build a kind of United States of Europe.*

At the Hague in 1948, when addressing an unofficial gathering of enthusiastic Europeans ('the Congress of Europe'), he sounded similarly enthusiastic. There he pressed for the establishment of a European Parliamentary Assembly at Strasbourg, and answered fears about any loss of independence. Accepting that there might be 'some sacrifice or merger of national sovereignty', he preferred to think in terms of

> *a gradual assumption by all the nations concerned of that larger sovereignty which can also protect their diverse and distinctive customs and characteristics and their national traditions.*

Such speeches made a great impact upon those who listened to them, and they aroused the hopes of enthusiastic Europeans, encouraging them to believe that Britain - or at least its most well-known and eminent spokesman - was in sympathy with their ideals. But in this they were wrong, for Churchill's remarks, lofty in aspiration but vague on detail, did not mean that he felt committed to many of the federalist notions which mattered most to them.

Given the freedom of opposition, his reflections were full of what **Peter Hennessy** calls 'glittering images of a future Europe', but he refused 'to lay down anything amounting to foundations for the new European home'. His grandiose ideas suggested a more constructive attitude than he actually possessed.

Britain's Attitude; 'We are with Europe, but not part of it'

Many British politicians in either party would have echoed Churchill's definition of Britain's relationship with the continent, as outlined in the title quotation above. He was not suggesting that Britain wanted to become a founder member of any new grouping, but rather that we were keen to see the continental countries working together in a new spirit of friendship. We could support their endeavours, and as was appropriate cooperate with them in any new ventures. But we also had other interests.

In the Fulton speech, he had referred to the special relationship of Britain and the United States, and even looked forward to the possibility of there being common citizenship between the two countries. That relationship was more important than the one with Europe, for there were traditional ties of race, language and a broadly similar culture which meant that Americans and Britons had a number of shared attitudes in world affairs. These ties had been cemented by the close cooperation of the wartime years. At this time Britain also had a large overseas empire and a growing Commonwealth, and the imperial tradition was one which Britain was reluctant to let go.

These connections made up the 'three circles' of British foreign policy in which Churchill believed. They meant that we still had a world role, and to

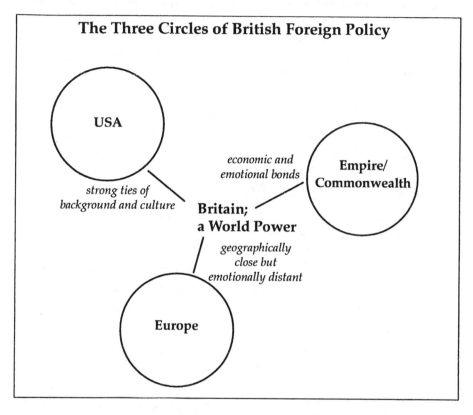

The Three Circles of British Foreign Policy

USA

strong ties of background and culture

economic and emotional bonds

Empire/ Commonwealth

Britain; a World Power

geographically close but emotionally distant

Europe

align ourselves too closely with Europe would intolerably restrict us as we fulfilled our global responsibilities.

The continent was one landmass, but Britain was an offshore island, and therefore attitudes were very different. As Churchill told de Gaulle,'France is the tip of a continent, Britain an island, America another world'. Europe was the other side of the Channel, separated by geography but also distinctive in language, culture and outlook. A headline in *The Times* expressed a common view of the way the continent was regarded; 'FOG IN CHANNEL: EUROPE CUT OFF FROM BRITAIN'.

Moreover, the nations of Europe had been a prey to internal upheaval in times past, and more recently had been defeated or occupied. By contrast, Britain had emerged battered and weakened, but nonetheless victorious. With help from the Empire and backing from the United States, she had thwarted Hitler's ambitions and proved invincible. It was easy for the British to believe that whilst other less successful nations needed to change, we were all right as we were.

Such notions of superiority were perhaps not too surprising in the circumstances of the time. Britain was proud of its history and traditions. It had not been successfully invaded for nearly nine hundred years, and had evolved by evolution rather than revolution. European nations had a good reason to unite, but for Britain there was no similar sense of urgency. It was easy to be complacent.

The attitudes of the British to peoples overseas were varied and complex. There has long been an element which has regarded all foreigners as in some ways suspect, believing that civilisation ends at the British coast. According to this attitude, foreigners are equally suspicious, be they from Paris, Berlin or Peking. It is best that we should remain apart from them, in splendid isolation. We were certainly very conscious of the 'foreignness' of those who lived on the Continent.

Many influential people in public life and from either party would have shared Churchill's attitude, and been reluctant to commit ourselves too fully in one direction. In the early years of closer European cooperation, they were happy for Britain to cheer from the sidelines, whilst remaining aloof and detached. We wanted to see a European recovery, and could see the case for greater European unity. But we were not prepared to go as far as the other European nations, or travel at the same speed.

Early Postwar Attitudes in Europe to Integration; Federalism v Functionalism

There were differing theories about the way in which European unity might progress. Essentially the conflict was between the **federalists** and the **functionalists**. At different times in the postwar era, proponents of either approach have had the upper hand. Between them, however, they provided the impetus for integration.

Federalists believed in a swift movement to unification, and were inspired by the phraseology of Churchill in his Zurich speech. They wanted more than a series of functional economic agencies. They argued that all layers of government, local, regional, national and European should cooperate with and complement each other.

Functionalists believed that greater unity in Europe would develop through a more piecemeal and gradual approach of which moves towards economic union would be the first stage. The organisations which were to be formed were not seen as an end goal in themselves, but rather steps on the way towards building a new Europe. Such an approach would involve a more gradual transfer of national sovereignty to a European level.

There were also **intergovernmentalists**, representatives of those states which wished to retain as much national sovereignty as they could cling on to (France in the days of de Gaulle, Britain since its membership and Denmark more recently have adopted this attitude to European organisations).

In the early days after 1945, there was much idealism in Europe, and statesmen sought to create new structures which would enable cooperation and union to flourish. In those days it was the rhetoric of the federalists which carried the day, and from 1948-54 their ideas inspired the bold moves that were initiated, from the Council of Europe (1949) through to the proposed creation of the European Defence Community and of the European Political Community (both 1954) which between them would look after political and military union.

But already by the early fifties, concrete steps were being taken which were more in the functionalist mould. They were more cautious in their immediate goals, but more practical and achievable. The plan to pool French and German coal and steel supplies was the first of these, and this functionalist phase was to be culminate in the signing of the Treaty of Rome (1957).

The Outlook and Approach of Jean Monnet

> *Europe will not be built all at once, or as a single whole; it will be built by concentrated achievements which first create de facto solidarity*
> *Jean Monnet, 1950*

Jean Monnet was noted for his belief in carefully coordinated planning in France. Unhampered by any concern for the faded glories of the past, he was intent on the modernisation of his country, to be achieved by coordinating the plans for individual industries and launching new ones. He placed France's needs for reconstruction in a European context. As he wrote in his **Memoirs** (1978); 'The countries of Europe must turn their national efforts into a truly European effort. This will be possible only through a 'federation of the West'.

Jean Monnet

He was clear about the end target which he wished to achieve in his European project, but recognised that there was scope for disagreement on the means by which the goal might be reached. In a broad sense, he is usually described as a federalist, and his writings are littered with references to the term, although he rarely spelt out what this might mean in practice. The ambiguity and vagueness were deliberate, because his preferred approach was to take concrete steps towards ultimate unity. He later acknowledged that;

> *The Community we have created is not an end in itself. It is a process of change. I have never doubted that one day his process will lead us to the United States of Europe; but I see no point in trying to imagine today what political form it will take.*

But when that union eventually came, he wanted a situation in which 'no state can secede by its own unilateral decision'. Nations would commit themselves to it 'with no limit in time and no looking back'.

To arrive at the ultimate goal, he was concerned with what was politically possible at the time. If appropriate, it might sometimes be wise to adopt an intergovernmental approach, for progress had to reflect what was possible 'at that time and that stage in men's thinking'. Generally, he was out of sympathy with mere cooperation between governments for this was an 'intrinsically weak' form of partnership.

He favoured a pooling of sovereignty in a particular area, for this would sublimate national rivalries and tensions. The hope was that eventually via such closer economic integration, there might develop closer political union if the results seemed good. As he put it;

> *Little by little, the work of the Community will be felt...Then the everyday realities themselves will make it possible to form the political union which is the goal of our Community and to establish the United States of Europe...Political Europe will be created by human effort when the time comes on the basis of reality.*

He did not believe in rushing his fences, and was unenthusiastic about moves which had not been well-planned and for which there was no strong backing - hence, his early doubts about the desirability of establishing a European Defence Community. Because of this commitment to a step-by-step method of building European union and his willingness to accept a variety of approaches en route for the federal goal, some commentators find it difficult to locate him firmly in the federalist camp.

Jean Monnet (1888-1977); Career Details

1888 Born at Cognac into a family trading in brandy

1919 Became Deputy Secretary-General of the League of Nations; travelled widely in public role and for family and banking interests Noted for his grasp of international finance; much involved in developing investment opportunities in China

1940 Initiator of plans proposed by Churchill to French Prime Minister Reynaud for fusion and joint citizenship of Britain and France

1939-45 Involved in liberation struggle and organisation of supplies from America to Britain and Free France

Postwar Committed to reconstruction and modernisation of France. As head of French Planning Commission, charged with task of reequipping country, and in 1947 inspired and coordinated an extensive programme of capital investment, working through commissions dealing with every sector of French economy
Convinced of need for European integration. Inspired Schuman Plan which led to formation of ECSC. Became the first President of the High Authority which ran the ECSC, 1952-56, but was reluctant to be a candidate for newly-established Commission in 1957
Instead, keen to influence development from sidelines, acting as, in **Holland's** phrase, an 'independent counsellor and source of ideas'. His thinking was reflected in the Messina Conference and in the Treaty of Rome

1955 Formed Action Committee for the United States of Europe and served as President until 1975, 25th anniversary of Schuman Declaration
A thorough-going internationalist, and one of the world's foremost supranational technocrats.

Burgess is critical of Monnet's contribution, noting its 'contradictory and diverse principles' which were sufficiently elastic that they could embrace 'incrementalism and intergovernmentalism'. He quotes with approval the verdict of Altiero Spinelli, an anti-fascist Italian who had a consistent record in support of federalism; 'Monnet has the great merit of having built Europe and the great responsibility to have built it badly'.

Burgess argues that despite the language the Frenchman sometimes employed, it is unrealistic to see him as a 'champion of the federalist cause in Europe', even if some form of federation was his ultimate object. He describes him as an 'economic functionary first and only secondly as an incremental federalist', by which he means one who advances towards his goal on a step-by-step basis. 'Incremental federalist' is a realistic description. He was certainly not a mere economic functionalist, for there was always a political objective to which he aspired, even if it was not one which was clearly formulated and elaborated.

In an interesting essay on the contribution of Monnet to the creation of modern Europe, **Duroselle** detects four themes in his approach;

- He was not a nationalist, and wanted to see the force of nationalism in Europe set aside
- He believed in a Europe of concrete institutions
- He wanted an 'open Europe', in which Britain would play a leading part
- In particular, he wanted a Europe linked with the USA - he felt the transatlantic partnership was vital, and noted that American governments were keen to see the European continent get its act together

Monnet's approach was not one which allowed much room for the expression of popular feeling. He worked with and through a small elite, and took the view that when the beneficial results of new initiatives became apparent then the public would willingly offer their support for any venture which the elite conceived. The paramount concern was to achieve a common approach between the leaders of opinion in the various countries concerned.

Essentially, he was a visionary, albeit a very practical one. Without being obsessed with too many details, he had a sense of mission and of history. He knew the direction in which he wanted Europe to travel. Peace in Europe was always fundamental in his priorities, the ultimate prize within the grasp of European statesmen. For him, a 'federation of the West' was the means by which past rivalries could be set aside.

?

What were the immediate and long term aims of the founders of postwar Europe?

What was Monnet's vision of the future of Europe?

Early Steps in European Unity, to 1950

The roots of today's European Union date back to the resolution of postwar statesmen to create a new structure in Europe based on peace between nations, political cooperation, economic recovery and a growth in international trade. In making this fresh start, it was hoped that progress might follow in three broad areas, military, political and economic union.

Early Military Cooperation After 1945

Soon after the war ended, the Western Powers saw more danger from the USSR than from a resurgent Germany, and many statesmen saw the need to create a military framework to complement other arrangements for the rebuilding of Europe. The Soviet Union had armed forces estimated at $4^1/_2$ million and she was credited with possessing 6000 planes. This represented a massive superiority over the military resources of the West. The surly attitude of the Russian leaders under Stalin, the Berlin Blockade and the seizure of Czechoslovakia served to confirm fears in England and

France that there was a 'red menace' in the East of the continent, and made it seem important to preserve Western Europe from the danger of attack.

In March 1947, France and Britain signed the **Treaty of Dunkirk,** and entered into a 50 year alliance, each promising assistance if either was attacked by Germany. This was expanded the following year with the accession of the Benelux countries, into the **Western Union,** and this time there was provision of aid against any armed attack. This was aimed against the Soviet Union, with whom France and Britain still had a legally valid military alliance.

In 1948, Britain, France and the Benelux countries (see p37-38) signed the **Pact of Brussels,** a vague commitment to set up a joint defensive system. No surrender of independence or sovereignty was involved, and this was essentially an intergovernmental step, albeit one in which the Pact did speak of the purpose of encouraging 'the progressive integration of Europe'.

Without assistance, the Western Union could not hope to resist a determined Communist attack. Hence the importance of the speech made by President Truman which laid down the basis of postwar American policy. He spoke of the need for 'containment' of Communist aggression, and promised American help for 'free peoples who are resisting attempted subjugation by armed minorities or by outside pressure'. General Marshall thought that the Soviet Union was uninterested in helping Western Europe, and more interested in expanding its influence there.

This was the era of the Cold War, a hostile relationship between countries or power blocks, but one short of outright war.

The Formation of NATO

The military significance of the Pact of Brussels was soon overshadowed by the establishment of the **North Atlantic Treaty Organisation (NATO),** in 1949. The governments of the USA, Canada and ten West European nations (Benelux, Denmark, France, Iceland, Italy, Norway, Portugal and the United Kingdom) agreed 'an armed attack against one or more of them in Europe or North America (should) be considered an attack against them all', and consequently that they would take such action as was necessary 'including the use of armed force' to cope with any such act of aggression. It was a mutual defence alliance, though each nation was free to decide the form of that assistance in the event of an attack.

The North Atlantic Treaty, April 4 1949

The Parties of this Treaty reaffirm their faith in the purposes...of the United Nations and their desire to live in peace with all peoples and all governments....the Parties separately and jointly, by means of continuous and effective self-help and mutual aid, will maintain and develop their individual and collective capacity to resist armed attack...The Parties agree that an armed attack against one or more of them in Europe or North America shall be considered an attack against them all.. signatories (include) Belgium, Canada, France, Luxembourg, the Netherlands, the United Kingdom and the United States.

Their action was prompted by the urgent need to combine against the powerful Russian army which was then seeking to drive the western allies from West Berlin. America had the vast industrial resources and a monopoly of atomic weapons which could counter-balance the military power of the Soviet Union and its satellites.

The Soviet Union interpreted the treaty differently, as the cartoon illustrates. In their view, it was aggressive in intent rather than defensive, a point well made in the cartoon overleaf, by the picture of Hitler and the goose-stepping march of the soldiers - of whom the American, Eisenhower, is the largest.

There were to be further steps in military cooperation, but before then there was a major move forward on the economic front - the creation of the European Coal and Steel Community (ECSC) - to which we must shortly turn. At this point, it is convenient merely to point out that in the early 1950s there was an attempt to create a European Defence Community (see p53-56). When this scheme failed to materialise, the **Western European Union (WEU)** was formed. It was an enlargement of the Brussels Pact to include Italy and Germany, and it was designed to ensure the better

coordination of defence arrangements between the signatories.

Early Political Cooperation

A Soviet view of NATO, 1952. The cartoonist shows NATO leaders goose-stepping, with the largest figure (the American, Eisenhower) carrying a portrait of Hitler. Reproduced by kind permission of the School of Slavonic and East European Studies, University of London

This was for a long while less marked than cooperation in the military or economic field. It was hoped that by integrating countries into a closer political community this would eliminate the possibility of war between member states. In 1948, supporters of the idea of a united Europe met at an unofficial congress at The Hague presided over by Winston Churchill. The Congress led to the establishment in 1949 of the **Council of Europe**. It served (and continues to serve) primarily as a forum for parliamentary opinion. Its purpose was 'to achieve a greater unity between its members for the purpose of safeguarding and realising the ideas and principles which are their common heritage'.

The idea was that the consultative assembly of 147 delegates from national parliaments of the Council would act as an embryonic European Parliament, but this did not prove to be the case. Individuals such as Adenauer, De Gasperi, Monnet and Spaak of Belgium were keen that it should work, but Britain was unwilling to allow it to assume any real power or influence. The Foreign Secretary, Ernest Bevin, saw dangers in an effective Council; 'Once you open that Pandora's box, you'll find it full of Trojan horses'. The remark was what **Hennessy** has called a piece of 'classic Bevinese', but it illustrated the British fear of anything more than a body of limited power, based loosely on voluntary cooperation.

We shall see that a major purpose of the statesmen who created the European Coal and Steel Community (ECSC) and went on to establish the European Economic Community (EEC) was to promote closer political union, though this was to be achieved by economic means. Similarly, the WEU was to be a political, as well as a military, union. Before we examine these later bodies, we need to see what was happening on the economic front soon after the war.

The Role of the Council of Europe

It was and is a debating body, lacking in legislative or executive power, and it does not discuss such matters as defence policy. It is concerned to safeguard the common heritage of European nations, and promote social and economic progress; mainly, it promotes cultural bonds between member-nations. As such, it is useful rather than very significant.

The Council was also responsible for drawing up the 'Convention on Human Rights and Fundamental Freedoms', which imposes obligations on all signatory powers. Coming into force in 1953, the Convention obliged members to respect and promote fundamental human rights and to recognise that individuals possess them under international law. In cases where these rights have been violated, it is possible for states and individuals to use the Strasbourg machinery to gain redress against the government responsible.

Currently (June 1996) there are 39 member states in the Council which is open to any European democracy accepting the rule of law and the protection of fundamental rights and freedom.

Economic Cooperation

In the search for closer economic cooperation in Europe, the two broad approaches, intergovernmental and integrationist, have been apparent. Monnet was keen to see step-by-step progress along the road to integration, but on the other side of the debate were many statesmen (notably in Britain) who were happy to think in terms of Europe drawing closer together but shrank from any binding commitment of the sort which he favoured.

In 1944 the governments of Belgium, the Netherlands and Luxembourg had agreed on the desirability of forming a free trade area between them, and in July 1947 an agreement on a customs union was concluded. Thereafter, they became known as the **Benelux** countries. The success of their venture encouraged further cooperation, and what made it particularly significant was that this was an experiment in integration as opposed to the intergovernmentalism of some other initiatives.

The Marshall Plan

> *The truth of the matter is that Europe's requirements for the next three or four years of foreign food and other essential products - principally from America - are so much greater than her present ability to pay that she must have substantial additional help or face economic, social and political deterioration of a very grave character.*
> *General Marshall, speaking on his Plan for Europe*

At the end of the war, the economies of Europe were shattered and in ruins. America was the only Power with a strong economy, and in June 1947 General Marshall announced that it would 'assist in the return of normal economic health in the world'. Billions of dollars were committed to propping up the states of Western Europe, for although the aid was available to all countries on the continent the Eastern bloc was uninterested in becoming involved. Bevin thought that the Americans were giving an 'inspiring lead', whereas the response of the Communist Party paper in Russia (Pravda) was less flattering. It discerned an attempt to interfere 'in the domestic affairs of other countries'.

American motives were mixed. Altruism played a part, but so did self-interest. It was in America's economic interests to see Europe prosperous again, for a flourishing continent could afford to buy American goods. In addition, there was a political motive, for Washington understood that hunger and deprivation made for popular discontent and disillusion with the democratic process. If aid could promote recovery, then there was less likelihood of Europeans being tempted by the communist ideas which were becoming entrenched in Eastern Europe. The position of West Germany was especially crucial in this regard, for it was geographically adjacent to the Soviet bloc. It was easier to sell the idea of assisting German recovery and rehabilitation to Western governments, if it was part of a wider programme of economic assistance.

Several leading Americans saw that integration in Western Europe was to their advantage if it could help to create prosperity and provide a buffer against Soviet westwards advance. They saw aid as a way of strengthening the West against further communist expansion.

It was one of Marshall's associates in the State Department, George Kennan (the brains behind the 'containment' policy), who came up with the idea that the offer of help would be 'in such a form that the Russian satellite countries would either exclude themselves by unwillingness to accept the proposed conditions, or agree to abandon the exclusive orientation of their economies'. In other words, they were never expected or intended to accept it.

Some $13.5b were made available and of this the largest share (over 3b) went to Britain, whilst France, Italy and West Germany also benefited considerably. The effect of the assistance was to help cement the divide between hostile economic groups, one linked to the United States, the other to the Soviet Union.

The allies also benefited from the economic boom in the United States, both in the rising demand for manufactured goods and because of heavy investment in European industry by private firms. By the early fifties, the West European economies were beginning to recover, much helped by the assistance given by the United States through the Marshall Plan.

It had been necessary to create an organisation to supervise the administration of this relief, and early in 1948 a number of countries joined together in the **Organisation for European Economic Cooperation (OEEC)***. This was a classic example of intergovernmental cooperation, valuable in itself, but quite distinct from the sort of mutual commitment favoured by the more enthusiastic federalists among European politicians.

*In 1961, this body was replaced by a new one with a much greater geographical scope, the **Organisation for Economic Cooperation and Development, (OECD)**. All the major industrial countries of what used to be known as the 'free world' are now members, including the United States and Japan - 25 states in all.*

No surrender of national sovereignty was involved, and Monnet diagnosed what he saw as the 'intrinsic weakness' of an approach which went no further than mere cooperation between governments; 'The idea that sixteen nations will cooperate effectively is an illusion'. It was true that in such a situation if there was no consensus, then there was likely to be little effective action, but this suited those who preferred to think in terms of cooperation rather than integration.

?

Why were the Americans keen to promote closer European cooperation?

Why was it difficult to achieve effective political co-operation?

The European Coal and Steel Community

For some time, Monnet had been looking for a way of bringing about economic integration in Europe. He was looking for some bold idea which would capture the imagination of internationalists in Western Europe. He was a visionary, but he understood that the politicians and civil servants in his own and other countries would only back his ideas if they were in line with their national interests and their postwar recovery programmes. In his **Memoirs**, he later recalled why his fertile mind alighted on a plan for future coal and steel harmonisation;

> *Coal and steel were at once the key to economic power, and the raw materials for forging the weapons of war. This double role gave them immense symbolic significance, now largely forgotten...To pool them across frontiers would reduce their malign prestige and turn them instead into a guarantee of peace.*

Problems in the Coal and Steel Industries

In the late 1940s, a crisis in the steel industries of Western European countries appeared to be likely, for there was the potential to produce vast quantities of the material. Europe appeared to be running into excess steel production, and it was estimated that by 1952 production would be approximately 69m tons, and consumption plus exports only 61m - hence the danger of a cut-throat price war or some new international cartel to keep prices artificially high.

Demand was low for with each country developing its own industry no adequate markets could be found, and prices were falling. The fear was that a deflationary movement would result, with its well-known effects, notably reduced investment, falling production and mounting unemployment. There was the further possibility of economic depression and political disturbance, especially in Germany which could then be a prey to communist subversion. A French socialist Deputy outlined the danger in 1950; 'Then the countries of Europe will be enfeebled by their internal contradictions and struggles, and will collapse, to become an easy prey and fall, one after another, like ripe fruit, into the hands of those who await the moment to seize our unfortunate continent'.

It was feared by the governments involved that producers would do as they had done before the war - create a cartel to limit competition. Ministers were keen to ensure that the effort of postwar reconstruction was not ruined by organised shortages to suit the manufacturers, for steel was too basic to their national economies. Economic policy for basic industries needed to be coordinated and a larger market established, with capital investment occurring in line with an overall plan. The future development of the iron, coal and steel industry was central to France's economy, but also to that of Europe as a whole.

Monnet was certainly aware that France had a clear interest in tackling the problem of excess capacity. As he wrote in his diary in 1950, 'France's continued recovery will come to a halt unless we rapidly solve the problem of German industrial production and its competitive capacity'. The problem needed to be tackled before German recovery enabled it to outstrip France and become a potential danger once again. It required new thinking, and he did not seek to 'solve the German problem in its present context. [We must] change the context by transforming the basic facts'.

Something had to be done, and Monnet's brainchild was to devise a plan for the harmonisation of the coal, iron and steel industries of France and Germany. The French Prime Minister, Bidault, was lukewarm, but the

42

Foreign Minister, Robert Schuman, was enthusiastic about the idea that there should be a new supranational organisation.

Robert Schuman and Jean Monnet

The Schuman Plan

Both Monnet and Schuman wanted to lay aside the age-old tensions between France and Germany, and a joint act would make this more likely. It had to be a programme relevant to the economies of the two countries, as action on heavy industry would be. Such a scheme would have the advantage that although limited in its specific scale, it was bold in its implications.

Schuman was responsible for the political action needed to implement the initiative. With his backing, Monnet drew up a plan for a coal-steel pool in Western Europe. Under what became known as the Schuman Plan, there was to be joint action. But the key decision was that rather than allowing governments to agree the development of the industries through negotiations and bargaining, the two men proposed the creation of a High Authority whose decisions would be binding on the two governments. This was a supranational step, for it meant that there was, in a limited sphere, a cessation of national control. It was also a realistic step, the way for Europe to proceed.

Though Bidault had at first been rather dismissive of the Plan and showed little interest in its details, the approval given by the French Cabinet on May 9 marked a turning point in the development of postwar Europe. Schuman could go public, and announce the scheme in a speech known as the **Schuman Declaration**.

Gathering Support

From the beginning, Monnet and Schuman could see that the proposal would be better if more countries were involved, so that it was open to others to join. However, the Plan had matured in secrecy, and it was sprung upon the relevant nations in such a way as to cause maximum impact. This would achieve a momentum, and get negotiations swiftly started on the right level of boldness and vision.

The French Foreign Minister announced that 'it is no longer the moment for vain words, but for a bold act - a constructive act'. He referred to the French initiative as 'preparing the creation of a united Europe'. The German Chancellor, Adenauer, was surprised at the news of the French project, but welcomed it and gave his country's approval, for it was 'a magnanimous step...making any future conflict between France and Germany impossible. It is a step of extraordinary importance for the peace of Europe and of the entire world'.

Adenauer was a shrewd politician who saw that the 'magnanimous step' was not only good for Europe, but also for West Germany. It provided him with the opportunity of rebuilding his fledgling state and giving the country enhanced respectability. To an aide he observed that the plan for an ECSC was 'our breakthrough...our beginning'. Speaking to Monnet, his language was less self-interested; 'I regard the implementation of the French proposal as my most important task. If I succeed, I believe that my life will not have been wasted'.

Agreement on the principles between France and Germany was the essential starting point, the precondition for securing assent from Italy and the Benelux countries. The French asked six countries to participate in discussions. Britain declined the invitation, whereas the others accepted. They signed the Treaty of Paris in April 1951.

The idea underlying the new Community was to establish a new body to manage all coal and steel production. There would be a tariff-free market in which there would be no customs-barriers to restrict trade in coal and steel across Western Europe. It began to operate in 1952, a date which marks the foundation of serious economic union in Europe.

The Treaty of Paris and its Importance

> *Let me make a point of declaring in so many words and in full agreement, not only with the French Government but also with M. Jean Monnet, that the importance of this project is above all political and not economic Konrad Adenauer, 1950.*

Like Bidault, others also took a long time to grasp the implications of what was proposed, and the American Secretary of State, Dean Acheson, wrote of his reactions to Schuman's exposition of its detail. He described it as 'so breathtaking that at first I did not grasp it. [Later] we caught his enthusiasm and the breadth of his thought, the rebirth of Europe which, as an entity, had been in eclipse since the Reformation.

The actual details of the ECSC are in many ways less important than its implications. Relatively small as it was, it opened up the way for a new era of good relations between two countries which had reconciled their differences. Beyond that, it was also a step along the road to European integration. What made this different to the other acts of cooperation which occurred around this time was that this was not intergovernmental liaison. This was an experiment with the federal principle, in Monnet's eyes 'the first concrete foundations of the European federation'.

The Operation of the Coal and Steel Community

Monnet saw the institutions of the new Community as significant, for 'only institutions grow wiser; they accumulate collective experience'. Four were established by the Paris Treaty;

The High Authority This was the key body for it was responsible for ensuring that 'the objectives set out in (this) Treaty are attained'. Supranational in character, it comprised nine members who were 'completely independent in the performance of their duties'. Monnet was its first President, to ensure (in Holland's words) that 'the neo-functional supranational objectives were honoured and enhanced at every opportunity'.

The Common Assembly This had only limited powers - to debate general reports, question members of the High Authority and in certain exceptional circumstances to dismiss it. As a non-elected body with membership drawn from the national legislatures, it had no democratic legitimacy.

The Special Council of Ministers At first, Monnet made no provision for the inclusion of such a body, which was designed to represent the national interests of the member nations. It was a concession to the principle of national sovereignty, in recognition of the anxieties of some of those who took part in the discussions which led to the signing of the treaty. At this early stage in the development of the Community, the creation of the Council shows the tensions which were inherent in the approach to cooperation - should it be supranational or intergovernmental?

A Court of Justice The Court had the responsibility for adjudicating on any action by the High Authority, and this involved examining any action to see that it did not infringe the rules laid down in the treaty.

Monnet was candid about his end goal. Addressing the Common Assembly for the first time, he stated that; 'We can never sufficiently emphasise that the six Community countries are the fore-runners of a broader united Europe, whose bounds are set only by those who have not yet joined. Our Community is not a coal and steel producer's association; it is the beginning of Europe'. The **Preamble** to the Paris treaty makes this clear;

> *Considering that world peace can be safeguarded only by creative efforts commensurate with the dangers that threaten it.*
>
> *Convinced that the contribution which an organised and vital Europe can make to civilisation is indispensable to the maintenance of peaceful relations...*
>
> *Resolved to substitute for age-old rivalries the merging of their (The Six) essential interests; to create, by establishing an economic community, the basis for a broader and deeper community among peoples long divided by bloody conflicts;...*
>
> *Have decided to create European Coal and Steel Community*

When the ECSC was formed, there was a choice of routes available. Europe could opt again for the intergovernmental approach in which national sovereignty was retained, or it could instead take a significant new departure and over a limited area abandon any notion of national control and go for the supranational. It chose the latter, and it was this course that meant that, whatever its broad sympathy, Britain was not likely to be able to find itself content with the new arrangements.

British Objections

Under Attlee as Prime Minister, Britain was not interested in joining the ECSC, though The Six would have liked her to do so. The invitation received an official welcome. But the note struck in the response was one of reserve and caution. A Memorandum of 27 May stated;

> *If the French Government intend to insist on a commitment to pool resources and set up an authority with certain sovereign powers as a prior condition to joining in the talks, His Majesty's Government would reluctantly be unable to accept such a condition.*

They were opposed to anything other than an intergovernmental body to coordinate the plan. The Labour Party believed that any pooling of resources would lessen the opportunities for socialist planning of the economy. Labour disapproved of the supranationalist implications of the ECSC, and was anyway in the process of nationalising the iron and steel industry. There seemed little point in taking over a 'commanding height' of the economy only to surrender control to Brussels. Therefore, Britain played no part in the discussions setting up the body.

There were wider objections, for the attitude of Labour was not dissimilar to that of many other politicians of the time. In the years after 1945, when the European dream of a more closely united Western Europe first appeared, Labour was sceptical of any moves in the direction of a unified Europe. Though a few individuals were well-disposed, the bulk of the Party wanted nothing to do with integration, even though fellow-socialists on the Continent were much involved in the early moves. Attlee showed an insular approach, when he wrote in 1948;

> *The Labour Party is a characteristically British production, differing widely from continental*

The Schuman Plan; a British Perspective (Punch)

*socialist parties. It is a product of its environment, and of the national
habit of mind.*

Europe was not a priority, and the Attlee Government thought in terms of
Britain as a world power, with American and Commonwealth ties. His
Foreign Secretary, Bevin, favoured a strong bond with America, and was
keen to see US involvement in the defence of Europe, as in the NATO
scheme; this was more important than cooperation with Europe. Bevin was
lukewarm publicly, and in private negative and on occasion actively
hostile. According to Acheson, he 'bristled with hostility to Schuman's
whole idea'.

Cripps had stated the Government's position very clearly in a debate in
June 1950. He noted the French view that the proposal was 'the first
concrete foundation of the European federation', and argued that;

> *This approach involves the other partners in the scheme not only in
> commitments in regard to the coal and steel industries, but also in
> commitments in regard to the future political framework for Europe. In
> our view, participation in a political federation, limited to Western
> Europe, is not compatible either with our Commonwealth ties, our
> obligations as a member of the wider Atlantic community or as a World
> Power.*

What of the Conservatives?

In the Parliamentary debates, Churchill and his colleagues were more
enthusiastic about British participation in the talks. Yet they were in reality
little more enthusiastic than many in the Labour Party about committing
an important area of the British economy to that of the continental states in
the manner proposed. As for the larger objective of European federation,
most Tories shared Cripps' misgivings.

Churchill was too much of a nationalist to wish to see Britain surrender its
power to any form of political community involving supranational control.
It was easy to express grand visions in Opposition, but in office he was as
concerned to protect British interests as his immediate predecessor. In his
eyes, the global connections of Britain precluded membership of a

federation which would be exclusively European in character. A later Prime Minister, Harold Macmillan could express a more basic consideration in 1950; 'One thing is certain, and we may as well face it. Our people will not hand over to any supranational Authority the right to close down our pits or our steel-works'.

There was one other factor. Some of those who argued for more unity in Europe were prone to suggesting that this would create a third force in international affairs, standing aside from the USSR and the USA, and rivalling either in size and influence. To British statesmen, such a view was fraught with dangers for if the vision was successful, then over the longer term it would probably encourage the Americans to withdraw from their enthusiastic commitment to the continent of Europe - just at the very time when they had become (in Bevin's term) 'locked in' as an Atlantic Power and leader of the Western world. Such a return to American isolationism could be fraught with danger, for without American protection then Europe and Britain might be a prey to communist aggression.

So Britain was not a part of the first venture in European integration. As Dalton later wrote , 'Britain would not take the federal road to Europe, but let others take it if they wished and good luck to them'.

With hindsight, it is easy to see this as the moment when Britain missed the European bus. At the time, it was perhaps less evident that this was to be such a dramatic point in postwar history, and the politicians and civil servants in London were highly sceptical about Schuman and Monnet's fantastic vision of a prototype 'common market'. That phrase first surfaced in the discussions around the setting up of the Coal and Steel Community. It was to be a few years more before the significance of the Treaty of Paris became apparent, and the phrase began to feature more frequently in the thinking of British political parties.

Why was the ECSC such an important innovation in postwar Europe?

Why were British government reluctant to become associated with the ECSC and other early attempts to achieve closer cooperation?

Was Churchill a good European?

From the ECSC to the Treaties of Rome

In August 1950, the French Chamber of Deputies voted for the Pleven Plan, named after its author, the Prime Minister. It proposed the creation of a European army in which German units could be integrated. In October 1950, not long after the Coal and Steel Community had been announced, the French officially launched the idea of two new communities, one for defence and one for a political community. In many ways, this was a logical development of the neo-functional approach, for it was an expansion of cooperation sector by sector.

The European Defence Community (EDC) involved 'the creation, for common defence, of a European Army under the authority of the political institutions of Europe'. Only a couple of months after the Treaty of Paris had been signed and sealed, The Six signed an agreement (May 1952) to establish the new body. A parallel organisation, the European Political Community, was devised to complement the EDC and give defence policy a political dimension. It was a bold plan, and would have involved a directly elected 'People's Chamber' among its other institutions.

This was a remarkable burst of Euro-activity, and showed that once the momentum to closer integration had been started it was dificult to rein it in. Indeed, this was precisely what the British feared. They saw the ECSC as a step along a long road which, at varying speed and by different routes, would lead to the ultimate goal of a Europe united along federalist lines.

Five of the six nations ratified the twin proposals, but in August 1954 it was ironically the French who effectively scuppered the idea as a result of an adverse vote in the French Assembly. The Fourth Republic (1946-58) was notorious for its political instability, and governments changed with alarming frequency. A new one which had just been installed soon found itself in difficultes over the proposed developments, for the rightwing nationalists and left wing socialist/communist groupings were hostile to the measures, which were decisively defeated. As **Nicoll and Salmon** put it; 'It was the end of the European Defence Community, and the stillbirth of the European Political Community'.

The Americans and the British had a contingency plan for a failure of the French Assembly to ratify the EDC. They decided to widen the Brussels Treaty of 1948 so that Italy and Germany could join in an enlarged Western European Union. Furthermore, it was agreed that the occupation of Germany was to be ended and Germany was to be allowed to join NATO. This formulation was acceptable to the Americans, and the French were persuaded to accept it.

It seemed appropriate for Western defence policy to become more closely integrated than it had been before. In 1954 the potential power of the hydrogen bomb (the next generation of weaponry after the atom bomb) had been revealed. It was realised that Russia had the technical know-how to manufacture one. Such a consideration may have helped to persuade the French and other doubters that it was time for a strong Western defence policy. The Americans saw German participation as essential to ensure that there was complete unity in the western half of Europe.

Why Was the Plan for a European Defence Community Unacceptable in Britain and France?

> *If Churchill wants us to ratify the European Army, he only has to ...agree to Britain's entry into the European system of integration..."Impossible" says London, "we've got the Commonwealth". Quite. But France has the French Union - and the problem is precisely the same (Le Monde, 1953).*

Despite the initial vote in favour of the establishment of an EDC, there was decreasing indication of parliamentary support in France for such a step, and many politicans understood this. They hoped that by lobbying for British and American support they could persuade their fellow representatives to endorse their proposal. The Americans were keen on the idea of a German 'defence contribution', something which was bound to stir unease in France. For all of the remarkable cordiality of postwar Franco-German relations, many Frenchmen were uneasy about the prospect of a resurgent Germany becoming a military Power in Europe again. Germany had the potential to dominate the continent.

The USA tried to place pressure on the French to commit themselves to the scheme and threatened 'an agonising reappraisal' of foreign policy if France failed to join. It might back German rearmament (which the French would view with horror), or turn its back on Europe and concern itself with only 'peripheral defence', in a 'Fortress America' policy. Attempts to bully France had the opposite effect to the one intended, for they produced stronger opposition to ratification.

Among Frenchmen, and certainly in Britain, there were anxieties about surrendering national sovereignty to another supranational authority. Defence and foreign policy were so vital to the well-being of all countries tha this made the area an especially sensitive one. Moreover, past greatness, tradition and national feeling all pulled in a different direction.

British participation might have helped to persuade the French to go ahead, but this was never on the cards. Britain was prepared to work with an EDC, but not actually participate in one. Churchill actually urged The

Six to ratify the plan, and declared himself in favour of the immmediate creation of a European Army under a unified command. He offered to play 'a worthy and honourable part'. But that part was 'all support short of membership'. Again, all the factors we have previously described came into play - her island tradition, her Commonwealth associations and her commitments to the United States were all still too important in the British psyche. France wanted more than Britain was willing to offer.

In a way, the idea of an EDC suffered by being too ambitious, for as yet the ECSC had not been given a chance to demonstrate how well close cooperation along supranational principles could work. It was remarkable that it got so near to being successful as it did. That it failed suggested that the time was not yet ripe, and that pioneers of the new Europe were perhaps rushing their fences.

Failure was a setback to the dreams of the federalists, and had a significant impact on the character of future cooperation. **Duchêne** has argued that ever since that date 'political federation as such has never been on the Community agenda. In fact, the federal element in all European integration plans was cut to the bone'. Europe was certainly not ready for closer political integration which was too far-reaching for many of those involved. Step-by-step economic integration was to be instead the chosen route to unity.

Economic Progress; Preparations Towards a Wider Economic Community

The success of the ECSC inspired The Six to extend their cooperation over the whole area of economic activity, and at the Messina Conference in 1955 they decided to examine the possibility of a general economic union, and the development of the peaceful use of atomic energy. The intergovernmental conference was seen as an opportunity to relaunch the European idea, and to do so by extending the ECSC into a wider area of the economy.

The countries involved wished to see a structure develop which would increase the chances of their achieving recovery and growth. They thought in terms of an enlarged free trade area. This time, the initiative came not from the Franco-German axis, but from the Benelux countries which had shown how neighbours could work together and harmonise their policies.

The leading Belgian federalist, Paul-Henri Spaak, and Monnet were the statesmen who did much of the preparatory work for the new meeting. They ensured that there was an achievable agenda which would enable agreement to be made on basic and concrete steps. The Conference went well, and its participants were convinced, in the words of the joint resolution, that;

> It is necessary to work for the establishment of a United Europe by the development of common institutions, the progressive fusion of national economies, the creation of a common market and the progressive harmonisation of (their) social policies.

Spaak's draft treaty formed the basis of the intergovernmental discussions which took place in June 1956, talks which were as much concerned with the progress in moving towards an atomic community as they were with the creation of a free trade one. Yet it is the creation of the common market which is most remembered about this period.

The discussions were carried out in a way which has become characteristic of Community development, with gains for any country in one area being matched with concessions in another. The French were keen to see the atomic community develop along the lines they urged. The Germans were more committed to an enlarged free trading area. Neither side would have agreed to the other proposal without being able to achieve what they wanted in the area of their preference. That two treaties could be signed together made a 'trade-off' approach possible.

In the discussions on free trade area, agriculture was especially significant. For the French this was an area of enormous interest and importance (see p309 and after), for the sector was one which aroused strong feelings in rural France. The Germans were concerned to get a customs union covering goods, services and capital, and as long as they achieved this they were happy to allow agriculture a special position; Germany had its own farming community to appease.

In those negotiations, the leading figures showed that they had learnt from the failure of the defence scheme. Federalism was still to be the end goal, but in devising the machinery of the new arrangements more concessions were made to intergovernmentalism, so that national governments could always defend their country's overriding interests.

The Treaties of Rome; Euratom and the European Economic Community

In March 1957, two treaties were signed in Rome to establish the separate organisations, **Euratom** and the **European Economic Community**. The latter is by far the most important, and when commentators refer to the **Treaty of Rome** this is the one to which they are usually referring. Its purpose over the long term was clearly stated in its **Preamble**; to establish 'an ever closer union' between European peoples.

The more tangible objective was stated in article two;

> *The Community shall have as its task...to promote...a harmonious development of economic activities, a continuous and balanced expansion, an increase in stability, an accelerated raising of the standard of living and closer relations between the states belonging to it.*

The main Rome Treaty set out major guidelines for The Six, including;

- establishing a customs union, in which all internal barriers to trade would be removed, and a common external tariff applied to the outside world

- developing a common agricultural policy

- harmonising social security arrangements

- providing for the free movement of labour and capital

- developing regional and social funds to assist poorer areas of their territory to produce new products and retrain workers whose skills become obsolete.

With the fulfilment of these objectives, there would be a 'Common Market', comprising the three elements of the ECSC, the EEC and Euratom.

The treaties again contained elements of supranationalism and intergovernmentalism, and although the Preamble contains the wish to move to 'an ever closer union among the peoples of Europe' it does not specifically say that this must eventually be a federal outcome. At the time, national sensitivities were recognised, so that there was a need to balance the aspirations of pioneers of European integration with the necessity to enable states to protect their national interests.

The institutions were all-important, however, and like the ECSC they contained important supranational bodies, the European Commission (the equivalent of the High Authority) and the Assembly (later known as the Parliament) which initially had only very limited powers. As the Community has evolved, the decisions of the Court of Justice have also provided an important push towards integration, and the Economic and Social Committee, though only advisory, has provided a useful 'transnational complexion to policy-making by institutionalising the concept that European interests take precedence over national interests' **(Holland)**.

Of the supranational elements, the Commission was the most important. As with the earlier body, the Commissioners 'shall, in the general interest of the Communities, be completely independent in the performance of their duties...they shall neither seek nor take instruction from any Government or from any other body'. It was to be the Commission which dealt with the day-to-day functioning of the EEC, and had responsibility for implementing Treaty provisions and for making recommendations. The national interest was again intended to be safeguarded via the Council of Ministers which is responsible for Community-level decision-making.

In what ways had the OEEC and the ECSC paved the way for the creation of the EEC?

What similarities were there between the ECSC and the EEC?

The Development of the European Community, 1957-73; British Reactions

Britain played no part in the Messina talks, and therefore had no input into the early evolution of the Community. If it had done so, the EEC and other bodies would have assumed a different character, for in the bargaining involved Britain would have stressed the importance of intergovernmentalism and sought to achieve greater safeguards for national interests.

Yet in 1955, as on other times before, Britain had not wanted to commit itself to any such involvement. Because the EDC failed to materialise, it was easy to assume that the impetus to unity had slowed down. In making such a calculation, Britain misread the situation badly, and then, as on many occasions subsequently, it underestimated the determination of others in continental Europe to press ahead in pursuit of the European idea. The drive to unity would not go away because of one setback. The way in which progress has occurred in the Community is that, as the process stalls in one area, so policy-makers turn to another where the obstacles might be overcome with less difficulty.

Britain was surprised at the pace of development in 1955-57, and when the Community was up and running in January 1958 was caught off guard. It found itself in a not very splendid isolation, excluded from an economic grouping into which it was increasingly difficult for British manufacturers to sell. It did not wish to see a trade-split in Europe, and had hoped to persuade The Six to join with them in a wider association of countries which could then work towards customs-free trade in industrial goods. Once the details of the EEC were agreed, it concentrated on pressing a scheme involving all OEEC members. Britain submitted its suggestions as to how a free trade area might operate, but wanted significant policy exclusions in any new agreement, such as the maintenance of special rights for the Commonwealth and the absence of any initiative concerning agriculture.

It seemed as though this was all part of an attempt to undermine The Six in their bold venture, and when serious talks got underway in 1958 they soon ran into difficulties. The coming to power of General de Gaulle in June of that year had an important effect, for he was unsympathetic to any dilution of the Community's negotiating postion. The French announced to the press in November 1958 that no agreement was possible, and the other five nations acquiesced. The British attempt to secure a wider agreement had failed, and it was apparent that within a few years The Six would be imposing a Common External Tariff against non-members.

The Formation of EFTA

In 1960, Britain was instrumental in forming EFTA, a loose free trade association but one much demanded by industrialists in the seven OEEC countries involved. The seven nations involved in EFTA were peripheral to the continental mainland, Austria, Denmark Norway, Portugal, Sweden, Switzerland and the United Kingdom. They agreed that over ten years (to 1970) they would remove duties on industrial goods, though there was to be no free trade in agriculture and no common external tariff. This meant that Britain could continue to import Commonwealth goods without there being any duty upon them.

Those involved in the new organisation believed that although it was a body totally distinctive from the EEC, nonetheless it could work easily alongside it. But hopes of such 'bridge-building' were a delusion. The aims and practice of the two bodies were very divergent, and as Monnet pointed out; 'The Community is a way of uniting peoples, and the Free Trade Area...is simply a commercial agreement'. EFTA was an organisation which had none of the built-in supranationalism which was a key feature of the Treaty of Rome. It was purely intergovernmental in character.

In the architecture of the new Europe, there were thus two rival bodies, the **Inner Six** and the **Outer Seven**. It was soon apparent that the likelihood of any agreement between them was small, and it was the now well-established and larger Common Market which was achieving such impressive results.

Progress Within the EEC

Before we consider how Britain came to reassess its stance in regard to the Common Market and other bodies, it is important to note the developments which were occurring within the Community itself. Significant economic strides were being made which showed that the Community was a great success for its members. Quickly, 'big business' and especially large, multi-national corporations benefited, and many mergers took place.

In the first five years, the GNP of the Community rose 27%, as compared with 18% for the USA and 14% for Britain. Statistics for industrial production were similarly impressive. American investment in Europe, especially in technology, quickly developed, and trade within the Community was considerably expanded.

In fact, the years up until the early 1970s were good ones for 'The Six'. During that time, industrialists benefited from the large market of about 170m people, and Germany, especially, prospered via its membership. The Franco-German bond was a strong one, and this cooperation made progress possible in many areas. The creation of a Common Agricultural Policy (CAP) was agreed in 1962, all customs duties between 'The Six' were eliminated in 1968, and by then a common external tariff was applied to goods from outside the Community. In other fields, such as transport, industrial and social policies, progress was less impressive. But by the late 60s/early 70s, discussions began on ways of moving towards political and monetary union, but they were at this stage inconclusive.

In 1965, a **Fusion (Merger) Treaty** was signed in Brussels. As a result, the institutions of the three independent organisations (the ECSC, EEC and Euratom) were merged in 1967, with the Commission based in Brussels, the Parliament in Strasbourg and the Court of Justice in Luxembourg. The treaties and communities remained technically separate, but from then onwards it was common to speak of one entity, the European Community (EC).

France was now led by a statesman who dominated the Community, General de Gaulle, the first President of the recently-created Fifth Republic. His thinking on the role of member states was in some respects more akin to that of Britain than that of his EC partners, but until his retirement in 1969 he successfully blocked Britain's attempts to join with them in an enlarged body.

The Attitude of General de Gaulle to European Cooperation

In a world which was moving towards internationalism and interdependence, De Gaulle clung to a belief that France could fulfil its destiny as a great nation by exercising fully the traditional freedom of a nation-state. He viewed moves to integration in Europe as a danger to France, and disapproved of any loss of sovereignty to supranational organisations. Yet when he assumed office in 1958, his freedom of manoeuvre was restricted, for France had signed up to the Treaty of Rome. Although he had spoken caustically in the past, now was the time for France to honour its word - for he regarded himself as a man of honour.

France was committed to a Europe of The Six, even if the General was unenthusiastic about schemes for closer political cooperation. He was not sympathetic to those countries who were in the process of forming EFTA and looking for links with the EEC, and took little interest in the negotiations involved. But in his dismissive attitude, he reflected the attitude of most 'Europeans' in France and the EEC as a whole. Few of them were prepared to consider such links as a viable proposition, purely to maintain some friendly link with Britain. It was, however, de Gaulle who gave the coup de grace to any accommodation with the Outer Seven.

He was more sympathetic to 'rapprochement' (a restoration of good relations) with West Germany, even though the Gaullist movement had never been very well-disposed towards its neighbour in the past. Like Adenauer, he believed in national interests but he also saw that it was necessary to set aside the German problem. Moreover, neither man had much liking for the Superpowers, the USA and the USSR, and both were suspicion of the motives and behaviour of Great Britain. For the moment, it was convenient for the General to share the limelight with the German Chancellor, who was a much older than he, and was unlikely to be around for many years more. France would then have its chance to assume the leadership of Europe and to speak for The Six.

General de Gaulle and Konrad Adenauer

In his attitude to NATO, he asserted French rights strongly and he was determined to be consulted at least as an equal with Britain. He might have to tolerate American leadership of the Western world, but with him around there was no hope that Britain could be allowed to speak up for Western Europe. It was in NATO that he showed his willingness to act independently, for he viewed the Alliance as one which made France a dependent nation, and deprived it of its freedom of manoeuvre.

Within the Community, his views soon became apparent. In opposition before 1958, he had never been sympathetic to federalist notions and supranational authorities, and on his return he began to espouse his ideas of a 'union of states'. He had no liking for Monnet's visions of closer cooperation, and his own conception was of a 'Europe des Patries', a Europe of sovereign states who came together for their mutual advantage but who were free to act as they wished in pursuit of their own interests. Any plan for closer political cooperation was regarded as impractical as well as undesirable, the stuff of 'myths, fictions and Pageants'. Over several years in power, he was to exploit every opportunity to thwart any moves to federalism, and to move the Community along more intergovernmental lines.

He was unwilling to make any concessions which would have allowed an extension of the powers of EEC institutions. He opposed any development of the European Parliament which would have given it increased powers over the EC budget, and was markedly hostile to a strengthening of the Commission and to many of its attempts to extend its supranational powers into areas of French policy-making. The only constitutional development which he was prepared to support was the Merger Agreement.

His approach to European issues was very different from that of the other five members, even more so after the retirement of Adenauer in 1963. The rest wanted to strengthen the links between them, and move towards majority voting. This was a departure from existing practice, for it had been agreed that for eight years after the Treaty of Rome the Common Market would proceed only on the basis of unanimity. On January 1, 1966 it was due to move to a system of weighted voting, under which the three larger nations would have had more impact on the outcome of decisions than the Benelux countries.

France refused to go along with majority voting, and was prepared to call a halt to Community cooperation over the issue of how the EC would operate in the future. For a while there was a threat to the continued existence of The Six as an entity. Yet, faced by some hostility to his stance from within his own country, the General backed down and was willing for France to be represented at a meeting of Foreign Ministers in Luxembourg in January 1966. The outcome was a compromise, and one which was to have significant results for the future course of events.

Spaak drafted the **Luxembourg Compromise**, as it became known, and its words are worth quoting;

> *Where in the case of decisions which may be taken by a majority vote on a proposal of the Commission very important interests of one or more partners are at stake, the Members of the Council will endeavour, within a reasonable time, to reach solutions which can be adopted by all the Members of the Council, while respecting their mutual interests and those of the Communities...*
> *The French delegation considers that where very important interests are at stake the discussion must be continued until unanimous agreement is reached.*

The Compromise was not produced as a formal amendment to the Rome Treaty but rather as a convention. However, the French had successfully asserted the idea of national sovereignty in decision-making, and this was to be a key weapon in the armoury of negotiators for many years. They could act, except where there were explicit objections by a state or group of states to what was being proposed. Ultimately, however, there was a blocking mechanism, and this was a barrier to further progress to integration.

If integration was opposed by the French, so was enlargement of the Community, for de Gaulle showed his willingness to block further expansion - particularly the admission of the United Kingdom. It is to Britain's changing stance in relation to the EEC which we must now turn.

A Change of Attitude in Britain

Of the British parties, only the Liberals had been solidly committed to moves for unity in Europe, with Britain working from the inside to influence the outcome of decisions. In the other parties, there were many people who had long been hostile to closer integration in Europe. However, the British Government of Harold Macmillan was impressed by the progress of The Six which seemed to be doing them so much good.

For several years, Britain had been slow to adjust to its decline in status, and only in the late 50s did attitudes begin to change. In world terms, the enforced withdrawal from Suez in 1956, the loosening of Commonwealth ties as countries achieved independence, and increasing doubts about the 'special relationship' with the United States, highlighted a loss of power and influence. At home, there were balance of payments difficulties and a 'stop-go' economy, whilst on the continent The Six benefited from their expanded market.

As the new decade loomed on the horizon, many of the reasons for scepticism about the EEC seemed less important, and the British government saw the advantages of sharing in the industrial development of Europe with its large market of over 180m people and its impressive rate of economic growth. Membership might provide just the incentive needed to British manufacturers to become more efficient, and much was made of the dynamic effect of the 'cold blast' which competition might provide.

With Britain inside the Community, there would be a vast population of some 240m, comparable to that of the USSR and larger than the United States. Such an arena offered the prospect that as part of a more united Europe, Britain could have a more influential voice in world affairs, and deal with the USA more as a partner than as an increasingly poor relation.

The thinking behind the application was more political than economic. This became clear many years later when Cabinet records became available under the Thirty Year Rule. Britain was no longer a first class Power, and the Government had to consider how it could best maximise its influence.

*EEC countries benefit from the Rome Treaty
and Macmillan pleads for Britain to be able to
do so also (Punch)*

*De Gaulle and Adenauer as the ugly sisters,
with Prime Minister Macmillan as Cinderella
looking on (Punch).*

*A rejected Macmillan returns to the
organisations from which Britain had sought to
distance itself (Punch)*

Britain's Decision to Join the Common Market; Government Thinking

The Cabinet Papers for 1961 have revealed Macmillan's thinking about Britain and the EC. He frankly admitted Britain's declining role in the world, and noted the increasing importance of the Community;

> The countries of the Common Market, if left to develop alone under French leadership, would grow into a separate political force in Europe...Eventually, it might mean that The Six would come to exercise greater influence than the United Kingdom, both with the United States and possibly with some of the independent countries of the Commonwealth. This development was therefore a threat to the political position of the United Kingdom as a world power...Politically, our interests would be better served by working for a wider European association in which we could play a prominent part.

The Cabinet minute went on to refer to 'the surrender of national sovereignty', which would require careful thought. A Foreign Office note observed on this point that;

> Continental opinion would not think that we were in earnest in establishing a new relationship with The Six unless we were prepared to abandon a significant degree of sovereignty.

The same issues of loss of sovereignty and a federal/confederal future were being discussed by ministers then, as now. However, a note from the British Ambassador in Paris detected the trend of events; 'We shall become more and more Europeans'.

The Papers indicate how concerned the Conservative Government of the day was to persuade de Gaulle to accept British membership. It was even prepared to contemplate a sharing of nuclear secrets, and to provide France with bombs and technical know-how, to win his assent.

The First Application, 1961. The General says Non!

In July 1961, the Macmillan Government announced that Britain would apply for membership of the EEC. Three other states (Denmark, Ireland and Norway) were also making independent applications, and the remaining EFTA nations hoped to gain 'associate status'. However, the fate of expansion really hung on the attitude to the British bid to join. In October, negotiations got underway, with Edward Heath, the Lord Privy Seal, leading the British team. They continued for more than a year, and many controversial matters seemed to be decided. In January 1963, General de Gaulle used a press conference to announce that France was vetoing this application.

Despite the veto, the talks continued over the next two weeks, until on the 29th of the month Spaak announced that an impasse had been reached;

> *It will be extremely difficult...to continue to develop the economic Europe. As for the political Europe about which we had dreamed as a necessary consequence of economic organisation, I do not know when it will be possible to speak of this again.*

How is it that by the time that Britain was ready to join the club, de Gaulle was only too willing to exclude us from membership?

De Gaulle claimed that Britain was not yet ready to be admitted, for it lacked the 'political will' because of its global interests. It was distracted by the Commonwealth connection, and was too much of an Atlantic power to be truly committed to a European destiny. He also questioned whether Britain's industrial base, protected agriculture and Commonwealth trading links made her suitable as a European partner. In all these respects, 'the nature and structure, the very situation that are England's, differ profoundly from those of the continentals'.

What seems to have particularly disturbed him was the British decision to purchase American rather than French nuclear weapons, and more generally an unwillingess on the part of the British government to cooperate with France in the development of nuclear technology.

Certainly, there were many 'reluctant Europeans' in Britain for whom the driving-force of our application was a fear of being left behind in a highly competitive economic race. There was little sign of a desire on their part to think in genuine European terms. But more than this was involved. France had achieved a dominance in the Community. De Gaulle was a strong nationalist who wanted the Community to have a powerful voice with a French accent. France was on the point of achieving a dominance in the Community, and British membership would pose a threat to that hegemony and dilute the French role.

The Second Application, 1967

In 1967, under the Wilson (Labour) Government, Britain tried again, along with Eire, Denmark and Norway as before. The Labour Government was attracted by the potential of a large single market, and believed that joint research and shared development-costs in high-technology industries would prove beneficial to British manufacturers. It was suggested that British entry would give the Community a new dynamism, and that Britain's capacity for technological innovation would be an asset.

There were several people in both main parties who remained unconvinced about the merits of the case, and even among supporters of membership it was recognised that the economic benefits available in the short term were likely to be marginal. The political case looked the more compelling. The overwhelming preponderance among MPs (488-62) supported the application, many having come to recognise that membership offered the best route forward for Britain.

The attempt was nonetheless again frustrated by de Gaulle, although - as previously - the application was not withdrawn. This time, the French veto came before negotiations even began. No longer could Britain be said to be more concerned about Commonwealth interests, and the other members wanted Britain to join; the Commission gave strong endorsement to the idea. But this time, he argued that Britain was still too subservient to the USA, and that her ailing economy would be a drag on the rest of the Community. This was around the time of a British devaluation of the pound, in November 1967.

De Gaulle suspects Britain of driving under the influence of America (Punch)

De Gaulle resigned after an adverse vote in a French referendum in 1969, and died a year later. His impact on the Community was important, and many would portray him as a barrier to its development. His conception of the way in which it should develop was totally at variance with the vision of his fellow Frenchman, Monnet. The General viewed federalism and any surrender of national identity or soveriengty with distaste, and put the brakes on any moves in that direction and on any expansion which would have challenged French leadership in Europe. He thought in old-fashioned terms of national interest.

In speaking up for French interests, his approach reflected the resurgent nationalism of his countrymen. They appreciated his almost mystical sense of the greatness of France, but unlike some other statesmen he combined this strong patriotism with a shrewd and acute sense of practical reality.

It is, however, ironic that de Gaulle was able to exclude Britain on the grounds that it was

A German view of Britain's second bid to enter the EEC (Die Zeit)

too preoccupied with preserving its own national interests and not yet ready for Europe. He himself exhibited a powerful nationalism, and was more than willing to assert French national interests over those of the whole Community. He believed in and practised the very intergovernmentalism that was anathema to pioneers of European unity such as Schuman and Monnet, and for which British statesmen had a natural inclination.

The Third British Application

Soon after the French President resigned in 1969, it was agreed that there should be new negotiations on the enlargement of the Community. The passing of de Gaulle from the international scene boosted Britain's chances of successful negotiations. By now, Edward Heath was Prime Minister, and the French President, Georges Pompidou, was personally and politically sympathetic to him. At his first press conference, Pompidou indicated a change in French thinking, and gave encouragement with his observation that; 'We have no objection of principle against a possible UK application'.

This thaw in relations between Britain and France eased discussions, and these brought the attempt to join to a successful conclusion. In October 1971, the House of Commons accepted the principle of entry into the EEC, and, thereby, accession to the Rome treaties. The Treaty of Accession was signed in January 1972, and Britain joined a year later, along with Denmark and Ireland. Norway had also accepted entry terms, but in 1972, the Norwegian people rejected the agreement in a referendum, and so Norway remained outside the Community. The accession of three new countries marked the **First Enlargement** of the EC.

Why had things turned out differently?

This time round the negotiations were conducted differently. Whereas in earlier applications it had seemed as though it was seven states who were in discussion, in 1970-71 it was The Six (speaking with one voice through the President of the Council of Ministers), plus Britain. The Six recognised the applicants' commitment to joining and their willingness to abide by the treaties and all that had already been achieved by the Community. They were examining how they could ease the process of transition to membership, in the light of the difficulties which were obviously there concerning agricultural prices, the British budgetary contribution and the treatment of Commonwealth produce.

There was from the start a markedly more positive tone about the meetings, and the absence of the General and the personal rapport of the new leaders in Britain and France were all important factors. Heath was widely seen on the continent as a committed European, and because of this it was more difficult to question Britain's preparedness for a more European future.

Beyond this, French thinking had undergone a change of mood. It was recognised in Paris that, as a likely net contributor to the Community, Britain could be a useful member - the more so as its preference for intergovernmentalism was in accord with their own more recent suspicions of supranationalism. Furthermore, it was becoming ever-more-apparent that West Germany, with its economic strength, was becoming a leading force in European affairs, and a London-Paris axis might help to thwart any unpalatable initiatives coming from Bonn.

? Why do you think that General de Gaulle rebuffed the first attempts made by Britain to join the EEC? Were his fears about British entry justified?

Was the General a 'good European' or a 'good Frenchman'?

The European Community, 1973 - 1986

The years up until the early 1970s were good ones for The Six. Europe was peaceful, and business was thriving. Since then, things have been more problematic, with periods of tension and difficulty alternating with periods of creative activity.

The widening of membership in the First Enlargement coincided with the energy crisis and a developing recession in the western world. In October 1973, the Oil and Petroleum Exporting Countries (OPEC) quadrupled the price of crude oil, and the EEC, which imported 63% of its energy requirements, was badly hit. In its reaction to the oil crisis, the EEC was torn by schism, and individual countries began to make separate deals with the Arab states. There was little sense of a Community interest, but rather a situation in which members thought primarily in terms of defending their national position. This was to be the pattern of the 1970s and early 1980s which saw a number of internal disagreements.

Further Expansion

Greece had long hoped to become a member of the EEC, and in the early 1960s had made an Association Agreement. Any chance of full membership received a serious setback in 1967 when a military junta seized power and began what became known as the Rule of the Colonels. The Community froze the Agreement for the period in which democracy was suspended. When the Colonels were brought down in 1974, it was reactivated and within a year the new Government applied for full membership. Members were keen to encourage the democratic regime, and in 1979 Greece signed the Accession Treaty, and entered two years later. With this **Second Enlargement,** there was now a Community of The Ten.

Spain and Portugal were also unacceptable as members of the Community as long as they had authoritarian regimes. Both disappeared in the mid-seventies, and the EC was keen to recognise the new situation and in so doing extend its influence in the Mediterranean region. In both cases the negotiations took much longer to conclude than they had done with other countries, and although applications were made in 1977 they were not able to become members until January 1986. This was mainly because of internal problems within the EC which for several years in the early 1980s was preoccupied with consideration of its own budgetary arrangements.

As a result of the accession of two new members, this **Third Enlargement** increased the Community to twelve. The trend was towards a steady increase in the area of the Community. There was a modest setback to this progressive enlargement when Greenland, a Danish territory, voted to leave the Community in a referendum held in 1982. Greenlanders were unhappy about the application of EC fisheries policy and felt remote from the distant 'Brussels bureaucracy'. The territory officially left in January 1985.

Inevitably, enlargement was bound to transform the character of the Community. This made it necessary to review the methods by which it conducted its business, and to ensure that measures were taken to improve the position of less developed states to ensure that they did not become a permanent drain upon the EC budget. Living standards varied considerably. Of The Twelve, some were clearly more economically successful than others, so that Luxembourg, Germany, Denmark, France, Belgium and Holland had the highest average incomes per head, then came Britain and Italy, followed by Spain, and with Ireland, Greece and Portugal at the bottom.

Progress to Integration

Some EC governments began to contemplate bold initiatives, but inevitably there were divergent views as to how the Community should develop in the future. Some countries were especially keen to move forwards to ever closer union. The attempt to do so at a rapid pace had received a setback with the failure of the EDC, and thereafter it was apparent to most politicians and diplomats involved that progress would be made via economic cooperation. Yet whenever there was the opportunity to advance the cause of integration there were some statesmen only too willing to seize their chance. This could be done by extending the powers of the European Parliament in the budgetary area, as happened in 1970 and 1975. There were plans for more substantial changes.

In 1976, the Belgian Leo Tindemans produced a report on 'The high road to European Union', in which he argued for a common foreign policy, moves to develop a monetary and economic policy and reform of EC institutions including a provision for direct elections to the European Parliament. The proposals had little immediate effect, for in the mid-1970s European leaders were preoccupied with the aftermath of the oil crisis and this prevented any creative thinking about the future. However, one important change did occur in line with the Tindemans paper. This was the introduction of **Direct Elections** to the Strasbourg Parliament, in **1979.**

Within a couple of years, the first elected Parliament had established a Committee on Institutional Questions with the purpose of drafting proposals for a European Union. It was chaired by Altiero Spinelli, long-time federalist and a past Commissioner, and he was keen to see definite progress to closer integration. The Parliament accepted his report, and in February 1984 voted overwhelmingly in favour for the Draft Treaty Establishing the European Union.

The document was then sent to the governments and parliaments of member states for their response, so that it was becoming apparent to all involved that there was likely to be pressure for a further period of advance in Community affairs. The key step was to be the signing of the Single European Act, but before we consider the passage and imlliplications of the SEA we need to examine again the position of Britain in the first decade or so of its membership.

Britain's Position After 1973

When Edward Heath signed the Treaty of Accession in 1972 he saw it as an historic turning-point in Britain's fortunes. He was an ardent pro-European, whose first speech in the House of Commons had been to welcome the publication of the Schuman Declaration. He was not just logically convinced of the merits of British membership of the Community, but was emotionally committed to the whole enterprise. He saw, and continues to see, Britain's future as closely tied to that of our continental neighbours, and wanted to see Britain play a positive role. However, his Premiership was over within thirteen months of Britain's accession, and it was a Labour Prime Minister, Harold Wilson, who replaced him.

In opposition, after the 1970 election, Labour's underlying scepticism had come to the surface again. As Leader, Wilson had needed all of his considerable management skills to hold the party together. Faced with an almost unbridgeable gap, he had compromised by saying that the terms obtained by the Heath Government were not right, and would need to be put to the people in a referendum. There was to be a period of renegotiation before this could happen. In office, he honoured his pledge.

The Labour Renegotiation, 1975

Renegotiation soon got underway and some modest changes to the previous terms were made, though their impact was largely cosmetic. They were enough to enable British ministers to claim that they had won useful concessions to the British viewpoint, and the Government felt able to commend the revised terms to the British people in the referendum campaign.

The campaign was heated and focussed on the supposed impact on the British economy, the political issue of sovereignty and the effect on Britain's position in the world in the event of withdrawal from the Community. The question asked of the electorate was straightforward; **'Do you think that the United Kingdom should stay in the European Community (The Common Market)?'**. In June 1975, Britain voted by 17,378,581 to 8,470,073 in favour of 'staying in', a 67.5% 'yes' vote on a 65% turnout.

The referendum was won, and Britain remained in the EC. A leading 'anti', Tony Benn, accepted that his followers must abide by the verdict; 'I read the message loud and clear. When the British people speak, everyone - including ourselves - should tremble before their decisions'. But this was not to be the end of British hostility to developments within the Community. Over the following years, the British had the reputation in Europe of being half-hearted about membership. On a series of issues, British representatives defended the Government's position forcefully, but the tone of this defence sharpened notably after Mrs Thatcher's victory in 1979.

The Conservative Position After 1979

From the start of her term in office, Mrs Thatcher adopted a more minimalist position than Mr Heath had done. She could see the economic benefits of membership and wanted to see Britain stay in the Community. However, her outlook was more of a Gaullist one for she favoured a 'Europe des Patries'. For her, the EC was 'a partnership of nation-states each retaining the right to protect its vital intersts but developing more effectively than at present the habit of working together'.

To other members, her approach was seen as strident, if determined. There was some admiration for the way she defended her country's interests as she saw them, but much irritation and resentment about her manner which could be carping and hectoring. She wasn't easily open to suggestion, and at one meeting in 1980 told the President of the Commission so in no uncertain terms; 'Don't try persuading me, you know I always find persuasion very counter-productive'!

Two areas of dispute in the early years concerned the Common Agricultural Policy and Britain's budgetary contribution, problems which were closely linked. On joining, the British soon found themselves at odds with the CAP, which had long been roundly condemned on this side of the channel. They objected to the amount which they paid into the Community budget to support 'inefficient French farmers'. For a while the transitional arrangements negotiated by Conservative and Labour ministers in the early-mid 1970s had served to conceal the dificulties, but by the middle of the decade, the rising costs of the CAP were widely seen as becoming unmanageable, and in serious need of attention.

In the late 70s-early 80s, at least 75% of the EC budget was being used to support agriculture. Great Britain did not much benefit from this, for we had the lowest workforce engaged in farming in the Community (less than 3%). Effectively, the result of the system was that there was a transfer of funds from countries with small agricultural sectors to those in which agriculture played a more significant part; five of those were above average in Community prosperity. Overall two nations, Britain and West Germany, were transferring money to the other seven irrespective of their wealth.

Mrs Thatcher forcefully reminded her partners in meetings of the heads of government that her country was paying vastly more into the Community than it got back out of it. In respect of the years 1980-2, that excess amounted to £1,014m. There was a serious problem to address, although it has to be said that from the beginning it was always obvious that Britain was going to be a net contributor rather than a net beneficiary of Community funding.

It was perfectly reasonable to seek changes to the EC budget so that a larger share of EC income was spent on regional and social policy from which Britain might benefit more. It was also reasonable for the Prime Minister to defend national interests by seeking to reduce the heavy British contribution. What exasperated her partners in negotiations was what they perceived as her uncompromising and frequently bossy stance, and some of them were irritated by any attempt to placate her.

Roy Jenkins, then President of the Commission, observed her performance at close quarters, and saw the resentment it caused. He concluded that the loss of goodwill outweighed the financial concessions she eventually won, and 'made the disputes of the next decade more difficult to handle...the eight lost their faith in Tory Europeanism, and Margaret Thatcher became an instinctive Euro-basher'.

In 1983, Britain gained an ad hoc refund, but a more permanent correcting mechanism was needed. The dispute was finally resolved in 1984 at Fontainebleau, when President Mitterrand was helpful in producing a compromise formula by which Britain had a rebate of 66% of the difference between its VAT contributions and what it obtained back in benefits. In the words of **Nicoll and Salmon**, this 'took the sting out of the budgetary problem and laid a basis for the further development of the Communities'.

The Community Moves Forwards

The late 1970s and early 1980s were a period of stagnation and disappointment for those anxious to promote closer European cooperation. There was little sign of progress towards integration, so that in 1983, in a sceptical analysis of European decision-making, **Paul Taylor** could write that 'the challenges to sovereignty were successfully resisted, and the central institutions failed to obtain the qualities of supranationalism'. The Economist was more gloomy, its cover for an edition in March 1982 showing a tombstone on which were inscribed the words; 'EEC born March 25th, 1957, moribund March 25, 1982, capax imperii nisi imperasset' ('It seemed capable of power until it tried to wield it').

The disagreement over the EC 'budgetary imbalance' used up an enormous amount of time, and was endlessly discussed in gatherings of the Council of Ministers and in the European Council. Everything else assumed secondary importance, so that the questions of enlargement and of the future shape of the Community never received the attention which many European statesmen wished to give to them.

Yet the Germans and the Italians, among others, were active in devising new initiatives to carry the EC forwards into a closer union, with more distinctive political objectives. By the mid-eighties, the future of the

Community was under serious consideration, and during the Luxembourg Presidency in the second half of 1985 a conference was held to discuss amendments to the Treaty of Rome. It was here that arrangements were to be agreed for the next major step towards European integration, the introduction of the Single European Act.

After nearly a decade and a half of stagnation ('Eurosclerosis'), the issues of monetary, economic and political union came once more to the fore in the mid-eighties. The breakthrough came with the agreement on the Single European Act and the appointment of Jacques Delors as the President of the Commission (1985). The SEA and the Delors Presidency between them generated momentum not only for the creation of the internal market but also for the moves to closer cooperation to be resolved at Maastricht in 1991.

The Single European Act, and its Aftermath

The passage of the SEA greatly extended the scope of the Community. The Act provided for the completion of the single market by the end of 1992. What this meant was that all technical, physical and fiscal barriers to intra-Community trade, were to be eliminated, as were all barriers to the free provision of professional and other services. This was in line with the original concept of the Community, that there should be a Common Market, a free trade area without any restraints to trade. Yet some regulations and barriers had never been eliminated and others had developed in the enlarged Community.

In signing the Single European Act, The Twelve committed themselves to movement towards monetary union, which was a goal to be 'progressively realised'. The phrase is to be found in the Preamble, rather than in the main legally-binding clauses of the Act. As part of the main text, there was - in addition to details of the operation of the single market - a commitment to lessen disparities between the richer and poorer areas of the Community, known as the policy of 'cohesion'; more resources were to be allocated to the 'structural funds', for regional and social expenditure. Provision was also made for closer cooperation in the area of foreign policy and security, and for environmental improvement.

The Single European Act

The purpose of the Single European Act was to create a single internal market among The Twelve by the end of 1992. This would fulfil the original version of a tariff-free trading area without obstacles to the free movement of goods, services, capital.

Among other things, this involved;

i   The creation of a single market for services such as banking, insurance, credit and securities

ii The creation of a single legal framework for business

iii The standardisation of differing national technical requirements for products

iv The gradual harmonisation of indirect taxes so as to remove the need for tax adjustments at the border

v   The easing of restrictions on living and working in another member state, with mutually recognised qualifications and diplomas

The Objectives and Principles of the Treaty of Rome were amended by the new Act, and the Preamble agreed by the High Contracting Parties set out the new version;

Determined to lay the foundations of an ever closer union among the peoples of Europe. Resolved to ensure the economic and social progress of their countries

---

Among other things, four main innovations in Community procedure were agreed;

i   The extent of majority-voting was widened, so that unanimity was
    required only for sensitive issues on which there were strong
    national interests

ii Matters concerning aspects of energy, environmental,
    research/technological and social policy were brought within the
    authority of the EC

iii A new decision-making procedure was introduced. For matters
    concerned with the single market, there was in future to be a
    'cooperation procedure' which would allow the Parliament a greater
    say in the development of policy.

iv Parliament gained two important new rights - to give or withhold
    assent when asked by the Council for its view on the entry of new
    members into the Community, and when agreements were made for
    association status with the EC

The SEA required the agreement of each member country and had to be
formally ratified in all of the national legislatures, because it amended the
Treaty of Rome. Mrs Thatcher felt able to go along with the measure, for
her Conservative Government had a very market-oriented approach to
economic policy. Her ministers had worked for open trading conditions,
and had since 1979 allowed the free movement of currency into and out of
Britain. There was some opposition in Parliament to the measure, not least
among the Labour Party which had yet to embrace the European cause
with any enthusiasm.

There was an initial threat of a rebellion in the House of Lords, for, as in
other countries, there was some unease about the loss of sovereignty
involved. Because of these constitutional implications, Denmark and
Ireland held referendums prior to ratification (see p390).

Work Left Undone

There was disappointment with the SEA among those Europeans who
wanted to hasten the pace to integration, for it was a compromise. Some
member states were not too keen to see any further moves, whilst others

wanted to see faster progress. All could agree on the desirability of this one measure, but there was doubt about what would follow. Enthusiasts for a more federal Europe were keen to see the Community develop more boldly, and for a combination of reasons, both internal and external, the period from the mid-1980s onwards was to witness a burst of Euro-activity along the lines they wished to see.

Several issues had not been finally resolved by the new Act, although some partial steps had been taken. In the Preamble, there was the reference to Economic and Monetary Union as a desirable goal, and several integrationists felt that such a policy - and in particular a single European currency - would be a useful adjunct to a single market and allow it to work more effectively. There was a mention (in a new article 102a made part of the Treaty of Rome) of the possibility of an intergovernmental conference to achieve any necessary changes in this field. Such a possibility was also mentioned in article 30(12), a part of the Act dealing with political union.

Others were more concerned with the possible side-effects of deregulation. In a free market, the weakest peoples and the weakest countries might suffer - hence the need for 'cohesion' to protect the interests of the ailing regions. But what about the peoples of Europe whose livelihood could be adversely affected by the absence of controls? Did not the SEA need to be accompanied by a social measures to protect the living and working standards of the member states?

Again, there was the worrying question about the danger - if frontier controls were abolished on travellers - that 'undesirables' might be able to move freely throughout the Community. Drug-trafficking, international crime and terrorism were potential growth areas, and in addition there was the fear of an influx of Eastern European migrants entering into the EC and then finding a safe haven in one of the member states.

Institutional reform had not been addressed, and many issues were in need of attention. The role of the Parliament had been enhanced, but other than this increase in the powers of an elected body nothing had been done to tackle the 'democratic deficit' in the decision-making process. Lack of accountability was seen as a major weakness, and both supporters and critics of the EC could agree that there was an absence of effective democratic control over the work of the Commission.

Outside the Community, the face of Europe was undergoing dramatic change by the late 1980s. The fall of the Berlin Wall and the subsequent reunification of Germany created a country of such a size and potential strength that it could dominate the continent if it was not fully 'locked in' to the EC. To the East, Communism was collapsing in many countries of the old Soviet bloc, and by 1991 the USSR itself was to be no longer in existence.

The Twelve; An Enlarged Community

The fall of the Berlin Wall in 1989 brought about an increase in the size of the Community, but not an increase in the number of countries which belonged to it. Within a year, the two halves of Germany, very different in their economic and political characteristics, were united.

What had been the separate state of East Germany had ceased to exist. It could have been granted an Association Agreement, or become a thirteenth state within the EC. Instead, it decided to join with the Federal Republic, and as it was incorporated into a member country there was no legal alteration in Community membership. This addition was not technically an enlargement, for there was no Treaty of Accession. If it had been an entry following the usual negotiations, more specific provision would have been made to cope with the particular difficulties involved in integrating the less-developed economy of the old GDR into the more advanced West.

There was a need to think carefully about the implications for the Community of the transition to democracy in Eastern Europe, for some of the countries once dominated by Moscow would be keen to align themselves more closely with the West, now that they were free to do so. In particular, as the Cold War came to an end, the security policies which had been based on the Cold War need to be re-examined, and the whole role and strategy of NATO - effectively an anti-communist alliance - was in need of serious rethinking.

Some EFTA members were also queueing up to join the Community, and for EFTA as a whole there was the prospect of developing closer ties with the EC by the formation of a European Economic Area, a free trade area covering the nineteen states who belonged to either of the two organisations.

These were all weighty questions ripe for consideration, and once the passage of the SEA had been completed and work was in hand to achieve the single market by the end of 1992, there was the chance to reassess the position of the Community in changing circumstances. It was on the verge of possible - indeed likely - enlargement. Before this could happen, the prevailing view in some member countries was that there must be a deepening of Community bonds to prevent any dilution once membership increased.

To Widen or to Deepen?

In the 'widening or deepening' debate, there were many in the British Government who came down firmly in favour of widening first, in the hope that this might make any deepening impossible. For in the late Thatcher/Major years, there was a growing coolness within the Conservative Party about all things European. On most of the issues which arose for discussion from the passage of the SEA onwards, the majority of British ministers seemed to be seeking to stem the tide of European advance. They wanted to limit Community competence as much as possible, and keep to the idea of a Common Market with, maybe, a little intergovernmental cooperation tacked on - where this seemed appropriate. Such an attitude was far removed from what the makers of the European Community had always had in mind.

It was during the Presidency of Jacques Delors (1985-94) that the Commission began to develop policies designed to bring about a closer union extending well beyond anything achieved since the signing of the Treaty of Rome.

The Delors Programme

History is only interested in the far-sighted and those who think big, like Europe's founders. They are still with us today in the inspiration they provided and legacy they left.
J Delors, Bruges, 1989

Jacques Delors

As President of the Commission, it was Jacques Delors who had unveiled the proposals for a single market in 1992 to the European Parliament. Two years later, he had presented a new programme in which he dealt with the challenges created by the steps already taken - the prospect of moving onwards towards closer union, via increased cooperation on economic and monetary policy, and on matters of foreign policy. In addition, he saw a need to re-examine Community finances, and review the workings of the Common Agricultural Policy. He then began work on a plan for economic and monetary union which the European Council had asked a committee chaired by him to devise.

In April 1989, the Delors Report was published, and it was presented to the Council of Ministers two months later. It envisaged a three-stage progression to its ultimate goal of full monetary union, of which a common currency would be an important element. By a majority vote, the decision was taken that there should be an intergovernmental conference to examine this and other issues more thoroughly.

Delors believed that the EC was more than a common market. It was 'an organised space governed by commonly agreed rules that (will) ensure economic and social cohesion, and equality of opportunity'. In other words, there was a social dimension to the market, which involved the protection of individual rights so that the Community worked for the benefit of all its citizens.

In May 1989, the Commission produced a draft **Charter of Fundamental Social Rights'** in connection with terms of employment; this was the Social Charter, later to become the Social Chapter. It was a bold document, but largely as a result of pressure from the British Government it was much watered down in its next version. Even this was unacceptable to the British who alone refused to go along with the proposals.

The Approach to Maastricht

The intergovernmental conference was due to be held in 1991, with the key decisions reserved for the meeting of the European Council to be held at Maastricht, in December. In the months leading up to the summit, issues such as the Social Charter, the common currency and the democratic deficit, were much argued over by politicians and in the press. There was to be a settlement of a number of European matters, with a view to signing a treaty which would, among other things, set out the target dates for achieving the next stages of the Delors Plan.

Many British Conservatives expressed strong hostility to the author of these suggestions, for they realised that he wished to see a massive transfer of power to Brussels and away from individual governments. His comment back in 1988 that he expected to see 80% of all legislation in member countries coming from Brussels within ten years convinced many of his critics that the implications of any proposals from him needed to be carefully studied.

 To what extent had the hopes of the signatories of the Treaty of Rome been already fulfilled before the signing of the Maastricht Treaty?

The Maastricht Treaty

The Maastricht summit (December 1991) was an important step in the process of moving towards a united Europe. It laid the foundations for more radical moves towards a federal-style union which would follow later in the decade. The 'f' word was excluded from the agreement, but the commitment remained to work towards an ever closer union of the peoples of Europe.

The most important agreement was to fix a definite date for the achievement of economic and monetary union (EMU), 1999 at the latest, or 1997 if seven members met the necessary criteria. The French Government, backed by the Germans, were determined to set an irreversible date for the introduction of a single currency. Leaders in both countries understood that shifts in public attitudes could lead to a questioning of the idea, especially as the German people realise that their familiar D-mark will disappear. Tying the Community to a fixed date would, it was hoped, preempt the emergence of any such doubts. The commitment made to achieve union was strong even in countries such as Italy and Spain for whom achieving convergence looked to be a more daunting task.

As a quid pro quo (a 'something for something' bargain), the French backed the German desire for a powerful central bank which would be free from political interference. The Germans also gained their wish that there should be tough rules governing entry into EMU, involving strict criteria on budget deficits, interest rates and inflation. The effect of such conditions would be that countries with high inflation and low productivity would need to improve their performance, or become depressed areas of the Community.

In certain major areas, the Parliament was to have new powers of co-decision with the Council of Ministers, allowing it to reject a proposal if agreement could not be reached. This applied particularly to areas where the Council could decide matters on the basis of majority voting. Co-decision making covered issues relating to the internal market, and common policies for research and development, training and consumer affairs, among other things.

The Parliament could also request the Commission to draw up proposals where it decided, by a majority vote, that new EC legislation was needed. In addition, the Commission and its President would be subject to Parliamentary approval at the beginning of their mandate.

Some progress was made towards a common foreign and security policy. In foreign policy, the principles would have to be agreed unanimously, but it could be unanimously agreed to use weighted majority voting for their implementation. NATO was accorded the key role, but defence arrangements might be gradually Europeanised, with the WEU becoming the vehicle for implementing EC policies. For those 11 nations which were signatories to it, the Social Chapter (formerly the Social Charter) meant that they could embark on new measures as soon as they were agreed. No longer would they need to fear a British veto when they were seeking significant improvements in workers' rights.

What Maastricht Was All About

The concrete result was agreement on the text of a Treaty of European Union. In the words of the **Preamble**, it was designed to achieve 'an ever closer union among the peoples of Europe where decisions are taken as closely as possible to the citizens'.

The agreement marked a new phase in the life of the Community, establishing a Union based on three separate sections, or 'pillars'.

i. The New European Community

The first pillar built on the existing EC Treaty, and was a development of what was already occurring. In many ways, it formalised the Community's commitment to what happened in practice. In addition, it extended its scope to cover such matters as economic and monetary union and the growth in power of the European Parliament.

Maastricht took the SEA further. Internal frontiers were already due to be abolished by January 1993, and the new Treaty decreed that citizens of member states would automatically become members of the European Union. As such, they could live and work in any member state, stand for municipal office or for the European Parliament wherever they live, and vote in the country of residence.

The key clauses are concerned with the irrevocable path to economic and monetary union (see p273-285). Other important developments were that;

- The Council of Ministers would be able to act on a qualified majority vote. in some new policy areas, effectively removing the national veto
- The Parliament was to acquire greater powers
- A Parliamentary Ombudsman was to be established

ii. The Other Two Pillars

The other two pillars were based on intergovernmental cooperation, outside the scope of the existing treaties. In both cases, provision was made for reporting to the Council and Parliament.

The Second Pillar. The new arrangements on foreign and security policy were important. In the SEA, there had been a formal mention of European Political Cooperation, a process which was already in existence and which referred to the search for a Common Foreign and Security Policy (CFSP).

At Maastricht, this term was used and the cooperation involved was strengthened.

The pillar was intended 'to assert the Community's identity on the international scene'. It covered all aspects of European security, and included provisions for the eventual framing of a common defence policy, and perhaps a common defence force. Decision-making would generally be through unanimity, though the governments could decide to take implementing decisions by majority voting. Policy-making was to be through the WEU, but would not conflict with NATO obligations.

The Third Pillar. This was concerned with policing and immigration control, and dealt with matters ranging from asylum and illegal immigration, to the fight against drug-trafficking and terrorism. The intention was to agree a common asylum policy by the beginning of 1993, and to develop police cooperation to combat drug-trafficking and organised crime, through EUROPOL, the new international police unit.

The three Pillars, as described, were set out in Title One of the Treaty of Maastricht. Title Two, the longer section of more than 100 pages, was concerned with the complex but necessary legal amendments to the Rome Treaty.

In addition to the main document, there were 17 protocols and 33 declarations attached to the Maastricht Treaty. One important protocol was that on Social Policy, which was designed to improve working conditions and industrial employment practices. This is better known as the Social Chapter.

The texts, much criticised for their obscurity and complexity, were subject to ratification by all twelve national Parliaments of the member-states.

The Three Pillars of the Maastricht Treaty

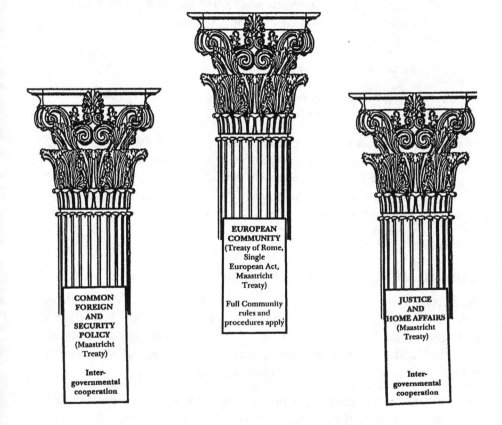

COMMON
FOREIGN
AND
SECURITY
POLICY
(Maastricht
Treaty)

Inter-
governmental
cooperation

EUROPEAN
COMMUNITY
(Treaty of Rome,
Single
European Act,
Maastricht
Treaty)

Full Community
rules and
procedures apply

JUSTICE
AND
HOME AFFAIRS
(Maastricht
Treaty)

Inter-
governmental
cooperation

New Ingredients in the Maastricht Agreement

i A common currency

ii An extension of the role of the Community, into, among other areas, such matters as justice and home affairs. The importance attached to some existing areas was to be increased, as in environmental protection and the social arena

iii The introduction of a common foreign and security policy

iv Increased powers for the European Parliament, especially over the appointment of the Commission

v Rights for European peoples in member countries. In the future, they would be 'European citizens', with a right to vote and stand in municipal and European elections in any other member state - eg, a British citizen could stand as a candidate for the European Parliament for a constituency in Italy

Immediate Reactions in Europe

The Germans were pleased to see a start made towards a common Foreign Policy, though progress towards political union and in the strengthening of the European Parliament was less than they would have liked. Above all, they welcomed the moves towards currency integration, and were pleased that the Bank was to be modelled on German lines.

For the French, the most significant step was the timetable towards monetary union, with the deadline for the single currency. They did not get the commitments on majority voting for the Council on matters of foreign policy which they favoured, nor the development of a defence policy more independent of the USA.

Spain, Portugal and Greece obtained the concession of more funds for the poorer countries of the Community, and Greece was to be allowed to enter negotiations with a view to joining the WEU, the future defence arm of The Twelve, in 1993.

The Netherlands, in its Presidency of the Council, had brokered an agreement, despite the odds. The fact was that everyone wanted an agreement, so that concessions were made all round. The text was designed to ensure that there was something for everyone, for each national leader obtained some trophies to take back home so that he could claim some national benefit and Community progress.

There was disappointment and irritation about special treatment for the British, for as the Dutch Premier put it; 'The United Kingdom is very much the same, except that this Prime Minister does not have a handbag'. Progress was less than some would have liked, and the British again seemed to have applied the brakes. But the majority could comfort themselves with the thought that, in the end, those nations which initially lag behind in their commitments, do usually eventually catch up with the others.

Immediate Reactions in Britain

British tactics had been influenced by short-term considerations, such as not upsetting the Tory Right. Most Conservatives were highly relieved by the outcome of the summit, for after all of the inter-party strife which led up to it, the result was one which many of them could accept. A damage-limitation exercise was needed, and they felt that, by a deft performance, John Major had secured a negotiating triumph and won 'game, set and match'.

British national interests had been protected, for many of the things they feared most had been omitted from the Treaty. Majority-voting on key issues of foreign policy had not been approved, so that Britain still retained a theoretical right to act alone if it so wished. The 'f' word had been dropped, so that Conservatives could reassure themselves that they were no longer on a conveyor-belt to a federal future. Above all, no irrevocable decision had been made to join a single currency (Britain could 'opt-in' at a later date), and the Government did not sign up for the much-despised Social Chapter.

Though the British representatives felt that a victory had been achieved by these two 'opt-out' clauses, many commentators suspected that if the others did go ahead as planned on economic and monetary union, Britain would not be able to afford to stand aside from a single currency. But the outcome had helped the Prime Minister with his party difficulties in the short term. The Germans and French at least understood British anxieties over this matter. They were more surprised that the Government refused to sign up for Euro-social legislation aimed at providing minimum standards for working conditions.

The Prime Minister claimed that the most important achievement was to set a date for Eastern Europe to negotiate entry. This was in line with the Thatcherite belief that progress should be made to bring in the new democracies, however frail they were and however feeble their economies. Such a move might have the convenient spin-off of slowing down steps to closer integration in Europe. This seemed to ignore the realities of the post-Maastricht situation, for EMU would make it harder for such new nations to achieve membership.

To their opponents, it seemed that Britain was again travelling in the slow lane, doomed to become a second-division player on the European scene. Labour spoke of 'Euro-Luddites', politicians who feared social progress and were indifferent to workers' rights. It liked the minimum standards which the Social Chapter contained, for the programme offered extended maternity rights, better provision for child-care and fairer treatment for part-time workers.

The argument about the 'social dimension' assumed an importance in the British reactions which was almost out of proportion to its contents. To Conservatives, they had been saved from 'creeping socialism'. For Labour, Britain was left semi-detached from Europe and doomed to be the most backward nation in the Community in its social provision. Yet some of its content was a drawing together or 'codification' of existing practice in the more advanced members of the EC, and other sections were little more than an aspiration to be worked towards over an unspecified period of time.

The Long and Difficult Road to Ratification

The immediate outcome of the Maastricht summit was a feeling of satisfaction among many of the European leaders who took part, for each had come away with something which could be displayed to the electorate at home as a personal triumph of skilful negotiation. Public reactions initially seemed modestly encouraging, although there was little evidence of widespread popular rejoicing. Such Europhoria as there was among certain groups was to be much-tested prior to ratification (due for completion by January 1993) and in the years which followed as steps were taken towards the achievement of economic and monetary union.

Doubts in Denmark and France

For the Maastricht Treaty to come into force, it had to be ratified by all the Parliaments of all the member-states. The target date for ratification was given as Jan 1, 1993, so that the Treaty could be operative from 1994, with the title European Union then replacing that of the European Community.

The process soon ran into difficulties, though the Treaty was approved by the European Parliament early in 1992. In the debates, there was much criticism of the 'democratic deficit' in the Community. The Parliament wanted a substantial increase in its powers and warned the Council that it would not agree to the acceptance of any new members in the EC until this issue has been tackled.

By the Spring, however, it was becoming apparent that there were growing misgivings in several countries. In Denmark, the Treaty was approved by a strong majority in the Folketing, but in a referendum in June 1992, the Danish people narrowly rejected it. Although there were only 48000 votes between the two sides, the verdict caused a political earthquake. The effect was to kill the Treaty unless there was to be another vote which reversed the stand taken, for the Treaty had to be ratified by all member countries. This suggested that either there must be renegotiation to allay Danish fears, or that the other eleven must go ahead on their own.

Meanwhile, other countries pressed ahead with their own ratification. In Ireland, later in the same month, the electorate voted strongly in favour of

101

the Treaty. The 'Yes' vote exceeded expectations, and this gave a boost to the process of ratification after the shock of the Danish setback. For the President of the European Commission, Jacques Delors, the result was no surprise; 'Given their geographical position, their demographic growth and their population, their attachment to the European Community is vital, and not just for the money'. Nonetheless, as a net beneficiary from the EC, the Irish had a strong reason to favour the further development of the Community.

However, the mood of many people in France was becoming more sceptical, and opposition to Maastricht was strong on the far Left and far Right. The situation was worsened by growing discontent with changes to the CAP (see p319-321) which upset the farming vote and helped to fuel anti-EC feeling. In September, the French gave a very narrow (50.5%-49.5%) endorsement to Maastricht.

For the French to stagger over the hurdle so perilously was in some respects a surprise, for they had always been in the forefront of the move towards European integration. Nonetheless, that they did so at all created a huge sense of relief in other EC capitals.

Solving the Danish Problem

Attention turned to attempts to resolve the Danish problem. The Danish voters needed to be assured that, among other things, the EC would develop in a more 'user-friendly'and decentralised manner, so that the drift of power from national states to Brussels could be reversed (see the Note on Subsidiarity, p 104-105). There were cautious hopes that a formula could be found to enable the Danish Government to go back to the voters with a reasonable prospect of them giving approval to the Treaty.

In October, seven of the eight parties in the Danish Parliament agreed on a package which would enable them to recommend ratification the second time around. They wanted a declaration making it clear that the Danes were not bound by EMU, could opt out of the security provisions of Maastricht and would suffer no threat to their superior social and environmental standards. The EC was also expected to find ways of bringing about more openness in its decision-making processes, and a strengthening of its Parliament.

The Edinburgh Council, December 1992

During the British Presidency of the European Council, a summit was convened at Birmingham in October 1992. This dealt mainly with the problem of making the EC more meaningful and acceptable to the peoples of Europe, and among other things it spent some time on an elaboration of the idea of subsidiarity. It was left to a second gathering in Edinburgh to find solutions for the remaining problems.

i The Danish Problem Denmark gained the exemptions it wanted from the Maastricht Treaty, so that the way was cleared for a second referendum

ii Subsidiarity To effect the idea of subsidiarity, the European Commission was to withdraw laws in some limited areas

iii The Budget Budgetary disagreements were resolved in a seven-year deal, by which there was to be a phased increase in budgetary contributions to 1.27% of each country's GDP, more money was to be available for the Cohesion Fund, with particular help for the poorest four countries and Britain was to retain its rebate for the time being (the Delors Two package)

iv Transparency Certain meetings of the Council of Ministers were to be televised, more information was to be made available about the voting and the language of EC legislation was to be made clearer

v Enlargement Negotiations with Austria, Finland and Sweden were to begin at the start of 1993, and with Norway a few months later

vi The Economy An economic growth package worth £24b was to be used on infrastructure schemes to stimulate economic growth

vii The Parliament Membership of the European Parliament was to be increased, to allow for German unification; Britain was to gain an extra six new MEPs.

Much of this did not require renegotiation of the 1991 agreement, but rather rights of exemption and clarification of certain areas. The Danish issue was examined at the Edinburgh Summit in December 1992, along with a series of budgetary issues. The 'loose-ends' of the Maastricht Treaty were finally tidied up.

This was a settlement which all the twelve members of the Community badly needed. Several problems were resolved, and each country gained something suitable. John Major wanted a 'political success', after many doubts had been expressed about the success of the British Presidency.

A Note on Subsidiarity

The doctrine of 'subsidiarity' was first put forward by Pope Pius X1 in 1931. For him, it meant 'government at the lowest possible level'. The British Government placed much emphasis in late 1992 on the idea, for it seemed to be useful ammunition against those Tory rightwingers who feared that a 'federal super-state' was being created on the foundations of Maastricht. Subsidiarity could help to tame the so-called 'Brussels Monster', and bring about a decentralisation of decision-making.

Subsidiarity was written into the Maastricht Treaty, which insisted that decisions should be taken 'as closely as possible to the citizen'. In Article 3b, it was spelt out that,

> *In areas which do not fall within its exclusive competence, the Community shall take action, in accordance with the principle of subsidiarity, only if and in so far as the objectives for the proposed action cannot be sufficiently achieved by the Member States and can therefore, by reason of the scale or effects of the proposed action, be better achieved by the Community. Any action by the Community shall not go beyond what is necessary to achieve the objectives of this Treaty.*

Douglas Hurd, the then British Foreign Secretary, spoke in July 1992 about subsidiarity in this way,

In the wide areas outside the exclusive competence, the Community should ask two questions; is it necessary for the Community to act; if so, to what extent? Even in the areas where national governments have by treaty given the Community exclusive competence, the institutions of the Community should ask to what extent do we need to act to secure the full objectives of the Treaties, bearing in mind that excessive intrusion is one of the accusations most often brought against it.

Jacques Delors tried to reassure the British and others, by stressing that under the principle, matters such as internal security, justice, planning, education, culture and health should remain the responsibility of member states. Some continental MEPs expressed the concern that subsidiarity could be used as an excuse to weaken integration. They feared that the cloak of subsidiarity was being used to enable the British Government to 'kill off' environmental and social directives in which Britain lagged behind.

At Edinburgh, new procedures were agreed to 'fill out' the doctrine which only had much meaning when applied to particular policies. In future, national power was to be the rule, and EC power the exception. The EC was to act only when member states could not achieve the desired goal as well themselves.

There was no question of challenging the existing powers of the Community. However, the Commission agreed to withdraw or amend 21 pieces of actual and draft legislation, as opposed to the 72 favoured by Britain. They include matters such as the treatment of animals in zoos, the harmonisation of gambling regulations and certain food labelling directives.

See also p451-455, for a discussion of subsidiarity and its relationship to federalism.

Britain and the Ratification Process

The British Government decided not to have a referendum, and the Government pledged itself to go ahead with ratification despite signs of growing opposition in Europe to the Treaty. The Maastricht Bill was brought before the House of Commons and given a Second Reading in May, 1992. The Prime Minister sold it to his rightwing as a decentralising Treaty, emphasising what the Government had not signed up for. Labour broadly accepted the economic, social and political framework of the Treaty, but could not endorse the Government's position because of its double 'opt-out'. It particularly disliked the decision not to embrace the Social Chapter.

After the Danish setback, Mr Major promised that he would not return the Bill for a Third Reading until a satisfactory solution had been found to the 'Danish problem'. Meanwhile, he ran into an additional problem, for after a period of intense speculation in the financial markets in August the Government was forced to withdraw from the ERM (see p277-279), and allow the pound to float down. This only served to strengthen anti-EC feeling, and on the Right there were some Conservatives who were relieved to have escaped from the shackles of the ERM and saw the necessity for withdrawal as an indication of the problems caused when ministers tried to tie Britain in to European financial systems. A growing band were becoming distinctly anti-EC, although they often referred to themselves as 'Euro-sceptics'.

At the special Summit held in Birmingham in October to discuss how the European public could be better reconciled to the Maastricht process, the Prime Minister was urged to bring about a speedy British ratification. It was accepted that he had difficulty over the issue, and discussion was given to how he could be helped along - for instance, by 'beefing up' the notion of 'subsidiarity', which involved more precisely setting out the limits of Community action.

The passage of the Maastricht Bill was slow and, for the Government, agonising. The successful completion of a second Danish referendum (56.8%-43.2%) in May 1993 encouraged ministers as they fought for the measure against the hostility of the Tory Right and the opposition parties who saw a chance to discomfit the Government on an issue on which it was very vulnerable. The British were finally able to ratify the Maastricht Treaty in August 1993.

A legal challenge in Germany threatened to derail the ratification process, for some opponents argued that the Treaty fundamentally altered the German Constitution. This last-minute move also failed. As a result there were no further obstacles to negotiate. Ratification was completed in all member states, and on November 1 1993 the new European Union came into force.

Assessment

No-one could be sure of exactly where the agreement would lead, or that the necessary convergence of the European economies in preparation for EMU would come about. However, other members were intent on strengthening and uniting the Community. In an uncertain Europe, where the East was in confusion, and in France and Germany there was the possibility of a rightwing backlash, the wish of many Europeans was to see irreversible progress towards their ultimate goal. Their concern was to stop Britain from undermining the whole enterprise.

The future looked uncertain, with talk of a major world recession, and with the most important economies of the postwar years, Germany, Japan and the United States, all beset by difficulty. Whether the preparations for EMU could survive a sustained recession could not be predicted, but a downturn in the world economy was a threat to the Maastricht initiatives.

Yet although concessions had to be made to keep the British 'on board', the other nations were determined to ensure that the idea of European unity would not go away. A future European super-state might seem to be a mirage, but within a few years the signatories would almost certainly be ready to contemplate their next steps. For all of its uncertainties and ambiguities, this was what Maastricht was ultimately all about. There was a real possibility that it could launch the old European Community even more explicitly towards a federal-style union.

?

Why did the Maastricht Treaty, signed in early 1992, not come into effect until November 1993?

Would the pioneers of postwar European cooperation have been proud of the Maastricht Treaty?

Life after
Maastricht

In the aftermath of signing the Treaty on European Union, European leaders were much preoccupied with selling the Treaty to their often doubtful electorates. The Commission drew up its proposals to finance the measures which had been decided, and this package (Delors Two) aroused conflict because some states were unenthusiastic about paying more into the Community largely to finance the Cohesion Fund. Eventually, the spending plans were agreed at the Edinburgh Council (see p103). Otherwise, the difficulties of 1992-93 were mainly over ratification.

In the period since then, there has been growing disquiet in parts of the new European Union over its role and performance. Anti-Brussels sentiment has not been confined to Britain, though Euroscepticism has been a persistent feature of the Westminster scene. A small group of hard-core critics on the British political Right have caused regular difficulties for the Prime Minister, and to ensure a degree of unity within his party he has found it necessary to make concessions to appease them. Tory policy has edged to the Right, and the pressure on Mr Major to make it clear that there will be no single currency in the next Parliament if there is another Conservative Government has been strong.

British ministers have strongly supported the policy of enlargement of the Union, and in 1995 three new countries were admitted. Agreement on membership was reached with four countries, and in three of them the voters backed the decision in a referendum - Austria, Finland and Sweden. In the fourth, Norway, the electorate was unconvinced of the merits of joining and rejected this second opportunity to do so.*

Enlargement to 15 (the **Fourth Enlargement**) is likely to be followed in the coming years by the accession of new members, for there are several countries queueing up to enter the Union (see p439-445). The policy of widening the membership continues to appeal to the British Government because it makes it less likely that the deepening process can be easily accomplished. Many Germans are more doubtful about accepting new entrants, fearing that as paymasters of the Union they will be required to support the weaker economies of Central and Eastern Europe. However, the Government has remained committed.

Enlargement also makes it more difficult for the Union to operate on a unanimity basis, and many members are keen to see an extension of qualified majority voting. This and other issues are up for consideration at the Intergovernmental Conference in 1996 (see p435-437), when many features of the Maastricht Treaty are due for review. By then, another decision will need to be taken, concerning the timing of any move to a single currency, the key step in moving towards Economic and Monetary Union.

As preparations for the IGC got underway, two familiar faces were missing from the European scene. Both Jacques Delors and Francois Mitterrand had been much identified with the burst of Euro-activity in the 1980s. A new President of the Commission, Jacques Santer, took over in January 1995, and in the elections for a new French President, Jacques Chirac emerged victorious over his socialist rival.

* *The First and Fourth Enlargements left EFTA with a much reduced membership. Currently, there are four countries in the organisation, Iceland, Liechtenstein, Norway and Switzerland. The first three are members of the EEA, and thus have some of the benefits of the single market without the commitment of full EU status.*

Jacques Delors; His Contribution to the Development of the EU

Delors is French, a Catholic, a Socialist and a Federalist, and three of these made him a 'bete noire' to Mrs Thatcher. Despite British misgivings about his attitudes and role, John Major supported an extension of his Presidency, so that he served a further two years, after two four year terms. His acceptance of what he termed this 'crown of thorns' for an extended period was conditional on evidence that EC leaders would not abandon Maastricht or the goal of union. He might have preferred to retire gracefully after the initial Danish rejection of the TEU, but he decided that it was important to stay on and prevent the Maastricht process from falling apart.

During his ten years, he was an active and interventionist President who intellectually dominated his colleagues. He was driven forwards by a single-minded vision of European integration, and his work to promote the single market, economic and monetary union, the Social Chapter and his package of anti-unemployment measures (Delors Two) entitles him for consideration as one of the architects of the drive towards European unity.

He was much involved in the Maastricht negotiations, and believed it was the best Treaty that could be obtained in the circumstances - faced as the participants were by British 'intransigence'. But it was not the outcome that he personally wanted. He saw it as a mixture of obscure, technocratic and sometimes undemocratic elements which bore only the vaguest and most muted echo of the federalist ideals which had long inspired the goal of European union. In particular, he disliked the incomprehensibility of a treaty which had three separate decision-making 'pillars' built into it.

Yet the alternative to ratification was, he feared, a retreat to an inward-looking, impotent Europe plagued by the dangers of economic nationalism. In his bid to achieve backing for the TEU, he was fortunate in representing a large and committed member state, for the support of President Mitterrand (under whom he had once served as Finance Minister) provided him with a useful ally. Not that the two men always agreed. When Delors wished to streamline decision-making by creating a new 'political executive', it was too much for the French head of state; 'It's mad. What is he interfering for? No-one in Europe will ever want that. By being extremist, he is going to destroy what is feasible'.

The support which he did get enabled him to survive the often-stormy issues which beset him. His manner sometimes exacerbated his difficulties, for he preached Europe as a gospel, and was sometimes willing to override other European leaders who lacked his passion even if it caused offence.

Assessments of his contribution are usually generous to his reputation, although British Conservatives never found him to their liking. The tabloids were also hostile, hence *The Sun* headline below.

In 1995, on Mitterrand's retirement, French socialists hoped that he would stand as the candidate of the Centre-Left, for he seemed to be a likely winner. He did not, although the vacancy was his if he had wanted it. He preferred to play a quieter - perhaps academic - role, and lecture and write on Europe's present condition.

?

'No European politician since Charles de Gaulle has mattered so much in the domestic politics of neighbouring states. But whereas the General was a great national figure first and a European second. Delors is the exact reverse'

(The Guardian, 13.12.1994).

Do you agree with this estimate of Delors' importance?

Francois Mitterrand (1916-95); His Contribution to European Unity

After a long career in national politics under the Fourth and Fifth Republics, he became France's first socialist and longest-serving President, in 1981. He served in that capacity for fourteen years.

Mitterrand had a consistent attachment to the cause of Europe throughout his long career, and was concerned that the continent should acquire its own distinctive identity. He was also a Frenchman much concerned with traditional French interests.

He accepted the de Gaulle-inspired contours of French defence policy, symbolised by the independent nuclear deterrent, and ruthlessly pursued French aims if national concerns were at stake. Yet he was more willing than de Gaulle to concede a limited amount of French sovereignty in the European cause, for he placed much emphasis upon the importance of keeping Europe peaceful and prosperous.

 He was particularly fearful of any resurgence of German power, and believed that a united Europe could best make Germany safe and contain its ambitions. He tried to convince Frenchmen that European integration was the means to fulfil France's self-proclaimed mission to lead Europe.

Although he was helpful to the Thatcher Government over the budgetary dispute (see the Fontainebleau settlement), he often despaired of the British approach In 1987, he observed; 'Perhaps it was imprudent to admit Great Britain into the European Community in 1972, but since it is there one must make the best of it'.

In sending Jacques Delors to Brussels as a Commissioner, he took a decisive step, for it was the fellow-Frenchman who was to play a creative role from the mid-1980s onwards. Mitterrand generally backed Delors, and gave his blessing to the SEA. The verdict of Helmut Kohl was a shrewd one; 'He was a great patriot and a great European', the remark perhaps implying that there could be a tension between the two characteristics.

Francois Mitterrand

?

By the mid-1990s, there have been four enlargements of the Union. In what way have they changed its character?

Has Europe significantly advanced along the road to ever closer union?

Has British membership been good for the Union?

Why do you think that Delors was so disliked by sections of the tabloid press in Britain?

The Movement to Integration: A Theoretical Perspective

We have already briefly referred to the different theories which have been put forward to explain the development of postwar integration, federalism and functionalism (see p26-32). Monnet felt that intergovernmentalism was not enough, and that there was 'an intrinsic weakness' in a system of 'mere cooperation'. But as to whether he was himself a federalist or a functionalist is a matter of disagreement. **Burgess** took the view that he was 'primarily an economic functionalist and only secondly...an incremental federalist'.

The same difficulty has afflicted those commentators who have attempted to provide a theoretical explanation of the dynamics of integration - in other words, to explain how and why it has come about. The difficulty is all the greater because at different periods the Union has exhibited different tendencies, sometimes seeming to progress more by intergovernmental agreement, at others because of the inspiration of those who urge a federalist agenda.

The Union itself has undergone different stages of development. At some times, it has seemed to be stuck into a groove of stagnation and introspection, at others (usually when the economic outlook has seemed more promising) there are hopes for a further move forwards. In the periods of stagnation, little is heard of the long term possibilities and the dreams of ever closer union.

Theories of Integration; Why it Has Come About

In attempting to explain the transformation of Europe in the postwar period, various types of theories have been put forward to show why it came about;

- Some writers place their emphasis on the long-expressed search to establish the 'idea of Europe' in concrete terms, and see the events of the late forties as the fulfilment of a dream of European unity which has deep roots. Unity is therefore an expression of, or a search for, a distinctive set of European values. It was President Mitterrand who in 1988 observed that 'one day, Europe will have its own identity'. Europe is in this view seen as the 'cradle of civilisation', and postwar cooperation has attempted to restore the continent to its former glory and importance.

- Others see postwar cooperation as the result of the hostilities of World War Two which so shattered the economies of the main participants and made them aware of the need firstly to prevent such a war from ever happening again, and secondly to unite in a common bid to restore prosperity. Such motives were particularly strong in the early years after 1945, and for many writers they provided the inspiration behind postwar integration.

- A third explanation stresses that in the postwar world there has been a growing move towards interdependence, and that the progressive integration achieved by the European Union is a particularly good example of this. States have cooperated because of the necessity for this to be done. The problems they face increasingly require a response that goes beyond traditional national boundaries. Environmental problems, for instance, do not recognise traditional frontiers, and many difficulties in the financial markets require a coordinated response.

- Finally, there are those who stress the importance of national interests. They feel that for all the grandiose talk of the merits of cooperation and the dreams of the founding fathers, the main reasons for cooperation have derived from individual states pursuing their own advantage. On occasion - in fact on the continent, rather often - there has been obvious value in working together.

France and Germany had their own distinctive reasons for wanting a coal and steel community (see p41-45), and France today has good national reasons for wishing to see its past rival and now powerful ally locked firmly into a European entity strong enough to contain its power. In the same way, smaller states such as Belgium, Ireland and Luxembourg have sound reasons for wishing to see closer ties in Europe for as members of such an organisation they carry more clout in European affairs than would otherwise be possible. For many British politicians, the perceived advantages of close union have often been less apparent - hence their wish to pursue intergovernmental cooperation, as is appropriate for the task in hand.

Idealism and pragmatism have both been prominent features of the postwar era. For many countries in Europe the two impulses have gone hand-in-hand. They have wanted to see integration develop for the reasons we have reviewed. For Britain and at times other nations, the advantages of cooperation have often been less self-evident. Britain, Denmark (on occasion) and France (under de Gaulle), have detected more merit in the intergovernmental approach in which states work together as seems necessary and desirable. They favour a Europe des Patries, whereas most countries have been inspired by the early visionaries and attracted by a more federal future.

Such differing approaches have led **Nugent** to conclude that there has been no 'common and coherent integrationist force at work in Western Europe. Far from the states being bound together in the pursuit of a shared visionary mission, relations between them have frequently been extremely uncomfortable and uneasy. Even in the EC, which has been at the integrationist core, the course of the integration process has varied considerably'.

How the Drive Towards Integration Has Been Accomplished

Functionalism

Several of the early attempts to explain the development of the Community reflected the functionalist theories which began to flourish back in the interwar years. **David Mitrany** put forward an approach based on the idea of 'the common index of need'. There are many areas where the needs of governments overlap, and for him the best way of resolving them was to act in a way that cuts across national boundaries.

In Mitrany's words, it was 'not a matter of surrendering sovereignty, but merely of pooling so much of it as may be needed for the joint performance of the particular task'. There would be a shared agency which would have supranational authority over the specific policies included within its orbit.

Mitrany was thinking in terms of a number of such international agencies, not because he saw supranationalism as in any way preferable to the idea of the independent state but because he thought it was the better way of running services and fulfilling needs which cut across national boundaries. He was not thinking in terms of one supranational agency which could preside over several sectors. The schemes put forward after 1945 went beyond this form, for they were not merely a series of complementary functional agencies. They had an end goal in view, and this was a federal one - what **Martin Holland** has called 'functionalist principles with a political objective'.

Functional theory has recognised that once you go down the route of allowing the creation of several independent bodies in which several members participate, then this has an effect on relations between those countries which find themselves becoming increasingly interdependent. Moreover, the peoples in the nations involved become used to a situation in which cooperation extends across frontiers. 'They are weaned away from their allegedly irrational nationalistic impulses toward a self-reinforcing ethos of cooperation' **(Pentland)**.

Functionalism therefore accustoms people to a new way of thinking, and thereby helps to bring about attitudinal change.

Neofunctionalism

Later writers, who saw the way in which postwar Europe was developing, saw deficiencies in the functionalist approach as a way of explaining what was happening on the continent. **Ernst Haas** put forward his theory of **neo-functionalism** which was better attuned to experience of the way in which the European Community was operating when he wrote.

Neofunctionalism accepted that there was a process which might lead to federation, and that there would be institutions with supranational authority over several areas of policy, particularly economic ones. As a result of this growing cooperation, so greater political unity would come about by essentially secretive means. Haas was less concerned with achieving a change in popular attitudes, for he believed that the move to integration would come about as a result of the leadership of an elite. Popular backing would come later, when the beneficial results of the policies was widely apparent.

In the neo-functionalist perspective, closer integration would evolve as a result of **'spillover'**. The more cooperation there was in one area, so there would be a spillover effect into other areas for few policies operate in isolation. Decisions in one area have repercussions elsewhere.

Haas' theory is widely seen as having validity for the period through to the 1960s, but for the next two decades there was little sign of spillover and steps towards integration. Indeed, what was happening was that there was an assertion of national self-interest, and any attempts by the Commission to extend the area of central decision-making ran into national opposition which had to be resolved by mediation between the competing states. **Harrison's** work reflected this sombre view of the prospects of step-by-step integration, suggesting that there was 'no evidence...of the beguiling automaticity...of economic integration leading eventually to political integration'.

This more cautious view reflected the experience of the period until the 1980s, but then the pace of change accelerated and new developments came about. **Keohane and Hoffmann** have concluded that the Haas approach is about right, and that what we have now is a supranational style of decision-making in which member states 'seek to attain agreement by means of compromises' rather than by vetoing proposals unconditionally. In their view, such a bargaining process (as each side seeks to view its national interests in the light of the common interests of the Union) is a prerequisite to spillover. The more agreement that can be reached, the greater the chances of spillover occurring.

At the heart of this approach is **intergovernmental cooperation,** and change often results less from a burst of what Keohane and Hoffman refer to as 'heady idealism', and more because of 'a convergence of national interests'. Discussion at conferences where disputes are ironed out can help to promote a consensus, and as a result the process of integration can move forward. **Spillover is not enough to explain the process of integration; it requires among other things what Holland calls 'the bargaining process characteristic of intergovernmentalism'.**

Holland has concluded that neofunctionalism as an explanation for the way the Union operates is useful in that it stresses three highly relevant features;

i   It suggests that there is a connection between the process of economic and political integration, with the former being a key factor in helping to promote the latter - 'although the precise form of political union is left intentionally ill-defined' ii The process of spillover provides the necessary, but not automatic, link between economics and politics'

iii It acknowledges that that via the institutions of the union, the individual states have an important part to play at intergovernmental level in promoting integration, when it seems to be appropriate to their interests.

The issue of the form of political integration in Europe is on the agenda with the approach of the 1996 Intergovernmental Conference. As nations prepare for this, Holland detects that 'The theory of a supranational-style of decision-making where compromises enhancing common interests have superseded the veto principle of national protection, appears to be of utility once again'.

NB For a full discussion of federalism, and for further discussion of Monnet's outlook, see pages 28-30 and 451-455.

The Varying Pace of Integration

Whatever the dynamics which promote the development of the European Union, what is clear is that it moves in phases. Sometimes there appears to be a period of stagnation, at others one of great movement. Suddenly the circumstances are right and the opportunity presents itself for a new momentum and drive onwards, and when such opportunities arise, theory must always take second place. In the words of Jean Monnet;

> *The unification of Europe, like all peaceful revolutions, takes time - time to persuade people, time to change men's minds, time to adjust to the need for major transformations. But sometimes circumstances hasten the process, and new opportunities arise. Must they be missed simply because they were not expected so soon?.*

Such a view expresses the pragmatism of the man often referred to as the 'founder of modern Europe'. As we have seen (see p31-32), historians differ in their description of his approach to integration, for whereas some literature labels him as a federalist - because he shared the ultimate federal vision - other writings (such as that quoted below) place him in the functional camp, because he preferred a gradual, sector by sector, transfer of sovereignty to Community level. The description of him as a neo-functionalist recognises the final destination which he favoured, and the approach which he thought was best geared to achieving that long term aim.

Pascal Fontaine, a French Professor in Political Studies, has recently summarised the evolution of the Union in this way;

> *The vision of a new Europe which would transcend national antagonism finally emerged from the resistance movements which had sprung up to resist totalitarianism during the Second World War. Altiero Spinelli, the Italian federalist, and Jean Monnet, the man who provided the inspiration for the Schuman Plan...were the main proponents of two approaches, the federalist and the functionalist, which were to provide the impetus for European integration...Today, the two approaches have merged in a conviction that national and regional authorities [ie, the federal approach] need to be matched by independent, democratic European institutions with responsibility for areas in which joint action is more effective than action by individual states [the supranational approach]; the single market, monetary policy, economic and social cohesion, foreign and security policy.*

Differing Approaches to Integration Within the Union

Among The Fifteen, there are differing degrees of enthusiasm for the long term goal of closer union in Europe. Those who adopt the intergovernmental approach appreciate that there are benefits to be gained from cooperation, but wish to limit Union competence and go no further along the road to integration.

States have their own reasons for wishing to speed, delay or reverse the process, and this is related to the perceived advantages which membership brings. Those countries which have gained most out of the Union often are more willing to surrender sovereignty to it - especially if they are small countries which would count for little on their own.

Belgium, Holland and Luxembourg have less to lose for it is many years since they played a leading role in European affairs, even if they once had greater continental prestige. They are more willing to embrace supranationalism, and have not spent time in anguished debate on the question of a surrender of national independence. Such states (and indeed the majority of the others who currently make up the European Union) have been keen to see progress on several fronts, and are willing to push forward at greater speed towards an ever closer union.

Some large and powerful nations such as Germany and France have been strongly integrationist members. Both have found that they could reconcile national and European interests.

A minority, and sometimes a minority of one or two, have been anxious about the pace of development, and wish to call a halt to further moves to integration. They believe in the nation-state as the preferred means of protecting their national interests. They can see merit and perhaps necessity in developing cooperation of an intergovernmental type, but any loss of national sovereignty and independence is to them quite unacceptable. Britain and sometimes Denmark have usually adopted this approach.

Dr Klaus-Dieter Borchardt has attempted to distinguish between the two camps by labelling them as the confederalists and the federalists, the former favouring interstate cooperation and the latter integration;

> *Essentially the confederalist approach means that countries agree to cooperate with each other without ceding any of their national sovereignty...The...principle underlies what are known as the second and third pillars of the European Union...[this] does not...rule out the possibility of progress towards closer integration in these areas at some stage in the future.*

> *The federalist aims to dissolve the traditional distinctions between nation states...The result is a European federation in which the common destiny of its peoples...is guided and their future assured by common (federal) authorities.*

Theories of Integration; a Summary

Federalists

They wished to see a rapid movement towards their grand design, complete political unification - as implied by the term a 'United States of Europe'. Their vision and that of the neo-functionalists inspired the post-1945 generation. Spinelli was an enthusiastic federalist

Functionalists

More cautious in their approach, they preferred to work for unification sector by sector, as seemed necessary and appropriate. They favoured practical cooperation for the more efficient working of different economic and state functions, and would hand over power to a supranational body where this was the best way forward

Neofunctionalists

They expect integration to come about as a result of 'spillover', which may eventually bring about integration almost by stealth. Intergovernmental meetings can sometimes provide a push towards greater cooperation, via the bargaining process. Monnet could be fitted into this school, for he was always committed to a federal outcome, though he was often vague on detail - hence, the description of him as an 'incremental federalist'.

Intergovernmentalists

They favour cooperation between governments for their mutual advantage, a vision rather like de Gaulle's idea of a Europe des Patries. This is an essentially pragmatic rather than visionary approach

In postwar Europe, the main arguments over political cooperation have reflected the intergovernmental-supranational debate. Most continentals, be they outright federalists, functionalists or neofunctionalists, have seen the merits of closer union, and for many of them there has been the prospect that this may in time lead to some form of federal outcome. Others, the intergovernmentalists, have been wary of powers being transferred from the national to the Union level, and have sought to slow the pace of change and limit cooperation to the search for mutual benefit.

? .'Neofunctionalism has been the driving-force of the postwar movement to closer union in Europe'. Discuss.

Has idealism or pragmatism played a larger part in the move to unite Europe?

TEACH YOURSELF
To Recap

After 1945, Western European countries saw advantages in cooperation, for three main reasons,

   i   The need to rebuild their shattered economies

   ii To lay aside the old enmity of France and Germany, and bring about a more peaceful continent

   iii Fear of the Soviet Union and the spread of Communism

The main stages of this cooperation after 1945 were as follows;

	Economic	**Political**	**Military**
1945			
1946			
1947			
1948	OEEC		Brussels Pact
1949		Council of Europe	NATO
1950			
1951	ECSC		
1952			
1953			
1954			
1955	WEU		
1956			
1957	Treaties of Rome (EEC, Euratom)		
1958			
1959			
1960	EFTA		
1961	OECD		

Britain in 1945

In 1945, Britain was victorious; other (defeated or overrun) countries needed to change, Britain was complacent.

Three circles in British Foreign Policy,

   i   The Commonwealth

ii The 'special relationship' with the United States of America

iii Europe

Britain and The Six

i Talks leading to establishment of ECSC; Britain not involved in talks

ii Messina, talks leading to Treaties of Rome; Britain a spectator only

British Attempts to Join The Six

i 1961-63 Conservative attempt; blocked by De Gaulle

ii 1967 Labour attempt; blocked by De Gaulle

iii 1970-72 Conservative attempt; successful. E.Heath, PM

1972 Treaty of Accession

1973 Britain became a member of Community

European Community After 1973

The Six had become The Nine in 1973, with accession of Britain, Denmark and Ireland.

i In 1981, Greece joined.

ii In 1986, Portugal and Spain joined; The Ten became The Twelve.

iii In 1990, Germany united and the Community grew to 345m.

Early British Disputes Within EC

In 1975, a British referendum on continued membership of EC yielded a large 'yes' vote. Problems soon arose, particularly over;

i 'Unfair' budgetary contributions; settled at Fontainebleau

ii Common Agricultural Policy, which involved major share of EC budget.

1986 Single European Act

i Creation of a single internal market within the EC after 1992, in services such as banking, insurance, credit and securities

ii Standardisation of national technical standards for products

iii Easing of restrictions on living and working in another member state, with mutually recognised qualifications and diplomas.

1989 Delors Plan

Three stages to economic and monetary union. Britain fulfilled Stage One when it became a full member of European Monetary System, by joining Exchange Rate Mechanism, in 1990 (Left 1992).

British anxieties over idea of a single currency (then known as the ECU) and over the Social Charter, which was to become known as the Social Chapter. These and other issues to be resolved at Maastricht, in December 1991.

The Three Pillars of Maastricht

Foreign and Security Policy	The European Community, built on the Treaty of Rome and developing towards EMU	Justice and Internal Affairs

Problems Over Ratification

1992	June	Danish referendum; narrow defeat of Maastricht Treaty
	June	Irish referendum; strong support for Maastricht
	Sept	French referendum; support, but a very close shave

In Britain, serious internal problems within Conservative Party - especially on the Right. Many Conservatives disliked the idea of a 'federal' Europe, the single currency and the Social Chapter. Labour, strongly in favour of Social Chapter, not keen to 'bale out' a Government beset by problems.

Britain ratified in August 1993. New European Union in force from November 1, 1993.

In 1995, Austria, Finland and Sweden joined the EU, turning it into a Union of The Fifteen.

Membership of European Economic and Political Organisations (as in late 1995)

EU/EFTA members	Council of Europe	EFTA	EU	OECD
Austria	*		*	*
Belgium	*		*	*
Denmark	*		*	*
Finland	*		*	*
France	*		*	*
Germany	*		*	*
Greece	*		*	*
Iceland	*	*		*
Ireland	*		*	*
Italy	*		*	*
Liechtenstein	*	*		
Luxembourg	*		*	*
Netherlands	*		*	*
Norway	*	*		*
Portugal	*		*	*
Spain	*		*	*
Sweden	*		*	*
Switzerland	*	*		*
United Kingdom	*		*	*
Non-EU/EFTA				
Andorra	*			
Bulgaria	*			
Cyprus	*			
Czech Republic	*			
Estonia	*			
Hungary	*			
Latvia	*			
Lithuania	*			

Malta	*			
Poland	*			
Rumania	*			
San Morino	*			
Slovakia	*			
Slovenia	*		*	
Turkey	*			*
Non-European Countries				
Australia				*
Canada				*
Japan				*
Mexico				*
New Zealand				*
USA				*
Total	**34**	**4**	**15**	**25**

NB The EU/EFTA countries, other than Switzerland, together comprise the European Economic Area (EEA)

Questions to consider

1 Read the following document and answer the questions which follow;

Britain decides to join the EC.   Extract from the House of Commons debate, Oct.28, 1971, on the motion that, 'This House approves Her Majesty's Government's decision in principle to join the European Communities on the basis of the arrangements which have been negotiated'.

Tonight, the world is...watching Westminster, waiting to see whether we are going to decide that Western Europe should now move along the path to real unity - or whether the British Parliament, now given the choice, not for the first time...will reject the chance of creating a united Europe...it inspired the founders of the European Communities after the war...

The Commonwealth has, since then, developed into an association of independent countries...but the idea that it would become an effective economic or political, let alone military, bloc has never materialised...'

i. Why had Britain on previous occasions decided not to participate in the creation of a united Europe?

ii. 'Commonwealth or Common Market?'. Why did Britain decide to opt for a European future in the early 1960s?

iii. Why had previous attempts to join the EC proved unsuccessful? Why did the third attempt succeed?

2 Read the following extracts and then answer the questions which follow.

a *The Single European Act came into force on 1 July 1987. In place of unanimous decisions, qualified majority voting in the Council of Ministers was introduced. This was to enable the member states to speed up decision-making in many areas.*
Europe in Figures, Eurostat.

b *Thus the UK's acceptance of the Community was reflected in the absence of the EC as an issue in the 1987 national election campaign. However, there is a natural tendency both by the media and by politicians to use the Community as a scapegoat for the UK's own problems.*

The signing of the Single European Act shows how firmly embedded the UK has become in the EC. Its reservations were fewer than those of some other countries, though naturally there was some concern by the anti-marketeers, which was shared initially by the British government (especially over the extension of powers by the European Parliament and the extension of majority voting). But the outcome of the Single European Act was a pale shadow of the draft European Treaty, and the compromise disappointed the federalists since it omitted the word `union' in its title. Yet the anti-marketeers consider that the Single European Act has gone too far in eroding British sovereignty through the predominance of Community Law - even though this has arisen mainly from the Treaty of Rome rather than the additional provisions.

In both the House of Commons and the House of Lords, there was a large majority for the government. The British recognised, quite sensibly, that having joined the EC, the Single European Act offered an opportunity to exploit its potential further, in particular in the internal market in which majority voting suits the UK. Under the UK Presidency of the Council in the second half of 1986, many measures were pushed through to create an internal market, since it was recognised that these would occur anyway once the Single European Act was in force.

The Political Economy of Integration in the EC, Jeffrey Harrop

c   *Even in the UK very few people have a harsh word to say for the single market. Over half the company directors questioned in one recent analysis predicted a 5% increase in their turnover during the next five years consequent upon the single market. Three-quarters thought that the concept of a single market was likely to prove workable for British industry in practice. Simultaneously, general awareness was increasing in leaps and bounds. Strategic plans were being erected on all sides of this strange monolith marked `Europe: 1992'. Yet every survey so far conducted has revealed a frighteningly low level of planning amongst UK companies which do not already have strong links in other European countries. In other words, precisely the most vulnerable sector of UK Business.*

It is an odd paradox. We are looking forward to, expecting great benefit from, something that most of us know too little about. No-one can predict all the repercussions of 1992, though the basic objectives of the single market programme are well-known - to create a huge capitalist power, a true `Common Market' with a population of 320 million people, a market free of practically all restraint to competition, with no trade barriers and common industrial standards, an environment in which goods, services, capital and people can move freely across 12 very different nations.

And if this sounds alarming to businessmen who are used to operating only in domestic markets, it should be said that the process is quite inevitable and is already underway.

There are two predictions that one can make with confidence about the newly emerging Single European Market. First, it is likely to bring

accelerated economic growth. Second, it is certain to bring increased competitive pressure. The winners will be a large number of consumers. The losers will be a small but statistically significant and vociferous number of producers.
Business View no. 20, Ernst and Young, Winter 1988/89.

i What is meant by `qualified majority voting', and what advantages can it provide? Why is it contentious?

ii According to extract b, what evidence is there that the signing of the Single European Act indicated `how firmly embedded the UK has become in the EC'?

iii Why was the signing of the Act seen by its supporters as an obvious consequence of joining the European Community? What benefits were expected to follow from the passing of the Act? (Extracts b and c)

iv In what ways can the Act be regarded as a landmark in the development of the European Community?

v What anxieties did some people have about the possible consequences of the Single European Act?

3 Four Frenchmen have had an important impact on the development of Europe in the postwar era. Choose two of the statesmen listed, and explain their distinctive contribution and importance;

Jean Monnet   General de Gaulle
Francois Mitterrand Jacques Delors

4 'The Father of Modern Europe'. Does Jean Monnet deserve the title often bestowed upon him?

5 To what extent have the federal dreams of the early pioneers of postwar European cooperation been realised?

6 Identify and assess the changes introduced by the Single European Act?

7 'Maastricht marked an important turning point in the development of modern Europe'. Discuss.

8 'The membership of the European Union has substantially increased since the original signing of the Rome Treaties'. How and why has this happened?

9 Why have many Europeans wanted to see closer integration in the years since 1945? Why has integration been difficult to achieve?

10 Compare the functionalist and federalist approaches to the development of postwar European integration. Which approach has been more influential?

11 'The main impulse behind European integration has been functionalism rather than federalism'. Discuss.

12 What do you understand by 'intergovernmentalism'? To what extent, post-Maastricht, are we entering another intergovernmental phase? (ULEAC)

13 Is the description of the UK as a 'reluctant European' justified? (ULEAC)

Chapter Two:
Institutions

The Institutions of the European Union

The Treaty of Rome is the equivalent of the written constitution of the EU, and the other treaties and acts such as the Treaty of Paris, the Maastricht Treaty and the Single European Act are like amendments to the basic text. They lay down the structure of the main institutions and the rules by which they operate.

The Union decision-making process involves five main institutions, some of which are more supranational and others more intergovernmental in character. We will firstly examine those which are **supranational** before moving on to those which are intergovernmental.

The Commission

Organisational Details

This comprises 20 Commissioners, including 2 from the UK, nominated by the governments of the member states. It is expected that they are people 'whose independence and general competence is beyond doubt'. They serve for five years, and each Commissioner has responsibility for a specific area of policy and its development. The senior British representative is Leon Brittan who holds the key external affairs brief, and Neil Kinnock has responsibility for the transport portfolio.

Each Commissioner has the support of a 'cabinet' (the French term) or private office, a group of four or five advisers selected to form a personal staff and headed by a 'chef'. Some members of this personal staff may come from the Commissioner's own country and serve on a short-term basis, others are members of the Commission allocated to the Commissioner for his temporary use. These people help him supervise the range of his specific activities, and keep him informed about the whole work of the Commission so that he is prepared for its weekly meeting.

The President and Vice-Presidents of the Commission are chosen by the governments of The Fifteen from among the 20, for a two year period. Since the Maastricht Treaty, the appointment of all Commissioners is subject to the agreement of the European Parliament and they can only be removed by a special vote in the same body. The Commission can collectively be dismissed by the Parliament if a two-thirds majority of those present vote them out of office. Although there have been censure motions, no such vote has taken place, perhaps partly because the sanction is such a drastic one.

The Council of Ministers or the Commission can apply to the Court of Justice to have an individual Commissioner removed, if he 'no longer fulfils the conditions required for the performance of his duties or if he has been guilty of serious misconduct'. Without very convincing evidence of inability or misconduct, an individual Commissioner is hard to remove.

Whatever their background as active national politicians, they are expected as Commissioners to act as independent and loyal servants of the Union. They are bound by oath to act in the interests of the EU as a whole, for article 157 states that the Commission 'shall neither seek nor take instructions from any government or from any other body'. Past experience suggests that most have been able to make the necessary adjustment in their attitude and behaviour, and this has sometimes been the cause of some disappointment to the national governments which appointed them - hence, Mrs Thatcher's complaint that one of her appointees, Lord Cockfield, had 'gone native'.

It is the right of any member government to nominate and renominate its particular Commissioner. If he or she is perceived to have been overly committed to the integrity of the position occupied then membership may not be renewed. Lord Cockfield was not invited to serve for a second term.

The Commission meets weekly and takes decisions on the basis of unanimity where possible, or if not by a simple majority vote. While it is desirable that all are fully committed to any given policy, it is inevitable that there are differences within a large body whose members have dissimilar backgrounds and repesent different political traditions.

Based mainly in Brussels, the Commission has a staff of some 15,000, 5000 of whom are translators. (By comparison, the British Department of Education has 5500 staff.) The executive tasks of the Commission are spread among civil servants in 26 Directorates-General, each dealing with a different area of responsibility, such as energy and agriculture.

Role and Importance

The Commission is responsible for proposing Union policy and legislation, and then it implements decisions when they are taken by the Council. It supervises the day-to-day execution of EU policies, such as the encouragement of regional and industrial development, and the employment of young people; it also manages the Common Agricultural Policy. As the guardian of the Treaties, it monitors the application of Community law, and initiates legal measures against member countries which fail to comply with EU initiatives.

Its work as the watchdog of the Union is a task which can incur odium among some member countries. Where an infringement of the Treaties is judged to have taken place it can refer the issue to the Court of Justice for a ruling. Firstly, the Commission notifies the state of its view in a 'reasoned opinion' that there is a treaty violation and requests an explanation within one to two months. If the report is unsatisfactory or does not even come, then the Commission resorts to the Court whose decision will be binding. Few cases ever get to the Court, although the number of alleged infringements has been on the increase.

The Commission is similar in its workings and importance to the High Authority created for the European Coal and Steel Community, only in this case the responsibilities of the organisation it runs are much more wide-ranging (The two bodies became one as a result of the Merger Treaty of 1965). In both cases, the role as described sounds rather managerial, but the obligation to act as the guardian of the Rome Treaty is one of fundamental importance.

In several ways the Commission can have a substantial impact on the making of decisions in the EU. Its powers are extensive, for the various treaties have allocated several tasks as part of its broad purpose of providing for 'the proper functioning and development of the common market'. Among other things, it must 'ensure that the provisions of this Treaty [Rome] and the measures taken by the institutions pursuant thereto are applied', 'formulate recommendations or deliver opinions on matters dealt with in this Treaty, if it expressly so provides or if the Commission considers it necessary', and 'have its own power of decision and participate in the shaping of measures taken by the Council and by the Assembly [Parliament]'.

The Role of the President

The ECSC was shaped by the guiding impetus of Jean Monnet who became its first President, and he imparted a very political character to that role. This has been the case with the Presidency of the Commission. Under the vigorous and creative leadership of particular Presidents, notably Walter Hallstein, Roy Jenkins and Jacques Delors (see p91-93, 105 and 111-112), full use has been made of the scope which the office provides, although there have been some periods in between when less authority has been exercised. Much depends upon the personal dynamism and commitment of the individual chosen. Some have been able to adopt a high profile and have been particularly successful in imposing a sense of collective identity on their colleagues and providing a sense of purpose.

However strong the degree of leadership shown by past Presidents, they have been known as persons of high quality and national stature at the time of their appointment. Jenkins had been a Home Secretary and

Chancellor of the Exchequer in Britain, Gaston Thorn a Prime Minister of Luxembourg and Delors a Finance Minister under Mitterrand.

Making the Choice

The President is appointed by the European Council after a process of bargaining between heads of government. There is no necessity to ensure that at some time a representative of every nation has a turn in office, although informally it is assumed that there will be a fair allocation if agreement can be reached.

The appointment can be a cause of dispute, as has been the case in recent years. Surprisingly, Britain backed the reappointment of Jacques Delors for a brief third term (1985-89, 1989-93, 1993-95), perhaps in the hope that after a longer period of service its own senior Commissioner, Leon Brittan, a former Conservative minister, might be a likely choice as his successor. Delors was a forceful President and a difficult act to follow. He sometimes antagonised his colleagues by seeming to by-pass consultation with them and issuing personal statements which reflected his own views and those of his advisers rather than those of the Commission as a whole. Nonetheless, his ability to move the work of the Community forward was widely seen as a positive contribution.

Responsibilities of the President

The President has very important duties, including, among others;

- The allocation of portfolios to newly-appointed Commissioners

- Chairing meetings of the Commission

- Dealing with the specifics of policy, in setting out the annual programme in the European Parliament debate (January)

- More generally, providing a sense of direction to EU development

- Acting as the voice of the Commission at international gatherings, and at EU meetings, including those of the European Council and occasions when there is a need to resolve any conflict between the institutions.

Delors was a particularly high-profile President, and his comments and actions often prompted some dismay among the member states, not least in London. He was an unashamed federalist, at a time when Britain was led by a Prime Minister who was an unashamed nationalist, and the Thatcher Government expressed unease at the direction in which he was leading the Commission. He became a target for regular abuse at the Conservative Conference and in the tabloid press ('Up Yours, Delors', as the *Sun* so colourfully expressed it).

Some members of the Thatcher and Major Governments would have been happy to see some curbing of the powers of the President and of the whole Commission, for as a leading supranational element in the institutional structure the Commission exercised too much influence in their eyes. They would have preferred to see a new emphasis on the intergovernmental aspects of the Union, and particularly on the role of the Council.

In 1994, there was some acrimony over the choice of the new President, for several countries wanted Jean-Luc Dehaene, the Belgian Prime Minister whose views were too federalist for the British Government. Compromise eventually fell on Jacques Santer, whose views are broadly similar, if in the past less assertively expressed. As **Holland** observes, it is somewhat ironic that 'the focus for supranational authority is, ultimately, decided according to intergovernmental demands'.

For those alarmed by the alleged democratic deficit within the Union, one suggestion sometimes put forward is that the President of the Commission (and perhaps his colleagues) should be democratically elected by the same voters who choose members of the European Parliament.

Powers

The importance of the President rests on few formal powers, for he has no say over the choice of the people with whom he works in the Commission. His appointment of portfolios may be limited by the claims of more senior members of the team. If they have been reappointed, they become eligible for a senior position. Moreover, in making his allocation he may be subject to some pressure from individual governments. Neither can he dismiss a fellow Commissioner.

Jacques Santer

Mr Dehaene and I come from the same political family and we have the same commitment to European Union.
Jacques Santer, President of the European Commission, 1995-?

For many years, Jacques Santer has contributed to the building of the European Union. He helped set up the European Monetary System, introduced the Single European Act which extended the powers of the European Parliament and brought about the Maastricht Treaty.
Chancellor Kohl.

Mr Santer's policies and opinions on the future of Europe are indistinguishable from those of Mr Dehaene.
Jack Cunningham, then Labour's Foreign Affairs spokesman.

Mr Santer is a federalist [but] in the sense that he is a decentraliser and a great believer in subsidiarity...He is also a great opponent of harmonising taxes, and so am I. His support for a single currency will not affect Britain's opt-out on these matters. He is also a great believer in the nation state.
John Major.

President elevated to apex of commission 'pyramid'

Santer wins more power than Delors

The Guardian, 31.10.1994

Santer seeks supremo role

Call for stronger EU presidency infuriates London and Paris

The Observer, 25.2.1996

143

Yet in spite of such limitations on his freedom of action, the role is a crucial one for he will be judged according to the extent to which he can ensure the effective working of the Commission. He is charged with setting out its goals, and he is in a key position to provide a dynamic impulse to its work. He not only addresses specific policy objectives, but seeks to give a sense of direction to the Union as a whole.

Criticism of the Commission

There have long been critics of the Commission within the Community, and they are particularly representatives from those states which would prefer to reduce its role in favour of developing intergovernmental forms of cooperation. At the time of the 1991 IGC an attempt was made by some member states to distinguish between the old Community and the new Union, and to suggest that the latter should operate in a more intergovernmental manner.

Others took the view that there was a unity in all of the Community's activities and that the role of the Commission was central to achieving this. In its evidence for that IGC the Commission stressed that 'the Intergovernmental Conference should be guided by the basic thinking which has been behind the construction of Europe for 40 years now, namely that all progress made towards economic, monetary, social or political integration should gradually be brought together in a single Community as the precursor of a European Union'. At Maastricht, in the second and third intergovernmental pillars, the Commission was given a role but a much weaker one than in the European Community. This was not to the liking of those states who would have liked to see it marginalised.

The 'founding fathers' always envisaged that there would be a single focus within the Community's institutions, knowing that this would boost the process of integration. By seeking that more aspects should operate outside of the usual Community procedure, some nations hoped to slow down the route to integration. This was unacceptable, for it was always the intention of the pioneers that there should be a 'unitary character in the European construction', which would provide 'the unity, the consistency and, as a result, the efficiency, of its...activities'.

As the regular attacks on 'Brussels bureaucracy' and the 'dominant and/or centralising Commission' indicate, there are often challenges to its authority and to the scope of its activities. Whatever it might do to encourage the development of the Union along more integrated lines, ultimately its fate and that of the EU as a whole depend on the actions of member states. In other words, the success of Commission initiatives depends, in the final analysis, upon the backing of the Council.

As we have seen (see p8-9), some of the attacks are misleading and the stories used to illustrate them are ill-founded. The support staff of the Commission is not as large as is often suggested, and one third of its staff are involved in language work, rather than 'bureaucratic' activities.

? Is the Commission becoming too powerful?

The European Parliament

This is made up of 626 members, known as MEPs, who are elected from across the Community and who sit not in national groupings but according to their political leanings (see p208-209). The number of MEPs for each country depends on its size: Germany has 99; Britain along with Italy and France has 87, whereas Luxembourg only has six.

A Truly Supranational Body?

The European Parliament is elected by peoples from across the whole Union, and for this reason it can claim to be a supranational body. Yet the representative process is marred by certain features.

The electoral system by which MEPs are chosen is a matter for national governments (see p237), as is the decision on eligibility to vote. Some states allow proxy voting, others do not, some allow only their own citizens to

The Strasbourg Parliament in session

vote, some allow nationals of any Union country. The number of representatives for each country is determined on the basis of a national quota, based on an imprecise population ratio. Some would argue that in a supranational election the allocations of seats should not be based on national boundaries at all, and MEPs should not be seen as a British or a German contingent.

However, the way in which seating is organised and the behaviour of members stresses supranational rather than national concerns. Although some members see it as their task to be on the look out for things detrimental to the interests of their own state, there is a willingness on the part of many to examine issues from a more European perspective.

MEPs are elected in large Euro-constituencies every five years on the basis of universal suffrage. The first elections were held in 1979, and the next are due in 1999. For the moment, each state uses its own separate voting arrangements, though the Treaty of Rome envisaged the adoption of a uniform system (see p237).

Once elected, MEPs travel to Strasbourg for monthly plenary sessions of the Parliament. Much of the more specialist work is done in the committees which meet in Brussels. These then make recommendations to the Parliament as a whole, which debates them in the plenary sessions which are open to the press and public.

The Workings of the Parliament

Parliament holds about 10-11 sessions a year, all in Strasbourg. Some part-time sessions (as well as the committee meetings) are held in Brussels for easier contact with the Commision and the Council. Members speak according to their own inclinations and the wishes of their constituents, but also as representatives of their political group or as a *rapporteur* for a committee charged with the task of considering a particular topic. They regularly interrogate members of the Council and Commissioners at Question Time, in plenary sessions and at committee meetings. In 1994, they asked more than 4000 written or oral questions.

Much of the important work of Parliament is carried out its committees (as listed in the box on p 148) It can establish committees of enquiry wherever appropriate. One of its 20 specialist committees handles petitions from citizens of the Union, for every person has the right 'individually or jointly with others, to address written requests or complaints (petitions) to the European Parliament'. These are addressed to the President, and may deal with any matter of concern to the complainant (such as union representation at the place or work and equal pay) which falls within the competence of the Union.

The President of the European Parliament and 14 Vice-Presidents together constitute the **Bureau** which has responsibility for all of the activities of the assembly. They are elected to serve for a $2^1/2$ year period. The Bureau and the chairpersons of the political groups form an **Enlarged Bureau,** or **Conference of Presidents**, and this wider body is charged with the task of devising the draft agenda for plenary meetings.

The proceedings of the European Parliament are open to the public, and its debates, opinions and resolutions are all published in the Official Journal of the European Union.

The Committees of the EP

Parliament works through committees. All members belong to at least one of them, and in 1994 there were 20, as follows;

Agriculture and Rural Development
Budgetary Control
Budgets
Civil Liberties and Internal Affairs
Culture, Youth, Education and the Media
Development and Cooperation
Economic and Monetary Affairs with Industrial Policy
Energy, Research and Technology
Environment, Public Health and Consumer Protection
External Economic Relations
Fisheries
Foreign Affairs and Security
Institutional Affairs
Legal Affairs and Citizens' Rights
Petitions
Regional Policy
Rules of Procedure
Social Affairs, Employment and the Working Environment
Transport and Tourism
Women's Rights

From time to time, special subcommittes have been established by the parent body. Also, committees of enquiry can be established. These may deal with matters such as racism and drug trafficking.

The Changing Impact of the Parliament

The status of the Parliament has undergone some change in recent years, but is still usually portrayed as little more than a 'talking-shop'. The original name accorded it in the Treaty of Rome was Assembly, which seems to imply a forum or gathering of people who come together to express their view. For many years it had little authority. It was not elected, and the powers it could exercise were described in article 137 as 'advisory and supervisory'.

This was an essentially limited role, but one which could be developed much more when the Parliament achieved democratic respectability after direct elections were introduced. New MEPs became interested in acquiring a more worthwhile role, and looked for opportunities to expand their responsibilities.

This bid for a more meaningful position was recognised in the SEA which allocated the Parliament more powers. Further powers were incorporated into the TEU in 1991, and among other things these gave the Parliament new powers over the appointment of members of the Commission. However, for many members and for commentators who wish to see the Union develop along more democratic lines, progress has been insufficient. They feel thwarted in their aspiration to provide the Strasbourg body with a clearer identity and more meaningful tasks.

Parliament's Powers; A Summary

The Parliament has never been a law-making assembly, but it;

- Supervises and questions the Commission and the Council of Ministers

- Has a power of codecision with the Council in fields accounting for a quarter of all legislation, and influence over most other legislation

- Can sack the Commission by a 2/3 majority though it has not ever done so

- Has a say in fixing the Union's annual Budget jointly with the Council of Ministers; it can also amend or reject the Budget

---

Parliament and the Legislative Process

The major weakness of the Parliament has been its limited role in the legislative process. This was strengthened by the SEA, which introduced the assent and cooperation procedures, the former requiring the approval of Parliament before any treaties of accession or association are valid, and the latter allocating Parliament a constitutional role in the passage of legislation connected with the single market. The TEU gave the Parliament a power of codecision with the council over fields accounting for about a quarter of all legislation.

Despite the limits on its formal power, Parliament's voice on legislation is listened to with growing respect. There is a developing convention that the Commission will take note of any views expressed in Strasbourg when it is obvious that they are widely-held. Also, when a Parliamentary Committee points to some weakness in a particular policy area, the Commission is likely to investigate further. However, as **Holland** observes; 'The Parliament may react, influence and under certain circumstances even prohibit legislation, but it cannot direct the legislative agenda'.

The main power rests with the Council, since the TEU applied the cooperation procedure to legislation in the majority of fields, and while it gives the Parliament more influence over much Community legislation, it does not satisfy the principle of representative government, namely that legislative authority should be held by an assembly of the people's representatives' **(Pinder)**. But where there is codecision, the Parliament's role is stronger.

Parliament and Financial Matters

In the area of financial control, Parliament has a more substantial supervisory role given its twin rights to amend the shape of the budget and to reject it entirely. It cannot alter the total expenditure allocated to compulsory items (eg, running the CAP) although it may query individual aspects of the allocation. On other areas of expenditure such as the Social and Regional Funds, which have assumed growing importance in recent years, it has more effect.

Since the coming of direct elections, the Parliament has employed its budgetary powers more effectively. Rejection of the entire budget can be a useful device for it can force the Council into a revision of its budgetary plans, and this tactic has been used in 1980, in a first flexing of the muscles of a body which now had a new legitimacy.

A Worthwhile Parliament?

There is still much doubt about the merits of the European Parliament and even some doubt about whether it merits the name of a Parliament at all, given the limit to its law-making power. Although its powers have increased and MEPs are allowed to comment on many proposals, they know that in the end the Council may take very little notice of what is said. Hence the demand of many MEPs for a stronger role.

Some national governments, including Britain, have been very reluctant to see an increase in the powers of the Parliament for the very reason that it is a supranational body. They wish to see the national legislature act as the main democratic check on the workings of Union machinery. Nonetheless, Parliament continues to press for more power and opposes the element of intergovernmentalism to which some members adhere.

It is not a lively body in the way that the British Parliament often is. This reflects the seating arrangements which are less adversarial and confrontational than at Westminster. The fact that there are eleven languages recognised by the Parliament (and therefore so much translation has to be done) slows down procedure and makes organised reaction more difficult to achieve. The lack of passion also reflects the fact that Parliament over a wide range of issues, is not a law-making body in which ministers are defending their policies against hostile interruptions.

The lack of drama is particularly evident at Question Time, a Westminster import which lacks the cut and thrust of the genuine article, and is late-night and low key. It might more accurately be referred to as 'answer time', for the answers given to already-supplied questions tend to be very long and few in number.

Yet if it is easy to pinpoint deficiencies in the workings and effectiveness of the European Parliament, it is interesting to note that there are many politicians who are showing more interest in belonging to it. They sense that the wind is blowing in the direction of a stronger assembly, and this is why MPs such as Edwina Currie tried (unsuccessfully) to build a new Parliamentary career in Strasbourg, in 1994.

To some MPs, Strasbourg does appear to be the place where more of the interesting battles are taking place. A Labour MEP, John Tomlinson, has made the point that, even were there to be a victory for his party in the next general election, he would not be tempted to return to Westminster. He finds himself more attuned to the agenda which the Parliament is discussing, and likes the way that it operates. In his view, the noisy House of Commons, with its confrontational style, loses sight of the real issues. By contrast, in Strasbourg he admires the way in which a genuine consensus can emerge across party groupings and national boundaries

A Costly Parliament?

Some criticism of Parliament relates to its cost. Translation costs alone account for about 40% of its budget.

Though full sittings are held in Strasbourg, most committees meet in Brussels, and the General Secretariat is based in Luxembourg. This is a wasteful allocation of resources, as well as being inconvenient for Euro-MPs, and some 12% of expenditure is caused by this division of location (Each month, the Parliament has to transport a mass of paperwork for the 500 mile round trip between Strasbourg and Luxembourg). Salaries and expenses use up much of the rest of the money (see opposite).

With an annual budget of over £500m (1994 figures) and a staff of nearly 3500 officials, the Parliament is expensive to run, but perhaps not unreasonably so. The costs work out at approximately £900000 per MEP (or £1.80 per voter), compared with £261000 for a Westminster MP (£4.25 per voter).

The Salaries and Perquisites of MEPs

The salaries of MEPs vary between the member states. They are fixed at the level of those of their national counterparts, so that French and German ones are much better paid than the British or Irish representatives. Allowances are generous for secretarial costs, research and travel, and stories of large sums being paid have fed the imagination of some critics who condemn the European 'gravy-train'. The perks of being an MEP are good and the lifestyle is very comfortable, though for these rewards members have to be prepared to undertake a great deal of travelling.

Salaries in Selected EC Countries, as at June 1994

France	£54700	
Germany	48953	
Ireland	31203	
Italy	73051	(the highest figure in the EC)
Spain	21436	(the lowest figure in the EC)
United Kingdom	31687	

Expenses

Staffing	71951
Hotel allowances/expenses	26149
European travel	2310

Plus; car mileage, computer allowances and first class airfare.

The expenditure allowances are paid as a lump sum, with no proof of expenditure required. In recent years (especially at election time), some British MEPs have campaigned for stricter control of 'extras', including the need to verify journeys made and expenses incurred.

In relation to other assemblies on the international scene, the cost does not seem excessive. The American House of Representatives is of similar size, meets in one location and employs only one language - yet it spends twice as much (It does, of course, also exercise much greater power).

? 'Although it has growing influence and power, the European Parliament is not a sovereign body as is the House of Commons'. Is this true? In what other respects is the EP different from the British Parliament?

The Court of Justice

A further supranational element of the Union's machinery is the Court of Justice which meets in Luxembourg. Its decisions are binding, so that the rights conferred by laws passed by the decision-making bodies can be claimed throughout the Union, irrespective of the wishes of the national government. The passage of

Justice, by Giacomo Manzu, as portrayed in the Entrance Hall Court of Justice (European Commission)

common laws and their uniform enforcement across the fifteen member countries is one of the distinctive characteristics of the European Union.

This body of 15 judges gives a ruling in any dispute relating to Community law between countries in the Union, but these cases are rare for countries are reluctant to litigate against each other. In one case in 1980, the French successfully sued the UK over the latter's fishery restrictions.

More common is the Commission suing a state for failing in its duties under the Treaty of Rome, or another treaty. Thus the French Government was taken to the Court in 1980 for its failure to open its market to imported British lamb, as was Britain for its attempt to ban imports of UHT milk and Italy for its failure to admit imported gin and sparkling wine. In several cases, the Court has ruled against unfair barriers imposed by member states against imports from other EU countries.

The Court also passes judgement, at the request of a national court, on the interpretation and/or validity of Union law. If a legal action produces a contentious point of this kind, a national court can request a preliminary ruling from the Luxembourg judges. They give a ruling on what the law means, and send it back for the national courts to apply it in the case before them.

The Court is charged with ensuring that 'in the interpretation and application of this Treaty [of Rome], the law is observed (article 164)'. That it often does so in a manner which is sympathetic to the process of integration means that the Court makes a considerable contribution to the strengthening of the Union.

In some cases, individual citizens and companies can and do ask for a Court ruling. A number of cases have concerned matters arising from female employment, such as equal pay.

The Court has a heavy workload, one which has grown substantially in the last fifteen years. **Nugent** estimates that the average number of cases dealt with per annum has actually increased from around 50 a year in the 1960s to over 500 today. In part this reflects the increase in the size of the Community, although it also indicates the growing area of its competence.

In recognition of this increasing burden, it was agreed in principle at the time of the SEA that a Court of First Instance should be established to handle 'points of law only...certain classes of action or proceedings brought by natural or legal persons'. It does not handle cases brought by states or Community institutions.

Altogether, more than 9000 cases have come before the Court which has delivered over 4000 judgements. The texts of the judgements include the reasoning on which they are based, and they are made available in each recognised Union language.

The Composition and Workings of the Court

The judges are chosen 'by common accord of the Governments of the Member States' from amongst persons 'whose independence is beyond doubt and who possess the qualifications required for appointment to the highest judicial offices in their respective countries or who are juriconsults of recognised competence'. As each state nominates its own member of the Court, there is little opportunity for 'common accord' to make any difference. The only time when it applies is when there is an even number of states in the Union. To ensure that there can be a clear verdict in any case, the five largest countries will take part in a system involving the appointment of an extra judge, in rotation between them.

The Court chooses its own President, and for each case he appoints a judge-rapporteur who takes a lead in the deliberations. The case may be heard in full plenary session (requiring a quorum of 7 judges) if it is brought by a member state or Union institution, whilst on other matters it may work in smaller chambers.

There are also 9 Advocates-General. An Advocate General presents a reasoned statement before the Court setting out details of the submission made by interested parties and providing information on relevant Union laws and previous Court judgements. His opinion is not binding on the Court though it is often accepted.

The System of Union Law

Union law is of two types, primary and secondary. Many of the rules which the Court enforces derive from the founding treaties and any later revisions of them. This **primary law** sets out the main objectives of the Union.

They are supplemented by **secondary law** to provide a comprehensive legal framework. This secondary legislation can be of several types, as explained in the box on p 158-159. They include regulations, directives, decisions, recommendations and opinions.

The treaties set out the distinction between them. The regulations issued by the Council or Commission are the most important type of Union law, for they are a clear example of the supranational force of the Union. Their key characteristics are that they are directly binding and generally applicable. In other words, they apply in their entirety across the whole of the Union. They do not have to be firstly turned into national legislation, but apply from the day they are introduced, and replace any existing law in any member state. States must comply with them.

By contrast, directives are binding on the states, but are not usually directly applicable. The objective is laid down, but there is discretion on how the end is to be achieved. Nations can therefore seek to interpret the directive in a way which best fits in with their own traditions. This form of law-making is more acceptable to several states, for although they approve the principle of common policies they baulk at being forced to implement them in precise detail. As one EU pamphlet put it, directives can 'achieve the necessary measure of unity while preserving the multiplicity of national characteristics'.

They may be less rigid than regulations, and this is why they have been favoured as the preferred means of law-making in areas such as the completion of the single market. But they still have to be passed into national law by the nations's legislature. If this is not done, then the Court may be asked to intervene, and because it can seek to enforce compliance this means that directives also act as a supranational device. In a number of decisions of the Court in the last twenty five years, rights conferred by directives have also received full protection.

The treaties and legislation are the main sources of law. There is also a developing body of **Case Law,** based on decisions made by the European Court and by the higher courts over several years. These have interpreted texts and applied principles to new situations; they act as precedents to guide judges in coming to their decisions.

Types of Union Law

Regulations

These set out general rules which are binding and apply uniformly throughout the fifteen states. As they are of immediate application, no national legislation is necessary to implement them.

Directives

These tend to be more general. They are addressed to the member states, and are binding as to the result which must be achieved. However, they allow for more discretion. The choice of form and methods for incorporating them into national law is a national decision. These are the main type of measure used in harmonisation, as for the programme relating to the completion of the single market.

Decisions

These are legally binding on those to whom they are addressed, eg, a government, company or individual, and therefore they require no further legislation to implement them. Most are very specific, such as those to allow an exemption from existing measures.

Recommendations and Opinions are not binding, and strictly not, therefore, Union law. However, the Court of Justice often alludes to them, and so they are mentioned here.

Altogether, there may be 7-10000 measures introduced per annum, the bulk of which are non-political and non-contentious. Over half of them are usually regulations, many are decisions and relatively few are directives. The classification of acts is not quite as straightforward as it appears from the above categories. On occasion, the formal designation of a measure may be misleading, and the ECJ pays more attention to its substance rather than to its label. In particular, the distinction between regulations and directives is not clearcut.

Directives are addressed to member states, but in theory they are not necessarily applicable to all of them. Yet in practice, as most are concerned with harmonisation, they are usually addressed to all states. Again, often they are devised in such a rigid form, that there is little opportunity for national discretion in their implementation. Finally, in some cases, the Court has ruled that they are directly applicable across the EU - particularly in cases where national legislation has been slow to emerge or has strayed from the original intention.

The Status of Union Law; Some Past Cases

Union law must be applied in the national courts, for it has primacy over national law. Generally there is no conflict between them, and the national legal procedures are the necessary initial means through which European law is made effective in member countries. However, where the two systems are in any way incompatible, the direct applicability and superior status of Union law has been confirmed in several cases. It automatically overrides any existing legislation, and has 'a limiting effect on laws adopted subsequently'.

This 'superior status' of European law has been established in several cases, most notably;

1   The Van Gend en Loos Decision, 1962

The first statement of the Court on the issue was in this case, involving a clash between article 12 of the Treaty of Rome and a prior Dutch law. Its significance lay in the position it outlined on the nature of Community law;

> ...*The Community constitutes a new legal order in international law, for whose benefits the states have limited their sovereign rights, albeit within limited fields.*

2   The case of Costa v ENEL, 1964

This involved a Milanese shareholder in a nationalised electricity enterprise who refused to pay the full amount of his bill on the grounds that he considered that great wrong had been done to him. The Court noted that; 'Member states have limited their sovereign rights...and created

159

a body of laws which binds both their individuals and themselves'. It went on to declare that;

> *It follows...that the law stemming from the treaty, an independent source of law, could not, because of its special and original nature, be overridden by domestic legal provisions, however framed, without being deprived of its character as Community law and without the legal basis of the Community itself being called into question.*

It is this principle which strikes at the heart of the sovereignty debate, for in joining the European Community Britain accepted a curtailment of Parliamentary Sovereignty. The issue has become apparent in several cases, such as

3 The Aero Zipp Fasteners v YKK Fasteners (UK) Ltd, 1973

Here, the judge concluded that 'Common Market Law should be applied in this country and should, where there is a conflict, override English Law'.

4 The Factortame Case, 1990

Again, and more famously, the primacy of Community law was apparent in the Factortame case concerning the Spanish trawlermen who registered their vessels in the United Kingdom and then used them to fish in British waters. Despite the passage of the Merchant Shipping Act in 1988 which laid down stringent rules to prevent them from so doing, it was made clear in a Court ruling (1991) that parts of the British statute were invalid, as they contravened European law.

The case was a long and complex one, but it established two important precedents;

   i   National law can be made to bow to Union law even while a claim is
       pending

ii British courts do have the right to review and suspend British legislation. They can set aside a national law if they believe that Union law is being infringed.

Cases such as these led Lord Denning, an eminent British judge, to remark that; 'When we come to matters with a European element, the Treaty [of Rome] is like an incoming tide. It flows into the estuaries and up the rivers. It cannot be held back. Parliament has decreed that the Treaty is henceforward to be part of our law **(Bulmer v Bollinger, 1974)**.

Another judge, Lord Scarman, has recognised that the situation since 1973 has been a 'legal revolution...We are at this moment part of a legal system which not only confers a right but imposes a duty on the Court in certain circumstances to invalidate legislation' (1974).

In the early years, British judges tended to rely less on the Treaty of Rome and more on the European Communities Act of 1972, in coming to their judgements. However, by the end of the decade, commentators had noted an increasingly 'European' approach creeping into their decisions, one which reflected the spirit and letter of the Treaties, rather than the law by which Britain joined the Community.

The Enforcement of Union Law

Enforcement of Union law is mainly a matter for the individual states. Most disputes are aired in the national courts, where British judges enforce it. Generally, British courts have accepted that they must apply Union law if there is any conflict with national legislation.

Most disputes involving countries are settled well before the Court stage. The Commission offers a 'reasoned opinion' after taking evidence, and only if there is a lack of compliance does it take the matter to Luxembourg.

161

What weakens the effectiveness of Union law is the lack of any strong sanction if it is not enforced. Although the Court may instruct a member state or institution to apply Union law, it has lacked effective power to insist that its wish is fulfilled. At Maastricht, provision was made for the Court to fine member states which did not respect its judgements. The amount of any financial penalty was to be decided by the Commission, in its 'reasoned opinion'. Ultimately, however, the Court relies for its authority on the fact that in joining the Union any state acknowledges the authority of the Court as binding.

Britain and the Court of Justice

On the Tory Right and in the tabloid press, there has been an outcry against some of the decisions of the Luxembourg Court. Critics wish to see its powers curtailed.

The overturning of British law in the Factortame case (see p160-161) was unpopular, but the follow-up in 1996 provoked particular hostility in the popular papers. The *Daily Mail* was incensed by the ruling that the British Government was liable for compensatory damages of around £30m for the loss of business to those Spanish fishing boats which were briefly prevented *'from plundering fish quotas reserved for British trawlermen. That adds damages to downright robbery'*. It went on to speak of a *'judicial inanity'*.

The judgement opens the way for other groups and individuals affected by UK legislation which breaches EU law to make claims against the HMG. This has already happened over ex-service women sacked by the Ministry of Defence after they became pregnant. It might include the case of a citizen of the Irish Republic who was sent back to Ireland under an exclusion order, and therefore lost his job in Britain - without there being any opinion from an independent appeal authority.

Another decision by the Court of First Instance on working hours upset the British Government. It argued that - in spite of the opt-out from the Social Chapter - Britain must abide by the directive producing for a 48 hour week. Again, it seemed to ministers that the Court was grabbing the political agenda away from elected domestic politicians.

In the White Paper published prior to the IGC, moves were outlined to curb the Court's powers. These included limiting the period of time over which the judges can backdate their decisions, and the creation of a new appeals procedure. Others criticise the delays in delivering judgements. On average it takes two years, but it can be six or more.

Despite the public criticism of the Court and its activities, Britain has a record of compliance with European law. It has only been taken to court on 35 times compared with 67 cases involving Luxembourg and 297 involving Italy.

John Redwood, a prominent member of the Tory Right, has described the institution as a 'faraway court with way-out views'. He wants Parliament to assert its supremacy over the Court and quotes the example of Germany, referred to below.

The House of Commons could theoretically stop the Luxembourg judges in their tracks, either by;

i   repealing that section of the European Communities Act which enshrines Parliament's 1972 decision to allow the Court of Justice certain powers over British law or

ii by passing a law of the kind which one Tory MP, Iain Duncan-Smith, proposed to MPs in April 1996, which declares that Parliament has the power to stop any Court decision it dislikes.

But such 'cherry-picking', allowing some decisions and obstructing those deemed undesirable, would be equivalent to a frontal assault on the EU. Most members like its integrationist tendencies, and any state which rejected the current legal arrangements would be seen as breaking its obligations and thereby indicating its wish to be no longer considered part of the Union. There is a great deal of difference between working to achieve the difficult task of reforming the Court (by seeking to speed up its operation, reducing the governmental liabilities which it can impose and improving the consistency of its verdicts), and asserting Parliamentary supremacy over its jurisdiction. Effectively, this could only be achieved by withdrawing from the Union.

The Basis of British Discontent

At the heart of the Eurosceptic dislike of the Court of Justice is the feeling that it has been unduly activist. Many critics accept that a Court is needed to interpret the Treaty of Rome and ensure the application of EU law in a uniform manner across the Union. They suggest that it has gone far beyond the intentions of its creators, and that it has become an instrument of integration - its decisions taking the Union ever-further down the federal route. They also suggest that its 'wayward' and 'erratic' decisions have imposed undue costs on business and governement.

In a House of Commons debate on the role and powers of the Court (April,1996), several Tories suggested that Britain should declare that it does not accept the overriding supremacy of European law, as they claim Germany has done. This suggestion was based on the idea that when Treaty modifications such as those at Maastricht have constitutional implications, they require the approval of the Federal Constitutional Court. In Germany, a country with a very different recent past to our own, the exalted role of the judiciary is a consequence of history, and its attitude cannot be ignored in particular cases. But there is no general power to override the judgements of the Luxembourg justices.

Other member states take a different view of the Court's activities to that of the British Cabinet. They note that the Government is happy to resort to the Court when British interests are at stake, as in the beef crisis (see p412-415). Some Europeans believe that Britain is only willing to commit itself to EU legislation it likes, and that when the adjudication goes against it then it attacks the role and performance of the Court. Beyond any such considerations, however, there is a differing approach between many continental judges and their British counterparts in the execution of their task. Continental judges adopt a more policy-orientated attitude. They tend to interpret the law in the light of what they see as its intentions and thus shape the law in a particular direction, whereas in Britain judges have traditionally taken a more conservative stance and confined themselves to strict interpretation of what the law says.

Within the EU, the Court of Justice has acted to extend the competence of the Union. In its early days, its work was largely concerned with trade and commerce, and the man-in-the-street was left untouched by its deliberations. Today, on several occasions, judgements are delivered on issues of importance to workers in a variety of sectors. For some, this is welcome as rights on such matters as sex equality are extended. For critics of the Union, it represents a harmful extension of the competence of the Union into fields best left to national policy-makers.

See also the Beef Crisis, p 412-415

? Should the British fear the European Court?

The other main machinery of the European Union is primarily **INTERGOVERNMENTAL** in character.

The Council of Ministers

The Council of Ministers represents the intergovernmentalist aspects of the Treaty of Rome. It consists of one minister from each of the fifteen member states. The person who attends will differ according to the topic under discussion. If the Council discusses the Common Agricultural Policy, then the British Minister of Agriculture will attend. If the topic is the single currency then the representative of the British Government will be the Chancellor of the Exchequer who will meet with fellow European Finance Ministers. Some Councils meet every month (those covering the crucial areas of agriculture, finance and foreign policy), whereas others such as the one on transport meet less frequently. Altogether, in 1994 there were just over 100 formal ministerial gatherings.

The person who attends is seen by each country as the representative who is there to defend national interests. We have seen that in the discussions surrounding the establishment of the ECSC, Monnet conceded this intergovernmental feature of the institutional arrangements, in order that he should get what he really cared about, a High Authority with supranational powers.

Some member states are conscious of the fact that if the Union is to move onwards to closer integration then it is only through the Council that the real push to unification can be given. Because of this, their representatives act with an eye to European as well as to national interests. This is why Holland has been able to describe the Council as 'the Janus face of the Community, looking, simultaneously, towards both a federal and an intergovernmental future' (Janus was a Roman god with two faces, one looking forwards and the other back).

The headquarters and secretariat of the Council are based in Brussels. It meets in private, as does the Commission, and the Presidency rotates every six months between the The Fifteen. Italy held it in the first half of 1996, and thereafter it passed to Ireland for the remainder of the year - thence to the Netherlands and Luxembourg in 1997, and the United Kingdom and Austria in 1998.

The Presidency of the Council gives a country a chance to influence the direction which the Union takes. The country which presides is charged with the task of devising the agenda for the period of its stewardship, and by ensuring that some issues are kept to the fore (and others that pose problems for ministers are kept in the background) it can chart the course of policy. Depending on its outlook, it can - via more informal means and behind-the-scenes persuasion - do something to force the pace of integration or stress the importance of intergovernmental cooperation.

Of course, the Presidency only lasts for six months, so that any delaying tactics have a short-lived usefulness. Moreover, some issues become relevant for consideration whatever the wishes of the country which holds the reins. They may be already planned at a previous meeting of the European Council.

There is much criticism of the way in which the Council operates (see p192-195), because its proceedings are secret and it is unaccountable. Other criticism derives largely from those who would like to see swifter progress towards integration. The Council is the bastion of national interests, and if it often does seek to devise a policy satisfactory to all or most ot those present it is not under an obligation to behave in a 'Communautaire' manner, as is the Commission. For those who seek a more federal Europe, the Council can represent a barrier.

The Work of the Council

The Council is the principal forum for discussion of Union affairs, and it takes the final decision on matters of policy. It receives proposals from the Commission, and those attending discuss them in the light of their national concerns and with a regard to the interests of the Union as a whole. Its role is both executive and legislative, for it makes the key decisions which the Commission then seeks to implement. But although the Commission can act directly on matters of detail, it is the Council which makes law on more substantial issues.

On occasion, governments are represented by a junior rather than the relevant senior minister. This may happen because the workload is particularly heavy, as in preparation for the single market. When this happens, it can lead to difficulty in getting a decision, for the presence of a lower-ranking delegation may make it hard to agree on a binding decision. On the other hand, even if the senior minister is present and agrees to a particular initiative, this does not mean that the decision taken will automatically find favour with the rest of the government back home. Sometimes, ministers have been overruled by their domestic colleagues.

Usually, the spirit in Council meetings is cooperative rather than confrontational, and if the relationship between the ministers assembled is a good and established one compromise is reached without too much animosity. Most present realise that there has to be give-and-take, and, as politicians themselves, they appreciate that a member who is handling an issue sensitive in his domestic Parliament, needs to be able to go home with some concession that he can sell to critics. The preparatory work done by officials and working groups can pave the way for such an outcome. (See box on p 168).

In Monnet's view, the ideal outcome of any Council meeting was the emergence of a 'common view' rather than a compromise which represented the lowest common denominator in a bargaining process. Where possible this is done without resort to a vote, but on issues where agreement is impossible because of a sturdy defence of national interests, balloting becomes necessary.

The Council Secretariat

The Council has a support staff of over 2000, of whom about one tenth operate at the diplomatic level. They collectively form the General Secretariat whose task is to service the Council itself. This involves a number of responsibilities, including;

- Devising the draft agenda for Council meetings
- Circulating decisions of the Council to interested bodies
- Monitoring the implementation of Council decisions

Such functions are essentially administrative and coordinating ones, but they are very important. The Secretariat provides the element of continuity in Council work. It is permanent, whereas as ministers come and go and the Presidency of the Council changes twice-yearly. As such, it keeps the machinery operative, and the smooth running of the Council is much assisted by the ability of officials to keep in close touch with the President. They warn him of likely difficulties or obstruction, and advise on the way in which pitfalls might be handled.

Larger countries holding the Presidency may need to rely on the Secretariat less than smaller ones, for they have more back-up staff and resources on which their relevant minister can rely. Yet any country is likely to find that much useful preparatory work for individual meetings is carried out by the Secretariat, as well as by COREPER and its own state officials.

The Secretariat retains custody of all Council archives. Its Legal department offers advice to the Council on all issues of law.

The Voting System in the Council

It was the original intention of The Six that the Community would move forward to a policy of majority voting at an early date. However, the adoption of the Luxembourg Compromise (see p68) was a setback to this expectation, so that the weighted system which had been devised was not usually employed. It was not until the passage of the SEA that change occurred, for on policies which were connected with the single market a weighted or qualified majority vote (QMV) was to be employed. This led to the use of the QMV procedure in the many other cases stipulated by the treaties, though unanimity remains the rule on some sensitive matters such as taxation. On these, there must still be complete agreement in decision-making.

Qualified majority voting (QMV) is unpopular with the British Government, the more so as Mrs Thatcher's ministers believed that the Commission tried to slip other social issues in the health and safety directives which came within the orbit of implementing the arrangements for 1992. The Major Government has shown a similar suspicion of the procedure, and it remains an area where Britain takes a Gaullist position and sees the right of veto as essential for the preservation of vital national interests.

To other nations more committed to closer integration, majority voting is both desirable and necessary. It is desirable as it ensures that the pace of advance reflects the wishes of the majority, and prevents a single country or group of countries from holding up progress towards a more integrated Union. It is necessary, because without it there might be no agreed decision as the Union becomes ever larger. Unanimity between six or even twelve states may have been difficult to achieve, but was possible. Between twenty or even thirty states, it is unlikely. This is why the issue is likely to feature strongly in the discussions of the Intergovernmental Conference, in 1996.

The Council of Ministers often avoids a vote on sensitive issues. Is this a good thing?

Why might majority voting become more common in the future?

The European Council

The Heads of Government, and the Presidents of the Commission and Parliament, meet as a 'European Council' at least twice a year. The same country presides over the meetings, as happens in the Council of Ministers, and as these gatherings provide another opportunity for governments to be represented by their (in this case, main) political leaders this seems the most appropriate place to examine the institution.

There was no initial provision for such a body, but following the first enlargement, it was decided that a body was needed to ensure that there was some leadership in the larger organisation. In 1975, the Council began to meet, and from the beginning it was recognised that this was not the place where technical details should be examined. Rather, it was the forum for frank discussion of the broader issues and matters of principle which should govern the way in which the Community develops.

Today, any agreements on closer cooperation are likely to be mooted at this level. Members provide the drive to move the Union forward, laying down guidelines on such issues as reform of the CAP, and economic and monetary union. At worst, such summits can get bogged down in discussion of one issue such as the British budgetary problems of the early 1980s. Sometimes, on the other hand, the agenda is so wide, that discussion fails to reach a conclusion of any importance on anything at all. Yet at their best, some Councils have helped the Union to move forward on important issues which have benefited from a push by those charged with the main responsibilities for governing their respective states, and the decisions to establish intergovernmental conferences in 1985 and 1991 derived from such meetings.

The European Council is in a pivotal position, and it can shape the direction of the Union. If there is to be a move forwards to closer unity, it will probably derive its impetus from the Council. On the other hand, if the development of supranationalism in the Union is to be slowed down, and a new era of intergovernmentalism to begin, then this too will probably result from the mood of, and decisions in, its deliberations. It sets the tone, and depending on the character of the lead it gives will also depend the willingness shown in the Council of Ministers to move in a similar direction.

Two other bodies are involved in making Community policy;

A Council of Permanent Representatives of Member States (COREPER)

COREPER prepares work for the Council and carries out other tasks assigned to it. It also acts as a link between the Council and the Commission.

Its importance is considerable. Many Council decisions are taken at this level, for the national ambassadors who belong to COREPER are accorded the power to speak and act on behalf of their member countries on matters which are of secondary significance. If the matter is of primary concern, then much of the initial clarification of elements of agreement and contention is carried out by these ambassadors. Because of the way in which it sifts the decisions, **Nugent** has described COREPER as 'a sort of filtering agency for ministerial meetings'.

Backed by their teams of state officials in the various working groups and guided by the General Secretariat of the Council, its discussions are thorough and exhaustive.

The Economic and Social Committee (ESC)

The Economic and Social Committee was established under the terms of the Treaty of Rome. It assists both the Council and the Commission. It is an advisory body of 222 members, including 24 from Britain, which meets in Brussels. Its membership is meant to reflect the various interests who make up the economic and social life of the Community, so that it comprises representatives of the employers, employees, the professions and other interests such as consumers. These people are appointed for four years, and are eligible for reappointment.

Often, the ESC is asked to give an opinion before the Council of Ministers decides on any proposal. It has nine specialised committees to enable it examine matters in depth, and usually holds eight plenary sessions a year. It gives around 180 'opinions' over a twelve month period.

At Maastricht, its advisory role was consolidated, and it was henceforward allowed to issue 'opinions' on its own initiative. It is thus able to make a real contribution by expressing the views of individual citizens through the intermediary of their economic and social representatives, and making these available to the other institutions.

Further significance lay in the fact that this is another institution which by its composition and task is designed to strengthen the transnational element in the machinery of the Union. It emphasises the European interest rather than the national one.

Recent Developments:
The Court of Auditors, The Committee of the Regions and The Ombudsman

The Maastricht Treaty had an impact on the workings of several existing institutions, including not only the most well known ones but also the much less discussed **Court of Auditors**. The Court now has fifteen members, one from each state. Its brief is to audit all revenue and expenditure of the Union and assist Parliament and the Council in checking the implementation of the annual budget. At Maastricht, it was granted the status of a full EU institution whereas formerly it had been one of the 'other bodies' referred to in the Treaty of Rome. This upgrading of its position was a recognition of the importance of the task of checking fraud and waste within the Union.

The Court's special reports are acknowledged to be a valuable input for Parliament's debates, and the use which is made of them indicates a wish to strengthen the role of financial management in Union life. The TEU required the Court to go further and provide Parliament and the Council with a 'statement of assurance as to the reliability of the accounts and the legality and regularity of the underlying transactions'.

Two new institutions were agreed in 1991. Under the TEU (article 198), a new **Committee of the Regions** was planned, its structure and role to be modelled on the ESC. It also has 222 members (appointed by the Council of Ministers), and it meets in Brussels.

Member states nominate people to represent each area of their country, although the criteria on which selection is made will vary across the EU.

Some states are strongly regionalised, or even, in the case of Germany, have a fully developed federal system of government. Others such as Britain have much less powerful county and district councils. Regional and local authorities are represented on the Committee.

Its creation was a recognition of the importance of the various regions of the Union, and of their right to have a voice in decisions which impact upon them. It must be consulted by the Council of Ministers on matters affecting regional policy, and it may also make representations to the Commission or Council wherever it feels that 'specific regional interests are involved'. In the first years of its operation, from March 1994, some 40 'opinions' had been given, and these early observations were characterised by a common concern for the theme of subsidiarity.

Although its powers are as yet limited to advisory ones, it has already served to reinforce the regions as a potentially influential lobby. From the UK, the Scottish and Welsh representatives have used the Committee as a way of making common cause with German Länder and other regions which have been accorded a greater degree of devolution in their own country.

Its reputation received a setback in late 1995, when allegations of nepotism and sleaze began to surface, in the suggestion that some 80 or so people had been appointed on the basis of political favours. Set up to bring the Union closer to the people, it seemed ironic that many citizens who held positions in local and regional authorities were being denied the opportunity to serve on the Committee because places were being allocated on the basis of patronage.

At Maastricht, it was also decided that Parliament should appoint an **Ombudsman** to look into instances of maladministration by any EU institution other than the Court of Justice. Where he finds that this has arisen, he will draw up a report for the institution concerned after receiving its view. However, because of 'procedural delays' within the EP, no appointment was made until mid-1995. Jacob Söderman, a Finn, was given the job, and he and his staff were soon kept busy. In the first year they dealt with nearly 700 complaints - the largest number coming from Britain - but most were ruled inadmissible.

The institutional structure of the Union envisaged under Maastricht combined existing Community bodies with new creations. Some of these are connected with specific policies, such as the European Central Bank which forms part of the machinery associated with EMU. Other EU machinery such as the European Investment Bank has existed since the Treaty of Rome was originally implemented. Technically, again it is not an institution of the Union, but one of its arms. These arms are best considered in the section of the book which deals with the policies with which they are concerned.

Decision Making in the Union

The process of decision-making in the European Union is complicated, and the procedure varies according to the issue being discussed. As **Nugent** observes; 'A host of actors, operating within the context of numerous EU and national-level institutions, interact with one another on the basis of an array of different decision-making rules and procedures'.

Broadly, this is the general pattern of what happens, but there are variations at stages ii and iii;

   i   The Commission proposes new legislation

   ii   The Council consults on the proposal with the Parliament which scrutinises (and may suggest amendments), and with the Economic and Social Committee which advises

   iii The Council decides whether to go ahead

   iv The Commission implements the proposal

   v   The Court of Justice arbitrates on any infringement of the law.

The Commission remains the starting point of the decision-making process. The powers of the Parliament have been increased, however, in particularly by introducing the co-decision procedure and extending the scope of the cooperation and assent procedures. Finally, the use of qualified-majority voting in the Council has been extended to new areas.

The Community's Decision-Making Process

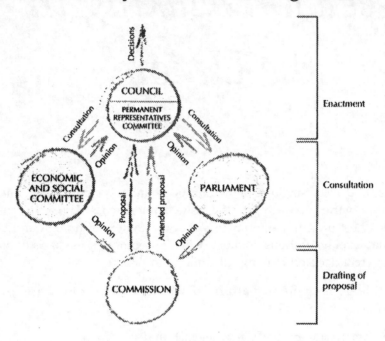

Democracy at work in the European Union (European Commission, 1994)

The Main Policy-making Procedures

In 1970, **Lindberg and Scheingold** wrote of policy-making in the following terms;

> *It is no exaggeration to view the whole policy-making process in the Community as a dialogue between the Council, representing national cabinets, and the Commission, appointed originally by the governments but acting autonomously in terms of its own view of the 'interests' of the Community as a whole.*

Since then, the policy-making process has moved on, for with the passage of the SEA and the TEU what was a dialogue between two institutions has become more of a partnership between three of them, for Parliament has now acquired a growing role in the process. **How then does it work?**

There are four main procedures, other than that for handling budgetary matters (see p265-267);

1 The Traditional Consultation Procedure

This is the procedure which has applied since the European Community was launched, and it means that Parliament gives an opinion on Commission proposals. The use of this method of policy-making has gradually been reduced with the introduction of the cooperation and co-decision procedures, but it still covers important fields such as the CAP, taxation and and certain aspects of economic and monetary union.

How a Proposal Develops

Much of the work of the Commission is concerned with the implementation of policies approved by the Council, but new initiatives are continually being suggested by the Commission.These may derive from suggestions of one or more of the member states, or from the discussions which are regularly held with leading interest groups with which the Commission has a strong association. They may result from thinking within the Commission itself.

Once conceived, the idea will be formulated into a draft proposal by the appropriate Directorate(s)-General, and this early version will then be sent to any organisation which might be thought to have a valid input to make. Such outlets include national governments, interest groups, committees of the Parliament, the Economic and Social Committee and - depending on its relevance - to the Committtee of the Regions. Once any suggestions have been considered (and rejected, incorporated or refined), then a formal draft document is published. It is sent to the Council and other institutions, perhaps including the Committee. At this stage, the pressure groups will be involved in active lobbying of the institutions and their personnel.

The Council will refer the proposal to one of its study groups which comprise civil servants from the various states. These officials will consult with national parliaments and groups, and then send an analysis of their findings and views to COREPER. COREPER will seek to establish common ground on the proposal, via consultation with the member states and with the Commission. At this stage, procedure varies, depending on the article in the various treaties from which the legislation derives, but usually the Council then discusses the proposal and the advice it has received - having taken into consideration the views of the EP, ESC and, maybe, of the Committee. It makes a decision, which it is then the task of the Commission to implement.

2   The Cooperation Procedure

The passage of the Single European Act extended the role of the Parliament, although the Council still has the final say. In the TEU, cooperation was taken further, and now covers areas such as the common transport policy and some aspects of EMU.

Again, the Commission initiates a proposal, as described in the section above. However, rather than consultation alone (the first reading), under this procedure, the Parliament acquired more of a legislative role; it was given a second opportunity to examine any proposal. The agreed position of the Council was to be submitted to it for scrutiny during a second 'reading'. For up to three months - or four if the period is extended by the Council - the Parliament can discuss the proposal.

Parliament has a number of options. It can;

i   Accept the proposal, or do nothing about it. In this case, the Council can go ahead and adopt it without further delay

ii   Amend it. If the Parliament decides (on a majority basis) to modify the proposal, then within three months, the Council must either accept Parliament's modification, accept the amended version of the Commission, or amend the revised version from the Commission

iii Reject it. If this happens, the Council can override the objection of the Parliament, but only on the basis of a unanimous vote.

3 The Assent Procedure

The SEA also introduced another device, the assent procedure. On any proposed enlargement of the EC, or on any association agreements, the assent of Parliament is needed.

Parliament may give or withhold its agreement on the proposal laid before it, but it has no power to amend it. Assent covers any international agreements as already mentioned, but in the TEU (article 228) it now covers other items such as policies with important budgetary implications for the Union as a whole, and matters connected with citizenship or reform of the Structural or Cohesion Funds.

In its analysis of the workings of the TEU (May 1995), the Commission indentified 32 proposals which had been adopted under the assent procedure, 20 of which were before the ratification of the Maastricht Treaty. In 7 cases the procedure had been completed, 5 concerning international agreements, one the accession of a new member and the other on a piece of legisation concerned with the Cohesion Fund.

4 The Co-decision Procedure

Article 189b of the Maastricht Treaty introduced a further legislative procedure, that of co-decision. This covers some matters previously dealt with under the cooperation procedure and certain issues concerned with the workings of the single market.

Under the co-decision procedure, Parliament and the Council adopt legislative initiatives on the basis of joint agreement. Parliament has an absolute right of veto if it rejects the approved position of the Council, though in a conciliation stage a committee made up of representatives from the Parliament and the Commission can look for a compromise satisfactory to both institutions. The conciliation procedure can also be utilised if Parliament wishes to amend a Council proposal covered by co-decision in a way which the Council cannot accept. In the absence of agreement, the policy initiative fails.

Although there were fears about the likely time and complexity of co-decision making, it has worked well and enabled decisions to be taken reasonably quickly on a number of issues. The Commission document referred to above suggests that the average time involved in the procedure is under 300 days, although as to whether this will remain true is difficult to say for there is as yet little evidence to go on. It only identified two occasions where the procedure failed to produce a decision.

The Early Experience of Co-decision Making

Proposals	124
Procedures completed	35
Proposals accepted	33 (incl. 15 after conciliation)
Proposals rejected	2

When the proposal has been approved under whichever of the four procedures is relevant, it is then introduced in the form of a regulation, directive or decision (see p158-159).

Comment on the Decision-Making Procedure

In preparation for the IGC, the Commission itself has concluded that there are three main deficiencies in the decision-making process;

i **The continuing divergence between legislative procedure and the budget procedure.** Parliament tends to push through measures under the budgetary procedure which more appropriately come under the auspices of the legislative procedure. The converse is that the Council tends to use the legislative procedure to introduce its financial plans when they should really come under the budgetary procedure, on which Parliament has greater power.

ii **The complexity of the legislative procedure.** There was a time
when decision-making followed a simple pattern, but this has
not been the case since the introduction of changes in the budget
procedure in the 1970s. The introduction of cooperation, assent
and co-decision, as well as special arrangements for EMU, CFSP
and JHA, have added to the confusion.

The addition of new layers of responsibility has led to a growth
in procedures and there are now more than 20 different
variations in existence. Sometimes, there is delay whilst
discussion occurs as to which procedures should be employed.
Moreover, some are particularly complex and this only adds to
the difficulty of understanding. Procedures need to be clearer
and more precise for those not actively involved in the process,
for this would provide for greater openness and transparency.

iii **The lack of logic in the choice of the various procedures and
the different fields of activity where they apply.** Different
procedures apply in three equally important sectors, agriculture,
transport and the internal market, consultation, cooperation and
co-decision respectively. Sometimes, several procedures may
apply in one area such as cohesion and the environment.

Decision-making is now complex to an unacceptable degree. This suggests
the need for a radical transformation of the legislative processes, so that
there is a clear hierarchy of issues, and an appropriate procedure to deal
with each layer. The 20 or so procedures in use at present need to be
reduced. The Commission itself envisages only three main forms in the
future - the assent procedure, a simplified co-decision procedure and
consultation. Simplification of decision-making in budgetary matters (see
p00) is also desirable to ensure that the institutions cooperate in a more
genuinely interinstitutional manner.

Criticism also focuses on other aspects of the policy-making process,
however.

181

The Search for Agreement; the Method of Voting in Council

One of the problems is to get agreement in the Council on issues which require unanimity. As we have seen (p 168-169), the Council worked on this basis for the discussion of important and controversial topics after the adoption of the Luxembourg Compromise, although the passage of the SEA introduced qualified majority voting in all areas connected with the single market. The QMV procedure has also been used for other questions stipulated in the treaties, apart from those where they provide for unanimity, such as taxation and the free movement of persons. However, even where qualified voting is employed, there is still a search for consensus, on the basis that agreed reforms are more likely to be good for relations between the states and are more likely to be implemented fully.

It remains the fact that one of the major barriers to any reform is the sturdy (some would say stubborn) defence of national interests offered by some member states which are unwilling to compromise. Agricultural reform is an area where the French are particularly unwilling to make any concessions, for fear of the outcry which it will provoke in the national agricultural lobby.

The Commission favours an extension of qualified majority voting, seeing it as an 'effective tool' in the decision-making process. Since Maastricht, it covers new fields of activity, including consumer protection, public health, visas and vociational training, among other things. It also applies to some areas of EMU and to the environment and social policy.

Where it is difficult to reach agreement an extra push can sometimes be provided by a meeting of the European Council. This may then enable agreement to be reached within the Council of Ministers.

The decision-making process is not only concerned to achieve agreement between representatives of the national governments. The procedure in all cases is designed to achieve consensus, that is agreement between the institutions involved. This may result in an ineffective policy, for compromise may be on the basis of the lowest common denominator. Pleasing everybody may mean actually doing very little, and in the area of common transport policy or especially reform of the Common Agricultural Policy it has been particularly difficult to achieve substantial change.

Implementation

Even where the policy is agreed much depends on the political will to implement it and some countries have a notably poor record at doing so. In many areas, Britain has a good rate of compliance, though less so on environmental matters including water safety. In some countries, EU regulations and directives are regularly flouted. Implementing measures is the responsibility of the Commission, in partnership with national government departments, and, where the law is concerned, of the Court.

The Lack of Transparency and Democracy

> *A Union that is closer to the people has to be a Union where decisions are easier to comprehend, whose actions are better justified, whose responsibilities are clearer and whose legislation is more accessible.*
> *The Commission, in its evidence to the Reflections Group, 1995.*

The Union's decision-making rules and procedures should also serve to make the institutions more democratic and help them to operate effectively. Central to the criticisms which are often made of the way the Union operates is the lack of transparency and democracy in its working arrangements.

How effective is decision-making in the EU? Can it be improved?

Democracy in the Union

When Monnet and his co-founders launched the idea of the ECSC and then formulated the Rome treaty, they were not primarily concerned with the issue of democratic legitimacy. They were concerned to get the communities off the ground, and to see effective supranational practices established. Yet Monnet always envisaged a move towards democratisation, as his **Memoirs** show. There, he described his task as '...to ensure that in their limited field the new institutions were thoroughly democratic...the Assembly should be elected by universal suffrage within a federal system...In this way, the pragmatic method we had adopted would also lead to a federation validated by the people's vote'.

Yet he and others of the period had a tendency towards elitism within their approach, and tended to assume that for the while they knew best what was needed to bring about peace and prosperity in Europe. As **Holland** remarks; 'Europe was being constructed by a cohesive and remarkably small elite; while public support was welcomed, it was never a prerequisite for Monnet's Europe'.

Although it was always intended that the Parliament would eventually be directly elected, the time was not then ripe for a democratic experiment. From 1953 until 1979, individuals who sat in the Strasbourg assembly were selected from the membership of their national legislatures. After its accession, the attitude of the British Government was seen as a barrier to holding direct elections for the assembly. But finally they were introduced and from 1979 (give or take certain quibbles - see p145-146) the Community could claim to have a new democratic authority for one of its supranational institutions, Parliament.

However, concern for the lack of democracy in the operation of the Union remains. Maastricht laid the foundations for a move towards a more federal-style union in the future, with whole areas of policy now being carried out by intergovernmental cooperation. It is a worrying feature that there is still no very credible system of democratic control within the Union. There is no effective accountability of the Council or Commission to either the national Parliament or to the European one. This is why critics (and also often supporters) of the EU speak of its glaring 'democratic deficit'.

Sir Leon Brittan, the senior British Commissioner, identified this concern in a speech in 1994. He noted three reasons for the 'widespread sense of unease' about Brussels, and what it stood for;

- The feeling that Brussels was interfering where it should not do so

- The absence of knowledge of what was going on in the central decision-making bodies

- The belief that Brussels lacked sufficient democratic legitimacy.

To correct these perceived failings, he recognised the need for the vigorous pursuit of initiatives in three areas, subsidiarity (devolution of decision-making to the most appropriate tier of government), transparency (more open and accessible decision-making) and democracy (correction of the democratic deficit).

Correcting the Democratic Deficit

By the democratic deficit, we mean the lack of democracy and accountability in the decision-making processes of the European Union. **Philip Norton** has defined it as 'the limited input into the law-making processes of the European Community by directly-elected representatives of the people'. He sees three possible solutions to the problem, namely;

i   Strengthening the powers of the European Parliament

ii Creating a new EU institution comprising elected representatives from national parliaments

iii Strengthening the role of national parliaments, in the law-making process.

The second approach has not proved to be a popular suggestion among observers of the Union. It was urged by Leon Brittan, who felt that '...if voters felt their local MPs were lending a hand to the process of Euro-legislation, it would greatly strengthen the EU's democracy and enhance its credibility'. One way of achieving this goal would be the creation of an upper house or senate, made up of people from either chamber in their national state.

One of the problems is that this would create a rival body to the existing European Parliament which is still seeking to establish a greater role for itself. Any such creation might be seen to represent a dilution of the position and importance of the existing body. The outcome may be two relatively weak bodies, instead of one which is becoming more effective.

Control Via National Parliaments

Norton notes the view of the Danish Government; 'It must be recognised that a considerable part of what is known as the democratic shortfall is attributable to the fact that apparently not all national parliaments have an adequate say in the decisions at Community level'. The Danish chamber is better-placed than others in this respect.

Such a policy could be achieved in two ways, either by providing some opportunity for MEPs in the European Parliament to work more closely with their national counterparts or by creating new machinery in the legislatures of member states. President Mitterrand favoured the first approach. He called for such a dialogue in 1989, suggesting that members of national parliaments should be brought into more contact with Strasbourg. Jacques Delors echoed his view, and took the initiative in summoning the Rome Assizes in November 1990. The gathering brought some 300 parliamentarians together, with members sitting in party rather than national groupings.

At the end, there was much, if vague, support for greater cooperation via further conferences of this type. Judgements on the utility of the meeting tended to reflect reactions to this expression of support for closer cooperation in Europe. Most continental Europeans were keen for similar opportunities to be organised, whereas several British MPs were markedly cooler in their response.

In the TEU, a British initiative for 'the greater involvement of national parliaments in the activities of the European Union' was accepted. It was hoped that it would lead to closer ties between national representatives and MEPs, with better exchange of information and facilities, and regular meetings of a Conference of the Parliaments. As yet, no such Conference has taken place, for the European Parliament has no wish to see a potentially rival body created.

The alternative is the possibility of more control via national parliaments, a position strongly endorsed by British ministers.

From the 1980s onwards, most legislatures have made greater provision for dealing with European legislation and given their MPs or deputies more opportunities to acquire specialised information. In Britain, apart from the committees which have been established (see p148), there are occasions when MEPs are invited to meet with their national colleagues in party committee meetings and informally.

Yet keeping up with the burden of work coming from Brussels is a difficult task for the British Parliament, and one which has grown with the preparation for and implementation of the single market. If eventually much foreign and security policy, as well as immigration and policing, are handled in Brussels the task will be even more daunting.

The problem is all the greater if more and more matters are to be decided on the basis of majority voting, which is probably the only way for an enlarged Union to operate efficiently. If the British, or any other government, can be simply overruled in the Council, there is no accountability to the domestic legislature.

Control Via the European Parliament

Norton's first possibility for resolving the democratic deficit was that there should be greater control of the Council and Commission through the European Parliament. Its past weakness and present limitations have already been described (see p145-153), but it is already more than an advisory body and its powers could be increased further, as the majority of MEPs wish to see happen. Any such extension of its current role is, however, highly contentious.

How effective is the control it exercises, and how much democratic legitimacy does it now possess? Parliament is acquiring new powers steadily, but many would still dismiss it as primarily a talking-shop. Moreover, many of the areas affected by Union initiatives, such as the environment and consumer protection, are ones where the majority of MEPs would wish to see more far-reaching European action than has yet been taken. It makes it unlikely that the Parliament will therefore act as much of a check on the activities of the Council and Commission. Rather, in those areas it wishes them to go further.

As yet, the European Parliament still has an essentially limited role in the legislative process. In Norton's phrase, it is 'still only on the edge of constituting a legislature'. Moreover, its legitimacy, enhanced in 1979 by direct elections, still suffers because of the modest turnout on each of the occasions when the European public has been invited to exercise its judgement. In Britain, far more people vote in national elections than in European ones. Observers sometimes disagree on whether it is better to enhance the powers and status of the Strasbourg Parliament in the expectation that this will stimulate interest, or whether to await evidence of popular enthusiasm before granting any increase in powers.

The matter of accountability has not yet been satisfactorily resolved, but it is ironic that some of those in Britain who lament the 'democratic deficit' are those who are most reluctant to make the European Parliament a more effective watchdog. The Major Government is strongly opposed to any extension of the powers of the European Parliament, and sees control remaining firmly in Westminster hands.

Possible Moves to Greater Democracy

To tackle the democratic deficit, the institutions of the Union must be placed under proper democratic control. Almost certainly this does mean a much greater role for the European Parliament, with more decisions being made subject to its approval. In other words, there is likely to be an extension of the machinery of co-decision.

Some would argue that another way of making Parliament strong is to make it more representative. Parliament is already accessible to the public, for people can elect their MEPs and then approach them with suggestions and views. Low turnouts and large constituencies are indications of the difficulties inherent in this form of representation. Also, at present, Britain is the only member state not to use some scheme of proportional representation for the five-yearly elections. If member states were to agree to fulfil the requirement of the Treaty of Rome for a uniform voting procedure, then this would make it more accurately reflect popular opinion. However as in 14 states schemes of varying proportionality are already in use, it would be wrong to overestimate the benefits involved.

The Commission

Another approach is to seek to democratise the Commission, by making it more responsible to the Parliament, as is the case in other democratic systems. A start was made at Maastricht, in the provision that the Commission's appointment should be subject to Parliamentary approval.

This was a useful step forward, but more could be done to enhance its credibility and popular support.

There are two ways in which this could most obviously be achieved;

i   Parliament could be responsible for the initial choice of the Commission, so that it would no longer comprise nominees of individual states. Instead, it would be an executive chosen to reflect the particular balance of the assembly. In this way, elections to the Parliament would also, in effect, become elections to choose the body which initiates legislation.

ii A different route to the one just outlined would be to allow the public to vote for the Union's Commissioners rather than allowing them to be appointed by the national governments subject to the Parliament's approval. This could be done by the public being invited to elect one or two Commissioners in each country, on the day of the EP elections. Such direct election would provide the Commission with a powerful popular base, and enable it to share power with the Council.

In this scheme, the Commission and Parliament would then represent the European electorate, whilst the Council would represent the electorate organised through the member states.

At present, there is a lack of popular control over the Commissions's initial composition, and once in office it is difficult to remove a failing incumbent. It incurs suspicion, particularly in Britain, and is written off as a remote and rather oppressive bureaucracy. Either method outlined would introduce an element of accountability.

The Complexity of the Union

The debates in several countries during the process of ratification of the Maastricht treaty illustrated just how widespread was the concern about the way in which the Union operates. In the referendums in Denmark and France particularly, it was evident that many people felt detached from the whole Maastricht process, and were unsure over what was in the Treaty and what it meant for them. There is an obvious need to bring the Union closer to the citizenry of Europe, and to make it meaningful to the people and strengthen their role in the decision-making process.

There was much comment at the time about the obscurity of the massive Treaty document, and when the future British Chancellor of the Exchequer admitted that he had not studied the script there were many who could appreciate that this required grim determination. To many commentators, it was incomprehensible, and the complexity of the terminology was all the greater because the structures it established made the original Treaty of Rome the more difficult to follow.

There were until Maastricht three entities which together made up the European Community. To these have been added special intergovernmental arrangements for internal affairs, and foreign and security policy, along with a special set of institutions in connection with the move towards economic and monetary union. If the public find the new structure difficult to follow, this is unlikely to mobilise opinion in their support.

Openness and Transparency

At Maastricht, it was agreed that the new Union should act democratically, transparently and in a way which people can understand. To these ends, some progress has been made in the last few years.

At the Edinburgh Council in December 1992, an elaboration of the concept of subsidiarity was produced, a measure which helped to clarify the exercise of powers between the Union and the member state. Subsidiarity had already been written into the TEU (see p104-105), but some member states were keen to emphasise that powers must be exercised in a way which respected the different levels of decision-making, the Union, the states and the regions. They agreed that whatever action was taken in Brussels must be in proportion to the objectives pursued.

Members have their own view as to what subsidiarity is all about, and they have their own purposes in wishing to see it implemented. But all agree on its importance. A clear outline of the tiers of responsibility within the

Union for the pursuit of particular policies is an aid to making the operation of the Union more intelligible to those who are interested in its work. Too often, at present, the concept is used by countries seeking to dilute the effectiveness of the Union, yet it can be employed more positively to justify measures which are better taken collectively than in isolation.

Openness and transparency are similarly important, as an annex to the Maastricht Treaty clearly established; The Conference considers that transparency of the decision-making process strengthens the democratic nature of the institutions and the public's confidence in the administration.

The transparency promised at Edinburgh is, however, modest in its scope. The Council has changed its rules of procedure, and although debates are still held in secret there is now more information available about the way in which states voted, with some explanation as to the events which led up to the final outcome. Open debates were also planned, so that the Council now holds a six-monthly public debate on the programme to be enacted during the Presidency, and periodically, on other areas of public interest. 22 had been held by mid-1995, 9 of which were in Denmark in early 1993 in a clear attempt to boost the chances of a 'yes' vote in the second referendum there.

Open debates have also been held in Belgium, Greece, Germany, France and Spain, the countries which have held the Presidency in this period. They have covered matters ranging from the competitiveness of small businesses and the employment situation, to proposals on agricultural prices and environmental protection. Discussions have tended to be based on those matters where broad agreement exists, and there is scope to extend them into more contentious areas of policy-making.

The Commission has also published a programme of its work, outlining details of its legislative plans and of the consultation it proposes. It produces White and Green Papers, the former setting out its general approach in a given area, the latter establishing areas for reflection and discussion.

Guardian Newspapers v The Council of Ministers

In 1994, a journalist on The Guardian concluded that the Council operated under rules which were alien to the European democratic tradition. It denied access to documents which should have been available under its freedom of information code.

The power to decide whether legislation passes, and in what form it does so, resides with the Council in most cases. In this respect, it operates like a parliament. But unlike the parliaments of Europe, it issues no verbatim transcript. Even the condensed minutes of decisions were classified until recently.

The journalist asked for three sets of Council minutes and supporting papers from COREPER. He received one set on Social Affairs, but not the ones requested on agriculture and justice. They were withheld 'to protect the institution's interests in the confidentiality of its proceedings'. The Foreign Ministers rejected an appeal, and regretted that the Social Affairs set had been made available - due to a mistake 'owing to the novelty of the procedure for allowing public access'.

The case went eventually to the European Court, after support had been obtained from sympathetic governments (Denmark and the Netherlands), and the Parliament. The accession of new Scandinavian countries further boosted the cause of transparency. The Guardian won an outright victory, for without examining the wider case of 'the citizen's right to know' it concluded that the ban on disclosing minutes was illegal under the rules which had been agreed at Edinburgh. The Council had tried to argue that the decisions taken in Edinburgh and at other summits were 'policy orientations', rather than binding regulations.

This was a first victory in the attempt to nudge the debate on openness in the right direction. Plans are afoot to give the public access to the first and third readings of the Council's legislative proceedings, and these now appear to be attracting wider support, following the breakthrough in this case.

More can be done to ensure that legislation is intelligible and clearly drafted, and consolidation of laws on various areas of policy such as the environment is underway so that it is easier for people to find out what the law is and how it applies to particular individuals and groups. But such measures, and those to increase access to documents, are still in their infancy. If the principle of wider access is conceded as yet there is much to be done before transparency and accessibility can be said to be genuine features of the way in which the Union operates.

A former French President, Giscard d'Estaing, has urged the need for concerted action to rectify the 'democratic deficit'; 'The Community cannot continue to be governed according to procedures which are contrary to the imperative requirements it formulates itself in relation to countries which are candidates for membership'.

His remarks are echoed by many politicians and commentators. Certainly, EU support for growing pro-democracy movements in the Eastern bloc lies uneasily with its own barely democratic system of control of Union decision-making institutions. Democratisation of the Union in the process of becoming a more federal state and lying at the heart of a wider European unity seems to be an idea whose time has come.

? How can the European Union be made more democratic?

Can it ever be fully democratic?

TEACH YOURSELF

To Recap

Community Institutions

There are four main institutions,

The Council of Ministers;   One Minister from each of the fifteen countries. The major decision-making body.

The Commission;   20 members from the fifteen countries. The Community's main executive body and civil service.

The Parliament;   626 members (MEPs), elected every five years; sit according to political affiliations, not nationality. Limited, but growing powers.

The Court of Justice;   16 judges from the fifteen countries. Rulings are final and binding on matters of European law.

Remember also;

i   The Heads of Government meet in the EUROPEAN COUNCIL, usually twice-yearly, to chart future direction of EU and make broad policy statements; e.g. Edinburgh Summit, December 1992.

ii   COREPER, the Committee of Permanent Representatives, established to prepare the work of the Council of Ministers, and carry out any tasks which that Council assigns to it.

iii   THE ECONOMIC AND SOCIAL COMMITTEE represents various `interests' within the EU, such as employers and workers; it issues `opinions' on a range of Community matters.

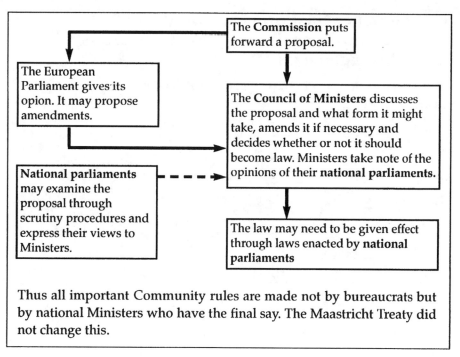

Thus all important Community rules are made not by bureaucrats but by national Ministers who have the final say. The Maastricht Treaty did not change this.

Source; The European Commission

Community Law

Derives from Treaties which are the Primary legislation of the EU. Secondary legislation includes

Regulations;   binding on all states in the form in which they are set out; no national legislation necessary

Directives;   binding as to result to be achieved, but can be implemented by states as best suits them

Decisions;   similar to Regulations, in that they are binding on those to whom they are addressed, be it a state, firm, or individual.

Recommendations and Opinions are not actually laws, and have no binding force.

The Council of the European Union (formerly known as the Council of Ministers); Voting Arrangements

Of the 87 votes allowable in the Council, the allocation under the weighted system is as follows;

Austria	4
Belgium	5
Denmark	3
Finland	3
France	10
Germany	10
Greece	5
Ireland	3
Italy	10
Luxembourg	2
Netherlands	5
Portugal	5
Spain	8
Sweden	4
United Kingdom	10
The qualified majority is	62
The simple majority is	44
The blocking minority is	26

The Presidency

The Presidency of the Union is held on a six monthly basis, rotating every January and July. Modification has been necessary since the Fourth Enlargement, and the following dates have been decided;

1996	Italy	Ireland
1997	Netherlands	Luxembourg
1998	United Kingdom	Austria
1999	Germany	Finland
2000	Portugal	France
2001	Sweden	Belgium
2002	Spain	Denmark

British Involvement in European Union Institutions

	Total membership	British membership
The European Council	15	1
The Council of Ministers	15	1
The Commission	20	2
The Parliament	626	87
The Court of Justice (also, Court of First Instance)	15	1
The Court of Auditors	15	1
The Economic and Social Committee	222	24
The Committee of the Regions	222	24

Questions to consider

1   Read the two extracts and then answer the questions which follow;

a

Mr Kinnock, the transport commissioner, points out the inconvenient truth at the heart of the Government's convenient Euroscepticism: 'It sometimes makes me impatient that the representation of this place is one of a great nosy-parkering bureaucracy issuing fiats left, right and centre. There is insufficient consciousness that there can be no European law without the assent of the ministers of the European states'

b

But accountability remains elusive. Sir Leon Brittan, a former Conservative cabinet minister and Britain's senior commissioner, says a touch smugly, knowing he will never again have to canvass on windswept doorsteps: 'I am a politician, not a civil servant. I think the foundation of the commission was extremely ingenious: it is because it is charged with putting forward proposals and giving a certain dynamism that it is a political institution. I personally would be quite happy to stand for election'.

Extracts written by Stephen Bates, The Guardian, 25.1.96

i   `The Commission proposes, the Council decides'. Is this traditional view of the relationship between the two institutions still appropriate?

ii   How are Commissioners appointed? Should they be elected?

iii On what grounds can the Commission be criticised?

iv   How can the Commission be defended?

2   With what justification is the European Parliament often criticised as being `weak and ineffective'?

3   Has the introduction of direct elections to the European Parliament led to a significant increase in its powers?

4   `Far from being irrelevant to the process of European integration the European Parliament has a central role in promoting it'. Discuss.

5   `The Commission is an unelected and uncontrolled bureaucracy. It is essential to curb its powers to make Europe more democratic'. Discuss.

6   `Real power lay with the Council of Ministers'. Discuss.

7   Why has the European Council assumed so much importance in recent years?

8   What are the powers and restraints affecting the Presidency of the Commission? To what extent does its importance depend upon the incumbent?

9   What is meant by the Democratic Deficit? How can it be removed?

10   What is meant by the `co-operation procedure' and the `co-decision procedure'? What do they have in common, and in what ways do they differ?

11   `Decision-making in the European Union is confused; there are too many ways by which decisions can be reached'. How could greater clarity and effectiveness be brought to the decision-making process?

12   Distinguish between the different types of European law. How has the supremacy of European over national law been demonstrated and made effective in recent years?

13   Discuss the view that the future evolution of the European Union is increasingly being decided by the way in which the Court is interpreting its laws and regulations.

14   Write a couple of paragraphs on the work and importance of two of the following bodies;

COREPER

The Court of Auditors

The Committee of the Regions

Chapter Three: Representation

Transnational Political Parties in the European Union

As the Union develops, so commentators begin to look for signs that national parties are becoming more 'European' in their outlook, in reflection of the general move towards a more integrationist approach. To what extent is a uniquely European party system likely to develop, linked to but distinct from the party systems prevalent in member countries? Or is it really the case that European elections can be interpreted only in terms of the impact on the fortunes of national parties in the various states?

At present, national political parties are involved in the affairs of the European Union in three ways, at the transnational level, via the transnational political groupings in the Parliament and via their activities back home where the agenda they pursue has become increasingly 'Europeanised'.

Transnational Parties

The three main political parties in Britain each belong or are affiliated to appropriate transnational confederations. These were created two or more decades ago, and they are loose associations which bring together broadly like-minded parties from member states in one organisation. Thus there is the Rightwing European People's Party (EPP), the Leftwing Party of European Socialists (PES) and the more Centrist European Liberal, Democrat and Reform Party (ELDR).

National parties have joined together in these confederations, for the purpose of coordinating their activities at the European level, enabling them to present common propaganda and to fight elections on a common platform. They are described as confederations rather than federations, for the bonds which unite them are not strong and there is little central direction or leadership. They see a mutual benefit in cooperation and the exchange of information, and could develop more in the future. But at present, other than organising and attending meetings, and producing election literature, their role is modest.

Nugent offers an explanation for this weakness. He makes the point that because they have no institutional focus (such as Westminster or the European Parliament) they are not involved in day-to-day political activities; 'They cannot develop attachments and loyalties. From this, other weaknesses flow; low status; limited resources...and loose organisational structures'.

If the three main transnational groups are only loosely coordinated, the smaller ones which have periodically emerged (for instance, the Greens) suffer even more seriously from the disadvantages of fragmentation and limited resources.

Transnational Party Groupings in the European Parliament

More significant are the party blocs which have developed in the European Parliament and which in many cases share the same name as the transnational parties already described. Their activities do have a specific focus, the assembly itself, and they can and do play an important role in its organisation and operations. These party groupings at Strasbourg are then a part of the wider transnational parties, but because they have a more definite role they are much more significant. The box detailing information about the European People's Party illustrates its organisation at both levels.

The organisation of the European Parliament emphasises its supranational leanings, for the representatives are not seated on the basis of their country of origin nor on the basis of whether they are British Labour, Conservative or Liberal Democrat supporters. They sit as part of a political group which shares a broadly common outlook, and is usually composed of members of more than one nationality. These groups are a recognised feature of the workings of the assembly. The drafting of the agenda, committee chairmanships, speaking rights, and other duties and facilities are allocated on this basis.

The minimum number of MEPs to be accepted as a group varies according to the number of countries from which its representation derives. In the Rules of Procedure as amended in 1993, the number of MEPs is set out, according to a scale which requires less members if they derive from more countries. If they represent only one member state, then 26 members are needed, whereas if they represent four or more then only 13 are required.

There are several groups, for the use of proportional representation in fourteen of the fifteen states means that diverse traditions in the national life of countries such as France and Greece can secure some representation. **Nugent** calculates that there have never been less than sixty different national parties represented in the European Parliament. In the 1994-99 body, there are almost 100.

These national parties are currently organised into 8 broad groups, though a few sit as Independents or are difficult to classify. Three main federations exist, the European People's Party (EPP), which comprises mainly Christian Democratic parties, the Party of European Socialists (PES) and the European Liberal, Democratic and Reformist Party (ELDR), but various other groupings exist either as a permanent or temporary feature of the political landscape. The two largest ones, the EPP and the PES, draw from

Transnational Political Groupings in the European Parliament, and the National Parties Within Them

Title	National Parties Involved	Comments
The Right		
Union for Europe Group (UFE)	French Gaullists Fianna Fail	Centre-Right, prefer to keep independent of EPP. Pro CAP
European People's Party (EPP)	Christian Democrats British Conservatives	Broadly Centre-Right and now affiliated federalist, now less cohesive on social issues
Europe of Nations (EN)	French National Front	Far Right, notably illiberal on racial matters
Liberal Democratic and Reformist Group (LDR)	Assorted Centre-Right parties, though some Leftish influences Includes 2 Lib-Dems	Very divided, lacking clearcut philosophy but strongly federalist
The Left		
Party of European Socialists (PES)	Members from 'socialist' parties in every country Includes British Labour Party	Various interpretations of socialism, some moderate and pragmatic, some more ideological; differences over future of Europe

European United Left /Nordic Green Left, (EUL/NGL)	Communists and other Far Left groups	Rather isolated from PES, less sympathetic to federalism
European Radical Alliance (ERA)	Scottish Nationalists	
Miscellaneous		
Greens	Environmental parties	Many, but not all members are pro-Left; not cohesive

NB *The UFE Group is a recent creation, the product of an amalgamation between the old European Democratic Alliance Group and the Forza Europa Group.*

membership across the whole Union, whereas some smaller groupings contain the representatives of only two or three member states. At present, the smallest blocs are the European Radical Alliance and the Europe of Nations group, each with 19 members, which draw from 5 and 3 states respectively.

The organisational stress on supranational rather than national interests has helped to create a sense of European identity in the Parliament, and many members do recognise a responsibility to examine issues on the basis of what is good for Europe rather than purely on the basis of what is good for their own country. After all, they share a broad similarity of outlook, and because of these common values they have a distinctive way of approaching European issues.

However, in any such grouping, there are bound to be differences reflecting differing national viewpoints and in some cases differences of doctrinal interpretation. In particular, the pace of European integration and methods of tackling racism on the continent tend to bring about less predictable alliances, and this is true of many other policy areas.

The European People's Party

The EPP is both a transnational political party organisation and a political group in the European Parliament.

A Transnational Party

The EPP organisation is a transnational party, a confederation of Christian Democrat and other Centre-Right parties from member states. Founded in 1976 in time to prepare for the first direct elections to the EP, it aims to promote closer liaison between the Christian Democratic Parties of the Union. Via its contact with the European Union of Christian Democrats (EUCD) it is also linked to the same cause in non-EU countries.

It operates at the governmental and parliamentary levels. Heads of government whose parties belong to the EPP organisation meet prior to summit gatherings, and those members of the European Commission of mainstream Centre-Right leanings have regular weekly meetings.

In recent years, membership has been widened beyond the CD movement, hence the admission of New Democracy (Greece) and Partido Popular (Spain). The accession of new members has brought other new non-CD parties into the fold, and it is now a much broader umbrella than was once the case.

Neither the British Conservative Party nor its MEPs are members of the EPP organisation; nor have they applied to join.

A Political Group of the European Parliament

MEPs from national parties belonging to the EPP organisation automatically sit in the EP as members of the Group of the European People's Party. The EPP Group contains some MEPs who do not actually belong to the EPP, but who are affiliated to it.

This is the position of the British Conservatives. The 18 MEPs (and the Ulster Unionist) are 'allied members', and as such are an important part (the third largest contingent) of the EPP Group. They enjoy the benefits of membership of a wider Centre-Right body, but are not bound by its policy statements.

Full members accept the EPP organisation's political platforms and programmes. Allied members do not. They accept the 'basic policies' of the Parliamentary grouping, not necessarily those of the wider EPP party organisation. The Conservatives are more Rightwing than most who belong to, or are associated with, the EPP, but it was considered on both sides that there were sufficient similar values and ideas between them for the British to be be partially integrated into the Group in 1992.

French socialists are more sympathetic to the CAP than are members of the British Labour Party, and within the EPP the differences on the future of Europe have increased since British Conservatives became affiliated to the body. The depleted British contingent is much less committed to the Social Chapter, and dislikes the federal goals to which the EPP is committed by its charter.

It is not uncommon for members of one bloc to share an affinity of outlook on key issues with members of another. Often the matters discussed do not easily fit into an ideological Left-Right battle between the supporters of Christian Democracy and those of Social Democracy.

This potential lack of unity is all the greater because MEPs are much lobbied by various pressure groups representing differing interests in Europe, and also because they often belong to **Intergroups** which cross the boundaries of the different groupings and espouse diverse causes. Intergroups range from the Friends of Israel and the Federalist Intergroup for European Union, to the Animal Welfare Group and the Media Intergroup.

These party groupings are not strong bodies as yet. They often lack money and resources, and are subject to internal division. There are inevitably differences in bringing about a united approach for members who share the same broad political principles may nevertheless find themselves much affected by considerations of national self-interest. This inevitably means that policy on key issues is sometimes fudged, and statements are often little more than vague platitudes.

The Trend Towards Common Action

Yet what is emerging, in a limited way, is a European party system mainly based on the series of transnational groupings at Strasbourg. These blocs adopt common manifestoes, and produce brochures which set out their policies and programmes, a development which moved forwards in the contests of 1989 and 1994.

The elections in 1994 were fought on the basis of national parties each standing in their own country, but those parties were affiliated to the Europe-wide bodies. Thus the Conservatives fought as Conservatives but also in association with the People's Party, and Labour fought a predominantly Labour Campaign but in their literature candidates asserted the party's membership of the Socialist bloc. The common European manifestoes and other electoral material were used more extensively, and this meant that more attention was paid to European issues and to the debate on the future of European integration.

The Change of Political Complexion in Recent Years

As in national parliaments, the attitudes of the political groups have a significant impact on the decisions taken by Parliament, both in committee and in session. The 1989 elections brought about a major change in the political composition of the Strasbourg assembly, for whereas parties of the Centre-Right had enjoyed the greater measure of success for the previous decade, it was the Socialist group which dominated the newly-elected Parliament. This brought about a new emphasis on social and environmental matters, for the PES often had the support of many environmentalists in a Red-Green alliance.

Thanks to the strong performance of the British Labour Party in 1994, this pattern continued. Although the composition is now more numerically balanced than before, the forces of the Right are more prone to fragmentation whereas those of the Left are more cohesive.

Whatever the party balance, however, many MEPs recognise the desirability, when possible, of seeking a common outlook which can be presented as a European Parliament view. Evidence of widespread support on any initiative enables greater pressure to be brought on the Council of Ministers and on the European Commission.

The Outcome of the 1994 Elections

Composition of the European Parliament (by Nationality and Political Group)

	A	B	Dk	Fi	F	G	Gr	Ir	I	L	N	P	S	Sw	UK	Total
PES	8	6	3	4	15	40	10	1	18	2	8	10	22	7	63	217
EPP	6	7	3	4	12	47	9	4	14	2	10	1	30	5	19	173
UFE					15		2	7	27			3				54
ELDR	1	6	5	6	1			1	6	1	10	8	2	3	2	52
EUL/NGA			1	1	7	4			5		3	9	3			33
GREENS	1	2		1		12		2	4	1	1			4		28
ERA		1			13		2							1	2	19
EN			4		13						2					19
IND	5	3			11				11						1	31
Total	21	25	16	16	87	99	25	15	87	6	31	25	64	22	87	626

NB The table reflects the composition of the groups in 1995. Some shifts of allegiance occurred in the months following the elections; eg, the Forza Europa Group and the European Democratic Alliance Group have joined to form the Union for Europe Group.

PES	Party of European Socialists	**EPP**	European People's Party
UFE	Union for Europe		
ELDR	European Liberal, Democratic and Reformist Party		
EUL/NGL	European United Left/Nordic Green Left		
Greens	Green Group	**ERA**	European Radical Alliance
EN	Europe of Nations	**Ind**	Independents

Future Prospects

What we have at the moment are the makings of a European party system, based on a series of party groupings in the Strasbourg Parliament. Among these groupings is a 'core' comprising two main blocs, the Party of European Socialists (PES) and the European People's Party (EPP). Between them, they currently control 355 of the 567 seats, 62.6%, a higher figure than the 55.4% of the 1989 assembly.

Their dominance is unsurprising, for they articulate the outlook of the two main forces in European politics, Christian Democracy and Social Democracy. Either of these 'core' parties is normally the senior partner in government in most of the member states.

The Logos of the PEU and the EPP

Two countries, Germany and the United Kingdom, contribute the bulk of their Parliamentary membership, just under half of their total representation. Labour now has the largest number of MEPs in the Socialist group, and the German CDU and the SDP are both well-represented (German membership is strengthened by the increased size of the country's representation following unification).

However, there has been a long term decline in the aggregate vote of these two German parties at federal level of the type which has occurred in several countries. It may be that if this continues it will tend to make the PES and the EPP less cohesive than they are at present.

The seeming erosion of support for the core parties has been matched by a growth of new forces in the Strasbourg Parliament. Since Maastricht, there has been an anti-integrationist mood in some countries. It has affected Germany and Belgium (among other nations), but it is in Denmark and France that the nationalist viewpoint has emerged most clearly. In 1994, two such Rightwing groups gathered 25.5% of the vote in Denmark, whereas in France Philippe de Villiers' anti-Maastricht party, L'Autre Europe, gained 12.3%.

Rightwing nationalism has also been evident in Greece and Italy. In the former, the Political Spring party has achieved some success, but in the latter the National Alliance/MSI and the Northern League are pro-Fascist and Forza Italia (30.6% of the vote) is led by a committed Euro-sceptic.

Of these groups, some may prove to be short-lived, but others may survive either as part of some other established party or as an independent force. The combination of this tendency to Rightwing splintering and the loss of electoral support for some established national parties, could be very damaging to the long term prospects of the two main blocs.

Both of those groupings are integrationist, committed to moving forward the political agenda of Europe in a federal direction. Other parties which have gained representation tend to think more in terms of national identity and adopt a less European approach. Any large-scale splintering of political expression is unlikely to be good for the cohesiveness of the European Parliament.

 What are the prospects for the development of a European party system? Is it desirable?

National Political Parties

It is national parties which select the candidates who stand in European elections, and who run the campaigns designed to bring about their victory. They may increasingly use the literature of the transnational groupings, but they fight primarily on national rather than European issues and they interpret the outcome very much in terms of what it means for their standing in domestic politics.

National parties have their own priorities, and use a range of policy issues in Euro-elections. Yet although they tend to see them as another opportunity to rally the faithful and inflict a defeat on their main rivals, nonetheless Europe is a key question with which they have to deal.

The Impact of the European Issue on British Political Parties

In no other country have the parties and politicians found the European issue so difficult to handle. Just as Home Rule for Ireland was a divisive question in the 1880s, and Tariff Reform was in the first decade of the C20, so Europe has been in recent years. Both parties have had to contend with internal divisions which have been difficult to handle, and the temptation has been to adopt short-term policies which have got them off the hook until the next election was safely out of the way.

 This was true of the **Labour Party** in the 1970s, yet whatever reluctance it showed in opposition the leadership came to agree with the Conservatives that Britain's place was in the Community as soon as it regained power. Today, it retains that approach, and has actually outflanked the Conservatives as the more pro-European party. This is something which a number of observers find amazing, for they recall the disunity in the party and the constant changes in Labour thinking over the last three decades or so. It is possible to discern six different eras in the party's attitude to European policy;

- Early 1960s At best, lukewarm; mostly opposed to EEC
- Late 1960s Leadership in favour
- Early 1970s Leadership opposed terms of entry
- Mid 1970s Leadership supported membership, after renegotiation
- Early 1980s Leadership opposed; 1983, favoured withdrawal
- Late 1980s Leadership embraced Community, as it has done since

Conservative In the same way, the **Conservatives** have found themselves preoccupied with matters of unity more recently, and have had to minimise the extent of the commitments they have undertaken in order to hold the party together. For John Major, the task was the more difficult as his predecessor was playing the nationalist card with some bravura. He has seemed to be the prisoner of the Right, to the dismay of more moderate members of his party.

If Labour's disunity was over the actual fact of membership, the issue for the Conservatives has been different. Few have felt that Britain could survive outside the Community, but many were and are uncertain as to the sort of future they want inside it. Most politicians and writers agree that there is little to be gained from espousing an anti-European viewpoint today. The debate has moved on, and even for most members of the Conservative Party there is no going back. All three parties are officially in favour of 'Britain in Europe'.

Indeed, the differences between them are considerable, but not fundamental. The Liberal Democrats are most committed, and see the merits of a more federal structure, although they are aware of the danger of policy being too far ahead of public opinion. They have in recent times been more cautious in their use of the 'f' word and in their view about the likelihood of Britain joining a single currency before the end of the century.

Labour sees an advantage in keeping a step in front of the Conservatve Party, though its past record invites some misgivings about the depth of its conversion. In its rhetoric, it is more enthusiastic about meeting the conditions of convergence which make a single currency viable, and it is happy to embrace the Social Chapter. Yet it too dislikes the word 'federal', and like the Government, it rejects a European defence force or majority voting for a common foreign policy.

The Conservatives generally favour membership, but there are varying degrees of commitment across the Left-Right spectrum, some of which are highlighted in the boxes on p 220-222. The differences within the party are greater than those between the leaderships of both main parties.

Apart from the tactical manoeuvering which has bedevilled the development of policy in both parties over the last few decades, there is more at stake in the European issue than the parties' perceptions of their short term interests. The issue of membership initially, but now of the future direction of the Union, poses real questions about the extent of British involvement in continental affairs, the loss of national independence which membership involves and the benefits, alleged or real, that it can bring. Many British politicians find it hard to commit the country more fully to a European future, for to do so means an admission that Britain cannot any longer achieve what it was once able to do on its own.

Chapter Three

Conservatism and Europe

Douglas Hurd (a former Foreign Secretary, party centrist and pro-European) has expressed concern about the threat to party unity and the danger of Britain being isolated in Europe. At the 1992 Conference, he reminded Conservatives that *'Our Party broke itself over the Corn Laws - and shut itself effectively out of power for ten years...(It could do so over Europe) with consequences which would deeply damage Britain and only comfort our opponents. Let us decide to give that madness a miss.'*

He was sure that there would never be a European superstate, and said that Conservatives wanted a wider and open free trade Community. Maastricht was based on the principle of minimum interference, and was not 'a blue-print for a centralised Europe'. He believed that it was essential for the Treaty to be ratified, for the alternative was *'...a sure way of shoving our country onto the sidelines in future discussions when the security and prosperity of Europe are being decided. We know in our bones, because of our history, that that's not right.'*

Michael Portillo (a prominent member of the Major Cabinet) addressed the Conference three years later, and made a much-publicised speech in which he outlined a strongly nationalist strategy, and denounced many aspects of Brussels policy. As he put it; *'I stripped away all the waffle and fudge and any Euro- speak, and I said that any Conservative government is not going to allow Britain to be drawn into a European superstate.'*

Emma Nicholson (a defector from the party in January 1996), mentioned the European issue as a reason for her increasing unease as a Conservative backbencher. Alarmed by Michael Portillo's speech, she observed; *The Government appears to have lost all sense of positive direction at a crucial time for the future of Britain. This is particularly true of the vital question of the development of a modern democratic Europe with Britain 'at its heart. How ironic those words of John Major's seem now in the light of the sorry saga of shilly-shallying on Europe that we have seen from the Government. I find that most of our continental European neighbours are in despair at the inability of the British Government to rise above cheap flag-waving populaism and get on with the real job of* *building the sort of Europe we want including, in the not too distant future, complete economic and monetary union.'*

Norman Lamont told the same Conference of his belief that the party must reject outright any notion of a federal superstate, otherwise the issue would *'continue to dominate our politics and poison the Conservative Party for many years to come'*. Having observed that Britain was a viable state on its own, he continued; I do not suggest Britain should today unilaterally withdraw from Europe. But the issue may well return to the political agenda.

The British Parties and Where They Stand; A Summary
The Conservatives

Leadership	Some closet Europeans in Cabinet, keen to promote the cause of closer involvement; such as Gummer and Heseltine. Mostly anti-federalist, and former pro-Europeans (Rifkind) sound increasingly Euro-sceptical
Bulk of MPs	Follow leadership, keen for unity, anxious about divisions and the threat to electoral prospects. Many are increasingly Euro-sceptical, anti-federalist, wary of a single currency and closer integration
Right-wing	Cool on EU. A few opposed in principle and talk of life outside the Union; more are Thatcherite and favour single market, but not moves to political unity; prefer a 'Europe des Patries'
Pro-Europeans	Mainly on Left, especially E. Heath, but some others who are pro-federalist, pro-Maastricht and keen to see greater commitment from British Government

The Liberal Democrats

Almost all MPs pro-European over many years, and keen to see closer integration and a more positive approach by Britain. Less overt stress of late on a federal Europe, for fear of electoral damage. Keen on idea of a Citizen's Europe, and favour a single currency when it can be realistically achieved.

The Labour Party

Leadership   In recent years, much more pro-European; Kinnock a convert, Smith always a supporter, Blair went along with 1983 policy but long a committed European

Bulk of MPs   Follow leadership in being broadly pro-Maastricht, but strongly disliking absence of Social Chapter. Some wish to exploit Governmental difficulties over European issues, but most wary of federalism, and common defence and foreign policies. Broad acceptance (whilst in opposition) of single currency, if criteria are manageable

Left-wing   Some committed 'antis', eg, Tony Benn. Most are reconciled to membership, but worry about deflationary impact of tough EU economic policies as nations seek to meet convergence criteria.

?

Why is European policy a problem area for British parties?

Why is Europe a particularly difficult subject for the Conservative Party today?

Lobbying Europe; Pressure Groups and The European Union

Over the last two decades, pressure groups in the member states have felt the need to modify their methods of operation to cater for their country's closer involvement in the European Union. They recognise that Europe plays an increasing role in national politics, and that the Maastricht Agreement and the completion of the internal market are moving the EU along the route of closer integration.

The Union has been increasingly active in a range of matters beyond those concerned with the creation of a tariff-free trading area, and these are of interest to particular lobbyists - for example, those concerned with the environment. As states have ceded a considerable degree of decision-making power to European institutions, it is not surprising that many groups feel the need to protect and promote their interests in Brussels and Strasbourg.

European regulations apply directly throughout the Union, while directives must be translated into national legislation within a given time.

Many of the measures introduced in the last decade have concerned the implementation of the Single European Act. Designed to eliminate the technical, physical and fiscal barriers to intra-Community trade, and the barriers to the free provision of professional and other services, they were and remain particularly relevant to pressure group activity.

For instance, some 60 EC directives in connection with the SEA had animal health and veterinary control implications. Others affected the veterinary profession, having implications for such things as the freedom of movement and rights of establishment of veterinary surgeons. In Britain, the British Veterinary Association and the Royal College of Veterinary Surgeons were inevitably going to be interested in such initiatives, whilst some of them were of relevance to the RSPCA, the NFU and the Euro-group for Animal Welfare.

Pressure Points for the Lobbyist

The European Parliament has limitations as a legislative body, and the legislative initiative comes from the Commission which puts forward proposals. But the outcome is the result of long discussions in several national and European governmental institutions, so that the scope for pressure group action is considerable.

Lobbying of the Union can be carried out via several routes;

- Via the Council of Ministers
- Via the Commission (Commissioners and Commission officials)
- Via the Parliament (and its committees, and those of party groupings)
- Via the Economic and Social Committee.

Once agreement has been reached in the Council, the legal validity of directives and regulations can then be challenged in the Court of Justice. In 1977, the manufacturers of Isoglucose managed to get a decision overruled in the Court, because the opinion of the Parliament had not been sought before the Council had come to its conclusion.

Via these institutions, there is a fertile ground for pressure group activity, and influence may be achieved in three main ways;

i   Lobbying the National Government, to encourage it to use its influence in the Council of Ministers

ii Acting through a Euro-grouping representing pressure groups from across the Union

iii Making direct contact with the European machinery, particularly the European Parliament and the Commission. Some groups will even have an office in the Union to further their interests.

Working Through National Governments

Many groups seek to influence the stance taken by their governments in EU discussions, and to influence the implementation of EU decisions. For several of them, this is the most effective means of influencing the Union. This is because they may find that their counterparts in the EU take a different line to their own on many issues, and also that lobbying in Europe can be an expensive operation.

British groups, especially those defending a sectional interest, already have access to Whitehall ministries. If, as with the TUC in the 1980s, they have found themselves excluded from such close consultation at the seat of power, they can still endeavour to influence the policy of the government through the parliamentary panel of sponsored MPs.

Naturally, a group with a European interest will seek to build upon the national channel of influence. If, for instance, the matter is one where there is a clear British interest, such as reform of the CAP and farm prices, it might expect the British Government to advance the cause in the Council of Ministers. The issue of agriculture is one where groups in all member countries are active in pressing governments to listen to their views. No German government would ignore the strength of feeling among the farming community in Bavaria, and French viticulturalists and farmers have always been active and often successful lobbyists.

Of course, with the completion of the single market and the decisions taken at Maastricht, the extension of majority-voting makes it more difficult for the ministers of any country to hold out against their European partners. Governments make concessions in the Council, and **Butt Philip** reminds us that 'the national pressure groups will be very much in the hands of government officials once the Council of Ministers' negotiations begin'.

Many British groups have preferred to operate via the British Government rather than make a direct approach to the Union. However, for the larger ones such as the Institute of Directors, this avenue is used in conjunction with others, the emphasis being on the one which is most likely to be effective in a particular case.

Euro-groups

Many British groups feel that in addition to taking advantage of their contact with their own governments, they wish to exert pressure via a European-level federation of national groups. Indeed, **Baggott** found that 75% of those he surveyed were members of such an organisation.

A number of these Euro-groups have sprung up, mostly based in Brussels, though some are in Paris, Amsterdam, London and Cologne. Many began to operate at the time the Community began its work (1958), or within a few years of its creation. In 1980, the Commission identified 439 with whom it negotiated. Of these, the best organised were the 165 concerned with representing the interests of employers. 148 represented agricultural and food interests, and the rest were an assortment covering consumers, trade unionists and environmental groups.

This figure of 439 is unrealistically low; even then, the Commission has contact with many others which did not seek a permanent relationship with it. For transport policy, it mentioned six with whom it had dealings, whereas the relevant Directorate-General listed 130 national and European bodies with whom it would consult. Butt Philip has put the present figure at more than 800 with whom the Commission has fairly regular contact.

Nugent has distinguished between those which are umbrella groups, covering companies in a vast sector such as industry or agriculture, and those more specialised ones which represent specific business groups such as pasta manufacturers. The Committee of Professional Agricultural Organisations of the

Unice's purpose is

• to keep abreast of issues that interest its members by maintaining permanent contacts with all the European institutions

• to provide a framework which enables industry and employers to examine European policies and proposed legislation, and to prepare joint positions

• to promote its policies and positions at Community and national level, and persuade the European legislators to take them into account.

European Community (COPA) and the Union of Industrial and Employers Confederation of Europe (UNICE) are of the first type, whereas the Federation of European Explosive Manufacturers (FEEM) and the European Spice Association (ESA) are in the second category. Euro-groups even exist for such highly specialised interests as mustard growing.

These Euro-groups can be used in several ways; to strengthen the case a national group wishes to promote, to put pressure on the government of another EU country to modify its own position, or to influence counterpart organisations in other countries, so that they might lobby their own government and collectively lobby the Commission.

They are vital two-way channels of communication between the Union and national groups. On the one hand, they keep the groups informed of important Union proposals, and on the other, they represent these groups to the EU. **Wyn Grant** quotes the example of the British Spice Trade Association which, working through the ESA, was able, in 1987, to gain special exemptions for herbs and spices from amendments to the Unit Pricing Directive.

Euro-groups and the EU Institutions

Pressure groups conduct their operations primarily at the place where the most power is concentrated. For Euro-groups, the Commission is the main object of their attention. It has the reputation of being an open bureaucracy. It does not conceal the fact that initiatives are being worked upon, and welcomes an input from pressure groups at an early stage. Some of the contact is informal, perhaps over a business lunch. Otherwise, much of it involves routine meetings with officials, or discussions on the phone. Some Directorates-General are particularly receptive to representations.

Communication with individual Commissioners is relatively infrequent, and may be less useful than regular dialogue with the officials engaged in the development of policy. Each Commissioner has a small cabinet of officials serving him, and lobbying can be done with the 'chefs de cabinet' who meet prior to the weekly meetings of the Commission.

Contact with the European Parliament is maintained, but staffing is a problem for many groups, so that meetings at this level have a lower priority, and ones with the ESC lower still.

Indeed, the effectiveness of some Euro-groups is limited by lack of resources, of which staffing is but one problem. Many are small-scale operations with only a handful of permanent staff, and these become active only when an issue of relevance to them becomes important. Very few have the resources to campaign over a long period, and Butt Philip could only identify 5/500 with 10 or more permanent staff.

These Euro-groups inevitably find communication with their many different members time-consuming, and for those with meagre resources the problem is compounded. More serious, especially for the larger umbrella organisations, is the difficulty of harmonising divergent national interests, once these have been ascertained from member associations. The temptation is to water-down proposals so that they command as wide an area of agreement as possible,

and in this process their effectiveness can be lessened. For those organisations such as ETUC and UNICE, which have a membership wider than the Union, it can be the more difficult to reach an acceptable common position. There is the additional risk that in operating on a wider scale their focus on the EU institutions is weakened.

Some Useful Examples of Euro-groups

The **Committee of Professional Agricultural Organisations of the EEC (COPA)** is perhaps the most influential Euro-group, and it has the resources and staffing to match. With some 50 full-time employees, it operates on a broad front and is in almost daily contact with one or other of the Union institutions.

COPA has made the Commission its main focus, and its secretary has regular contact with the Commissioner and his cabinet. It makes little use of the European Parliament, though it communicates its views on important matters to it. Neither does it have much to do with the Council of Ministers, though it may send telegrams when key matters are under discussion.

COPA is a high-profile group, though it is easy to confuse activity with influence. It has often succeeded in reaching internal agreement on significant and controversial subjects such as agricultural prices, and though deviating positions do occur, this is not a common feature; it realises that a united front is likely to strengthen its case. Where differences are apparent, members tend to forward their views more positively through their national government.

The **Eurogroup for Animal Welfare**, formed in 1980, is concerned to identify areas of concern in the treatment of animals and lobby for the introduction and enforcement of legislation in the European Union. It has an office in Brussels to liaise with the main institutions.

Its close cooperation with the Parliament and Commission has led to a number of important achievements, among which are the introduction in 1983 of an EC ban on the importation of skins from hooded and harp seal pups, and the adoption three years later of a directive regulating the use of animals for experimental and other scientific purposes.

Its present priorities for action include;

- Animal transportation, and protection of animals for slaughter
- Full implementation of the ban on the leghold trap in the EU, and on the import of furs obtained with such traps
- Minimum standards for the welfare of animals in zoos
- Reduction, refinement and replacement of tests involving animals

The **European Trade Union Congress (ETUC)** is an umbrella organisation which includes more than thirty affiliated national associations from more than twenty countries. Its size and range makes it difficult to achieve internal cohesion, the more so as its affiliates include some organisations with a communist tradition, and others with a socialist or christian one.

Direct Representation in the Union

Big business soon realised the importance of the EC, and lobbied it extensively and expensively. This made it all the more important for other groups to make their views felt. Lobbying at this level is usually done as a complement rather than as a substitute for action in the home country.

Direct contacts with Union institutions are becoming increasingly important for many national pressure groups. Almost all of them lobby members of the Commission, personally or by written submissions.

Some major groups have set up offices in Brussels, which were at first conceived primarily as listening-posts/service centres for national association members and staff attending meetings in Brussels. In recent years, these offices have become a more significant part of the groups' activities. Brussels is the place for them to be, for not only is the Commission based there, but also the committees and party groupings of the European Parliament meet in the city.

Some of the Leading Euro-Groups

Group	founded	Headquarters staff	membership	other info
COPA Committee of Professional Agriculture Organisations of the EC	1958	Brussels 35	22	Main agriculture group. Several specialist working-groups, eg milk, tobacco, etc.
UNICE Union of Industries in the European Community	1958	Brussels 25	13	Main employers' group. Several working groups, eg Industrial Affairs, Social Affairs
BEUC European Bureau of Consumer Unions	1973	Brussels 7	16	Main voice of the consumer associations. No permanent working groups
ETUC European Trade Union Confederation	1973	Brussels 28	17	Main trade union association. Some working-groups
EEB European Environmental Bureau	1974	Brussels 2	37	Lacks resources of more powerful umberella organisations. No permanent specialist groups.
FÉDÉRATION BANCAIRE Banking Federation of the European Community	1960	Brussels 6	10	Main voice of the commercial banks in EC. 3 specialist groups.

In Britain, the National Farmers' Union was one of the first groups to recognise the importance of the European dimension. It currently has an office manned by 3 policy-negotiators and 3 support staff. They lobby the relevant Directorate-General on detailed and often highly technical matters concerning the 'price-fixing' aspects of policy, such as the levels of agricultural support, as well as on matters of trade policy such as the GATT talks.

Likewise, the Confederation of British Industry quickly recognised the importance of the EC in furthering the interests of its members, and established its Brussels office before Britain had actually joined the Community. In the last decade, it has placed more emphasis upon developing its contacts with Europe, as its understanding of the Union has increased.

The workload deriving from the EU is a huge one for any major manufacturing group. Though only 6 CBI staff are permanently based in Brussels, many of the 70 or so executive staff of the London office spend up to half of their time digesting European legislation and thinking of its implications; some spend 90% of their time on this.

The bulk of its direct lobbying is done in regular meetings with officials of the Commission, but the CBI also lobbies the European Parliament, mainly via British MEPs. It is, therefore, an example of a group which uses all three available approaches. It has fully established links with civil servants and ministers in Whitehall and currently benefits from there being a sympathetic Conservative government. Though it has no panel of Parliamentary spokesmen it also lobbies MPs of all parties, according to the issue and their interest. It works through the Euro-organisation, UNICE, and it makes direct representations in the Community, via its own office.

Most national pressure groups cannot afford the luxury of a European office, not having the means to sustain such an outlet. They nevertheless recognise the importance of the Union, and use other means to conduct their lobbying of its institutions.

This contact may take several forms. Several national groups lobby MEPs, who may individually contact an official at the Commission, work through the political grouping or committee or even approach a Commissioner directly, formally or informally. Otherwise, he/she can draw attention to an issue by asking an oral or written question in the Parliament, or perhaps by initiating a debate there. Not many days are allocated for debates, and speeches in the chamber do not usually attract much publicity.

Greenpeace presents a petition to the European Parliament. EP News, 15-19 January 1996

For many groups, contact with the Union involves such an initial approach through an MEP. The MEP will often then liaise with the Commission, on their behalf. Larger and more powerful organisations will almost certainly make their own direct contact with the Commission, though they will probably keep the MEP involved in their deliberations. Usually, the links are with the officials in the Directorates-General, though some may have occasional meetings with a British or other Commissioner.

Animal welfare is an area of increasing concern in all countries, and some groups such as Compassion in World Farming are active lobbyists of the

Union. The British RSPCA seeks to influence European legislation, through the Eurogroup for Animal Welfare, by seeking the support of British MEPs, through contact with British Commissioners and through contact with the UK Ministers in the Council. It has been involved in lobbying at Strasbourg and in Brussels since 1979, and this field of activity has increased considerably since then, as the box below indicates.

In the last few years, much has happened in Europe which is of direct interest to national pressure groups, and the trend to a 'Europeanisation' of their activity has been gathering pace. In Britain, the traditional view of Whitehall/Westminster as the centre of attention is now becoming obsolete, and the same is true elsewhere.

The percentage of our work that is concerned with the EU varies according to the issue. In the present year, the RSPCA expects to work on a wide variety of EU-driven legislation, including draft legislation to improve the farm conditions for veal calves, battery chickens and pigs, legislation to prohibit the importation of furs caught in leghold traps and new laws designed to stop the testing of cosmetics on animals. Thus legislation on agriculture issues such as farm animals, tend now to emerge from the EU (eg, the 1995 Transport Directive). Legislation on wild animals and research animals is also EU directed to a great extent, whereas legislation on pet animals tends to be more nationally oriented (Letter to Author from the RSPCA, 5.1.96).

? Why do National Pressure Groups now lobby in Europe?

What are the uses and limitations of Euro-Groups?

Elections to the European Parliament

The European Parliament is the only EU institution to be directly elected by the peoples of the fifteen member countries. The first elections were held in 1979, thereafter to occur every five years. Although they were designed to provide the European Parliament with a new legitimacy and to introduce an element of democracy into the Community, the way in which voters use them often has little to do with what they feel about matters European. They have not stimulated a major political debate about Union policies and the future direction that the organisation should take. Rather, they reveal the usual characteristics of what **Curtice and Steed** refer to as second-order elections; 'low turnout, an anti-government swing and a relatively high level of support for small parties'.

Low Turnout, Anti-government Swings and Support for Small Parties

Turnout in 1994 was down by an average of around 2%, and is low compared to national elections if relatively high compared with US Congressional ones. In Britain, it fell compared with five years earlier, although it was still higher than in 1979 or 1984. The figures compare unfavourably even with voting in a typical local election, for in metropolitan districts over the last decade turnout has usually averaged at approaching 40%.

We examine the level of non-voting and the reasons for it later in the section (see p247-249). For the moment, it is necessary to make the point that people are influenced much more by what they think about the performance of the national government of the day than by any other issue. In 1994, they seized the an opportunity to express their reservations about the Major Government and its works.

A similar trend was exhibited elsewhere in the Union, for only in Italy did the governing coalition do better in the Euro-election than in the previous general election. The Italian government was still enjoying something of a honeymoon, only three months in office. In other countries, governments experienced a sharp reversal in their fortunes, and the British Conservatives - despite a lamentable result - actually performed better than did many other ruling parties.

Yet if elections are dominated by national issues, especially where the government is unpopular, nonetheless there is some consideration given by the parties to European issues. The European party federations adopt common manifestoes and produce brochures and material which address contentious topics concerning the future direction of the Union. If anything this European dimension was greater in 1994. The national parties made more use of the federation material which examined the question of integration in the light of the backlash against Maastricht in several states.

The third feature which Curtice and Steed pinpoint as a characteristic of second-order elections has traditionally had less application in Britain, for the electoral system has not been kind to small parties. In 1979, parties other than Conservative, Labour and the Liberals gained only 3.3% of the vote, in 1984 only 3.2%. Yet to be fair they offered few candidates to the electorate. When there was more choice as in 1989 and 1994, the outcome was different, for they gained 19% in 1989 and 11.1% in the last elections. The Greens contested every British seat in 1989, and in 1994 they were joined in this by the Natural Law Party which also contested all constituencies.

A Common Electoral System? The Use of Proportional Schemes in Europe

The Treaty of Rome (article 138) laid down that there should be 'proposals for election by direct universal suffrage, in accordance with a uniform procedure in all member states'. As yet, no such uniform system has been adopted, and Britain has clung to its First Past the Post (FPTP) method. The other countries all use some variety of proportional representation, and the method of election is currently being reviewed to see if the requirement of the Rome Treaty can be fulfilled.

In the Autumn of 1991, the Parliament voted by 150-26 in favour of a new, common system; of the British MEPs, 2 were in favour, 9 against, 29 abstained and the rest were not present. It was agreed that the Parliament would work on producing a scheme, and after two previous failures the emphasis switched to producing the principles rather than the details of any new arrangement. The Council will have to reach unanimous agreement before any scheme is accepted, and at Maastricht provision was made for the Parliament to approve, on a majority basis, any system adopted before it can be introduced.

For the 1994 elections, new electoral boundaries applied. At the Edinburgh Summit of December 1992, the EC states increased the size of the European Parliament to take account of German reunification. Britain gained an extra six seats, giving it a new total of 87. Nothing was done by the British Government about the allocation of those seats for six months and then a Bill was brought forward.

To the alarm of the Scots who are numerically over-represented in the EP, they were not given an extra seat. They felt that one should have been made available to boost the Scottish voice in Europe. One seat went to Wales, and five to England (see accompanying map of the Euro-constituencies, overleaf). The chance to redraw boundaries on the basis of proportional representation was not taken, although this was urged by some commentators. Though Labour policy is sympathetic to the use of PR for European elections, the party did not press the issue.

Key to the constituencies

England

1 Northumbria
2 Cumbria and Lancashire North
3 Tyne and Wear
4 Durham
5 Cleveland and Richmond
6 North Yorkshire
7 Humberside
8 Lancashire Central
9 Lancashire South
10 Yorkshire West
11 Leeds
12 Merseyside West
13 Merseyside East and Wigan
14 Cheshire West and Wirral
15 Greater Manchester West
16 Greater Manchester East
17 Greater Manchester Central
18 Cheshire East
19 Yorkshire South West
20 Yorkshire South
21 Sheffield
22 Peak District
23 Nottinghamshire North and Chesterfield
24 Lincolnshire and Humberside South
25 Staffordshire West and Congleton
26 Staffordshire East and Derby
27 Nottingham and Leicestershire North West
28 Leicester
29 Cambridgeshire
30 Norfolk
31 Herefordshire and Shropshire
32 Birmingham West
33 Midlands West
34 Birmingham East
35 Coventry and North Warwickshire
36 Northamptonshire and Blaby
37 Suffolk and South West Norfolk
38 Worcestershire and South Warwickshire
39 Bedfordshire and Milton Keynes
40 Essex North and Suffolk South
41 The Cotswolds
42 Buckinghamshire and Oxfordshire
43 Hertfordshire
44 Essex West and Hertfordshire East
45 Essex South
46 Bristol

47 Wiltshire North and Bath
48 Hampshire North and Oxford
49 Thames Valley
50 Surrey
51 Kent West
52 Kent East
53 Somerset and North Devon
54 Itchen, Test and Avon
55 Wight and Hampshire South
56 South Downs West
57 Sussex South and Crawley
58 Cornwall and West Plymouth
60 Devon and East Plymouth
61 Dorset and East Devon
62 London North West
63 London North
64 London East
65 London South East
66 London South Inner
67 London South West
68 London West
69 London Central
70 London North East
71 London South and Surrey East

Wales

1 North Wales
2 Mid and West Wales
3 South Wales West
4 South Wales Central
5 South Wales East

Scotland

1 Highlands and Islands
2 North East Scotland
3 Mid Scotland and Fife
4 Lothians
5 South of Scotland
6 Strathclyde East
7 Strathclyde West
8 Glasgow

Northern Ireland

Three members

238

European Constituencies in the United Kingdom

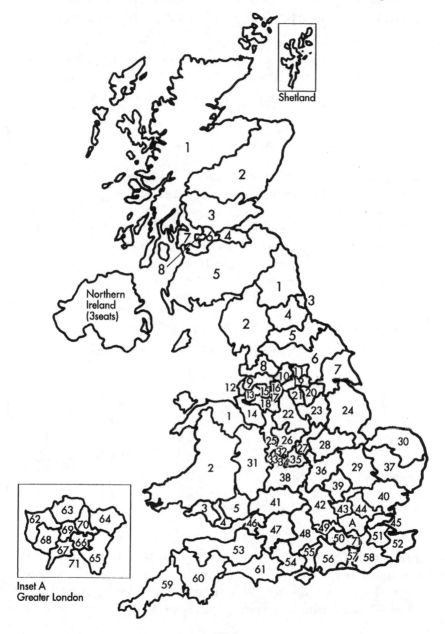

Shetland

Northern
Ireland
(3seats)

Inset A
Greater London

Chapter Three

The Workings of the British System in European Elections in 1989 and 1994; The Case for Change

> *In no other country could a party succeed in securing 74% of the seats on the basis of only 44% of the votes as Labour did in 1994, thereby ensuring that it had the largest single delegation of any national party in the European Parliament.*
> D. Butler and M. Westlake, 1995.

The case for a change of system in Britain is a strong one, whatever form it may take. There are 87 constituencies in the United Kingdom, and these are inevitably very large, with typical electorates of 70,000 or more; often they embrace 7-10 Parliamentary ones. The size factor makes the outcome even more distorted than is the case in elections to the House of Commons, and indeed in the elections of 1989 and 1994 the results well illustrate the anomalies that can occur under FPTP.

The Outcome of European Elections, 1989 and 1994

	Seats Won		% of Votes	
	1989	1994	1989	1994
Conservatives	32	18	35	27
Labour	45	62	40	45
Lib Dems	0	2	6	16
Greens	0	0	15	3
Plaid Cymru	0	0	1	1
SNP	1	2	3	3

In the 1989 elections, the Liberal Democrats were left totally unrepresented. The Labour Party had no MEPs in the South outside London, and the Conservatives had none in Scotland or Wales. It was, however, the fate of the British Green Party which pointed to the unfairness of the system, for a comparison with the representation of their counterparts in France and Germany showed how badly a small party could fare in the United Kingdom.

	No. of Seats	% of Seats	% of Votes
France	9	11.0	10.5
Germany	8	9.9	8.4
United Kingdom	0	0	14.9

An Analysis of the 1994 Result

In 1994, similar discrepancies were again evident. Whereas in 1989 both main parties were beneficiaries of the system, in that each obtained a higher percentage of seats than the number to which they were entitled, this was not the case five years later.

The Conservatives achieved their lowest percentage of the popular vote in any national election ever, and lost seats heavily. Having been the beneficiaries of the voting system in Parliamentary elections since 1979, it served them ill for they gained only three quarters of the seats they might have expected to win on the basis on their national vote, 18 as opposed to 24.

Partly this reflected the fact that the electoral system tends to greatly exaggerate the position of the winning party, Labour. But the distortion which worked against them was also related to another factor. Broadly, the turnout was down in Labour areas and higher in Conservatives ones, so that the Tories were able to acquire a respectable (if still embarrassingly low) share of the national vote but many of these votes were wasted. This said, they lost support heavily in their heartlands, whereas Labour turned in a particularly good set of results in the semi-South and Midlands, where they were best placed to translate extra votes into extra seats.

The Liberal Democrats did well where they had the best grounds for optimism. They made impressive advances in the South West and for the first time ever gained two seats in the European Parliament and narrowly missed a third one. In the past, it has often been pointed out by commentators that third parties suffer under the electoral system because their vote is thinly spread across the country. The converse is true that where the vote is more geographically concentrated they tend to fare better. Hence the impressive results in the area referred to, and their weaker performance eleswhere where they suffered from not having the resources to put into fighting on a national scale.

Under any other method of voting, Labour would have done much less well than it did, and the Liberal Democrats and the Conservatives would have done better. Labour would have benefited from any system to some degree, however, for on this occasion its vote was unusually geographically concentrated. It made little impression in the Deep South outside London, and did not pile up wasted votes in winning safe seats in Scotland and Wales.

By 1994, the Greens had lost the momentum they achieved in 1989, and they fared badly under the electoral system. Neither were the Scottish or Welsh Nationalists able to gain the percentage of seats which their popular vote merited on a strictly arithmetical basis. Third parties suffer particularly badly in European elections, because of the vastness of the constituencies. Their best areas of support can be submerged in a Labour or Tory sea.

Many candidates are elected on a minority of the popular vote. Wales North provides a good example of this. In 1989, the Parliamentary constituencies were held by representatives of all four main parties in Wales (3 Conservative, 3 Labour, 3 Plaid Cymru and 1 Democrat), yet in the Euro-election of that year the seat was held by the Conservatives with only 31.6% of the vote. Nearly 70% did not vote for him as their choice.

Other Reasons for a Change in the British Electoral System

Such anomalies are the more questionable because the European Parliament is supposed to be a forum in which differing shades of European opinion are reflected. It may be the case that FPTP for Westminster is preferable, in that it usually produces a government with a working majority. No government has to be formed out of the assembly in Strasbourg, and so arguments about PR leading to coalitions are irrelevant.

Similarly, the objection that multi-member constituencies would lessen the contact between an MP and his constituents has less force in European elections. The 87 areas are already so large that any such personal connection is out of the question. Such is the remoteness that few British people know the name of their Euro-MP at present.

The Experience of Northern Ireland. A Relevant Example?

The latest elections for the three seats in Northern Ireland were again held on a Province-wide basis under STV, and the outcome was a fair balance in the political representation of the unionist and nationalist candidates. The three largest parties each secured one seat, just as they did in 1979, 1984 and 1989.

The Results in Northern Ireland, 1989 and 1994

	% of First Pref. Votes		No. of Seats	
	1989	1994	1989	1994
Democratic Unionists	29.9	29.2	1	1
SDLP	25.5	28.9	1	1
Official Unionists	22.2	23.8	1	1

In 1989, there were ten candidates for three seats and a turnout of 48.3%, well above the British figure. The turnout in 1994 was a fraction down on the previous election. On this occasion 13 candidates stood for the same number of seats, and required a quota of 139967 votes to get elected. Whereas most parties in each election ran just one candidate to maximise the chances of gaining a representative, the Sinn Fein and Natural Law parties in 1994 (with no expectation of securing a seat) were more concerned to boost their total of votes and put up three candidates to widen the basis of their appeal. Of the other minorities, the Conservative Party vote collapsed from 4.8% to 1.0%, and the Alliance and Workers' parties also suffered losses.

Turnout in local and European elections does tend to be much better than on the mainland. Indeed, at 64.4% in 1984 the Irish performance was even better than the European average of 61.0%. Although it was marginally down in 1994, the figures are still respectable in European terms. It can be argued therefore that an electoral system which caters for all shades of opinion does tend to stimulate more people to turn out on polling day. Given a range of candidates, electors can cast an effective vote with a real chance of influencing the outcome. In 1994, they were again presented with a meaningful choice of would-be MEPs of differing shades of Green and Orange, whereas in Britain as a whole the alternatives were usually much more limited.

Of course, there may be other factors which encourage people in the six counties to exercise their democratic right. It may be that there is a greater interest in political matters in the province. Such an interest would not be surprising in view of the acute divisions in society and the contrasting views as to whether Northern Ireland should even exist as a separate entity.

Against a Change of Method for Voting

If Euro-constituencies on the mainland are already considered so vast that many people are unaware of the name of their MEP already, that situation would be further aggravated if even larger ones were necessary to create a multi-member system. Furthermore, accepting that PR may be particularly appropriate for Northern Ireland, there is the slippery slope argument which several sceptics might advance. Once the principle is conceded for one type of election, it is more difficult to resist for others where its disadvantages might be more apparent.

Critics might point out that in Southern Ireland where there are only four constituencies, STV does not always provide a very proportional result. Small parties did not fare well in 1984. In its two three-member constituencies, for a party gaining less than 20% of the first preferences there was little chance of gaining a seat. The winning party, Fianna Fail, gained a much exaggerated victory on a minority of the votes (53% seats, 39% votes). In 1989, however, six groups gained representation, a notably fairer outcome and the same victorious party won 33% of the seats for 32% of the votes.

John Curtice and **Michael Steed** have shown that even if the 1994 election had been fought on a proportional system, it does not follow that a party winning over half of the votes would have won over half of the seats. They show that the outcome 'could still have been signficantly disproportional' and base their calculations on the use of a regional list system which was mooted in the abortive European Assembly Elections Bill of 1977, under the last Labour Government. They conclude; 'In the context of the continuing debate within the Labour and Liberal Democrat parties about electoral reform, it is clear that the particular choice of proportional system can matter'.

Although a uniform system of election is often regarded as the ideal, most member states are content to proceed with their present method and there is little likelihood of any early standardisation. It has been difficult to find common ground on any agreed system in Council deliberations.

British Parties and a Change of Method

> *I fully support the party's commitment to a referendum on the issue of the electoral system for the Commons [and] existing party policy for both the European Parliament and an elected [second] chamber.*
> Tony Blair

The Conservative Party has no interest in any change of system, even though it suffered badly from the distortions produced by FPTP in 1994. The opposition parties take a different view. The Liberal Democrats would like to see a change of voting method for all elections, local, general and European, and since the publication of the Plant Report, Labour is more favourably disposed to change for certain elections including the European ones. Indeed, the 1992 Manifesto committed them to the adoption of an alternative system, but as yet it is not clear that change would be a priority of an incoming Labour government.

The Plant Report, 1993

It was Neil Kinnock who, as Leader of the Labour Party, asked Lord Plant to investigate the British electoral system and the possibility of reform. The discussions in the Plant team and the subsequent report helped to bring about a clear shift in Labour policy on the issue of electoral reform in general, and on the use of a different system in European elections in particular.

The Report did not dwell on the anomalies produced by the present system, or on the benefits to be obtained for any one party. It believed that there was more to the debate than matters of electoral expediency, and considered issues such as the representativeness of any assembly, its legitimacy and democratic standing. It suggested that a new system was a necessary condition for increasing the powers of the European Parliament and its degree of legitimacy. It noted that the other members of the Union employ systems which embody the principle of proportionality, although the actual methods differ. It also noted that there were strong pressures within Europe for a more uniform system of election, as required under the Rome Treaty.

There was general agreement in the Committee on the need for change, and the abandonment of FPTP for European elections provoked no obvious opposition. There was less agreement on the replacement, and the final verdict was a majority one. Some members would have liked to recommend the Additional Member System (AMS) for all non-Parliamentary elections, but felt that this would have been unsuitable for elections to a Second chamber and for the European Parliament. It would have failed to cater fully for the regional and national dimension within Great Britain, and it was felt that a regional list would do this more adequately. Moreover, such a method was used in several other countries.

Some Labour MEPs have let it be known that they favour retaining the FPTP method, their concern being the size of any multimember constituencies. They argue the need to retain direct constituency links, and to keep constituencies as small as is viable in the circumstances.

Turnout in Britain and in the Rest of the Union

The European elections have not aroused great interest or excitement in any member country. In the UK, the overall turnout is particularly low, as the figures below indicate. Even when they are better, as in 1989, it has more to do with national politics than real concern about the European Union.

1979	1984	1989	1994
32.4	31.8	37.0	35.9

The low British turnout may be a reflection of our geographical insularity from the continent and a consequent feeling of remoteness from European institutions. It may also reflect the doubts of the British people about the value of the European enterprise, or more specifically the ambivalence of governmental attitudes to Britain's position in the EU and the consequent lack of leadership on the issue. Certainly, the issues surrounding the EU and its future have failed to arouse the British electorate.

The British figures are markedly poorer than those for other European countries. Until 1994, the Danish turnout in 1989 (47.4%) was the worst figure recorded outside the United Kingdom, and as we have seen, this was far higher than the British performance in any of the four elections.

In 1994, turnout was down in nine of the twelve states, and in some cases it was worse than in Britain. The Netherlands had just had a series of elections and this may account for some voter indifference, though this is surprising in a country which has long been a firm believer in European integration. In Portugal, the polling took place in the middle of a public holiday. Southern Ireland, like Portugal an obvious beneficiary of membership and without either excuse, did little better than Britain, its turnout slumping from 68% in 1989 to 44% in 1994. France and Denmark bucked the trend, and this may have reflected the fact that in the referendums of 1992-3 the issues surrounding Maastricht were hotly contested.

Turnout in the European Community/Union, 1979-94

	1979	1984	1989	1994
Belgium	91.6	92.2	90.7	90.7
Denmark	47.1	52.3	46.1	52.5
France	60.7	56.7	48.7	53.5
Germany	65.7	56.8	62.4	58.0
Greece	78.6(1981)	77.2	79.9	71.1
Ireland	63.6	7.6	68.3	37.0
Italy	85.5	83.9	81.5	74.8
Luxembourg	88.9	87.0	87.4	90.0
Netherlands	57.8	50.5	47.2	35.6
Portugal	n/a	72.2(1987)	51.1	35.7
Spain	n/a	68.9	54.8	59.6
United Kingdom	31.6	32.6	36.2	36.5
European average	**63.0**	**61.0**	**58.5**	**57.0**

NB i. *Some of the twelve countries were not members at the time of the 1979 and 1984 elections. The three latest members joined a few months after the 1994 elections were held.*

ii. *Comparisons are not strictly accurate, for turnout figures quoted outside the United Kingdom include invalid votes, whereas they are discounted in Britain and Northern Ireland. In the Irish Republic, invalid votes may account for 1-2% of the figure given.*

iii. *Belgium has a provision for compulsory voting, so that the figures are artificially high.*

The latest elections would seem to confirm a steady decline in the participation of voters since the first direct elections. In 1979 and 1984, the average was at or above 60%. It fell in 1989 to 58.5% and again in 1994 to 57.0%. It may be that this is not so much a serious long term trend, more a reflection of the fact that in the early years there was some novelty in voting in European elections. Perhaps this created (in the words of **Gordon Smith**) 'possibly unrealistic expectations of what a model democratic Europe could become. Participation is actually rather high when one considers that in the eyes of most European voters, European issues feature fairly low in their priorities'.

The Outcome of the 1994 Elections in the European Union as a Whole

Whatever one thinks of the British electoral system and its performance in 1994, one thing is certain. The result that it produced has had an important impact on the relative strength of parties in the European Parliament. It provided nearly a third of the membership of the Party of European Socialists (63/198) and helped to ensure that the total number of 'Left' MEPs (268) was nearly equal to the number of 'Right' ones (272), who are in any case a less cohesive grouping. Labour's triumph compensated for poor socialist performances in France, Italy and Spain, and a disappointing one in Germany.

The picture on the Centre-Right is a different one, for the Right suffered from some turbulene as a result of a backlash against Maastricht, and the drive towards European integration. The British campaign was handicapped by divisions on Europe, but the anti-Maastricht case was particularly strongly articulated in France where the billionaire Jimmy Goldsmith financed a list headed by de Villiers which was successful in winning 13 seats. Overall, the Centre-right is much more susceptible to divisions and fragmentation.

If Labour had won the 44 seats which **Curtice and Steed** calculate they would have won under the regional list system rather than the 18 extra ones it achieved, the Right in Europe would have been in a notably stronger position. The Conservative disaster dealt a blow not just to the morale and standing of the party in the British Isles, it also damaged the standing of its allies in Europe as well.

Overall, there was a small shift away from the most federalist groupings in the European parliament and a slight increase in support for more cautious ones. But the number of seats gained by those who oppose European integration outright was much the same as before and actually fell as a proportion of the newly-enlarged Parliament.

Chapter Three

The Impact of the British Result on the Future of Europe

Finally, we may consider the impact of the elections in Britain on the whole question of the move towards European integration. Most of the successful Conservatives were Euro-sceptic by inclination. The weakening of the party's overall position means that there has been a further erosion of the Party's links with Europe at the very time when the Westminster Party is also becoming more lukewarm about British membership of the Union. By contrast, Labour's ability to build on its 1989 success has helped to confirm its connections with Europe, and the party now provides around a third of the MEPs of the Party of European Socialists (see p240-241). **David Butler and Martin Westlake** make the point that 'European elections were originally designed to help integrate Europe's citizens into a new political structure', but they conclude that;

[The elections] have helped to integrate the opposition Labour Party into Europe. But at the same time they have encouraged the isolation of the Conservative Government. True, Labour's support for Europe may help to strengthen the European Union in the long-run if it can ever win power at Westminster. In the short term, however, it is the reinforcement of Conservative scepticism which is of greater import. The hoped-for benefits of European elections are still far from being realised.

Does the European Union need a common electoral system? Will it get one?

TEACH YOURSELF

To Recap

Parties

Europe has been a difficult issue for the two main British parties. Labour has undergone more twists and turns since the time of British entry into the EC, but more recently the Conservatives have found the issue divisive.

Within Europe, transnational parties have developed, though as yet they are not particularly effective. However, within the Parliament at Strasbourg, party groupings reflecting these 'blocs' are well developed, particularly the EPP and the PES (broadly Christian Democrats and Socialists). British Conservatives are allied at MEP level to the EPP, but do not belong to it. Labour is affiliated to the PES. Both transnational parties have federal goals. Elements on the Left in the Parliament tend to be more cohesive than those on the Right.

Pressure Groups

National Pressure Groups have a new outlet, lobbying in Brussels/Strasbourg as well as in their national capitals.

Business and farming interests were soon active in approaching European machinery, particularly the Commission. Unions and environmental groups, as well as professions such as the BMA and Law Society, have become more involved.

3 main approaches can now be used by a national group;

  i. Lobbying the national government to persuade it to use its voice in Brussels, in support of the cause

  ii. Lobbying through a Euro-group, eg, UNICE for 'big business'

  iii. Lobbying European machinery directly, especially the Commission; maybe also (as with the NFU) via the use of an office in Brussels

Elections

The only elected EU body is the European Parliament, for which elections are held every four years. Each country uses its own electoral system, although the fourteen nations other than Britain use some variety of proportional representation. In Northern Ireland, STV is employed.

Turnouts are low in several countries, and this may reflect feelings of remoteness from European machinery and a feeling that Europe doesn't mean much to citizens. People who do vote tend to vote on national rather than European issues, and unpopular governing parties tend to be punished by the voters.

Questions to consider

1   Read the following passage, and then answer the questions which follow;

Who are the lobbyists?
(Taken from EP News, January 15-19, 1996)

One estimate puts the total number of lobbyists in Brussels and seeking to influence decision-making at the incredible number of 10000...a reflection of the importance in which the EU is seen by a growing number of organisations representing practically every interest under the sun from...seed manufacturers to the elderly...Lobbyists can be placed into two categories.

On the one hand, there are those representing powerful business interests who watch each proposal like a hawk and are ready to move to try and persuade MEPs to back amendments which would weaken the impact of any draconian legislation that could have an adverse impact on the industry they represent. The motor industry is a case in point, as it anxiously awaits further moves to tighten pollution control laws...

On the other hand, there are single issue pressure groups, often voluntary organisations, seeking parliamentary support for a particular cause, be it immigrants' rights, aid for the Third World or the environment.

Greenpeace is an obvious example here, and it maintains close links with the Greens in Parliament...

When it comes to budget time, the pressure hots up with other groups representing, for example, the elderly or handicapped, seeking funding for their particular priority.

In fact, the lobby is also active in Parliament through the various 'Intergroups' which have now grown to around 60, and bring together like-minded MEPs from different countries and political parties. Once again, the groups represent a wide range of interests and regions, including health, music, shipbuilding and even ceramics...the Animal Welfare Group...numbers around 90 members...It was extremely influential in working for the controversial ban on the import of furs caught in leghold traps.

   i What avenues are open to a group such as Greenpeace in its bid to achieve the maximum backing from MEPs?

  ii Explain how a typical national pressure group is likely to go about the task of advancing its cause in the European Union, other than via MEPs.

 iii Why do you think that animal welfare groups are increasingly active on the Brussels scene?

 iv Why do you think that the European Parliament is now becoming such an important part of the lobbying scene in the European Union?

2   Outline the differences of viewpoint in the British Conservative Party over policy towards the European Union.

3   Are there any signs of the development of a European party system?

4   Why are national pressure groups increasingly turning their attention to Brussels? Which types of group are likely to experience greatest success there?

5   Is there a case for the use of a uniform electoral system for elections to the European Parliament? Which scheme would you recommend?

6   Discuss the outcome of the European elections of 1994, and their likely impact on parties and policies over the next few years.

7   How, and why, does the European Parliament encourage the development of transnational groupings?

8   Why has the European issue proved to be such a difficult one for British political parties to handle?

Chapter Four:
Policies

255

The Range
and Extent of
Union Policies

The Treaty of Rome refers to three areas of policy as 'common' ones, those involving agriculture (article 43), commerce (113) and transport (74). However, in addition there are other references to 'common policies', and especially in the later treaties (the Single European Act and Maastricht) references are made to 'Community policy'.

Initially, the emphasis of the Community was upon the development of a common market free of trading barriers, and this aspect is still of fundamental importance. The Common Commercial Policy, competition policy and the Single European Act are all related to the promotion of what used to be called the 'Common Market', a label which some people still use when they refer to the Union today.

Today it is much more than a Common Market, for it was always the intention that close cooperation would extend into other sectors. Some of these are economic policies related to tackling wider issues than those of tariffs and their elimination. Others go well beyond the economic sphere, and deal with matters ranging from foreign policy to immigration, from broadcasting to combating crime.

Just as the range of policies undertaken by the Union is a wide one, so is the degree to which the EU becomes involved in their management. In some areas, such as agriculture, industry and trade, many important decisions are now taken at European level, which is why the National Farmers Union, the Confederation of British Industry and the Institute of Directors spend so much of their time on European policy.

In other matters, including some of those dealt with in the Second and Third (Intergovernmental) Pillars of the Maastricht Treaty, EU involvement is increasing. This is also the case with many aspects of social policy, particularly those relating to labour relations, working conditions and employment practices more generally, although the British exemption from the terms of the Social Chapter means that in theory at least it is not applicable in this country. In a few areas, there is little or no Union involvement in national policy. This is true of issues relating to policy on education, health and welfare.

The trend over the last generation has been for Brussels to become more involved in many spheres, including some in which its role was once limited. On foreign policy and the environment, the European machinery now has far more of a role than was the case even a decade or so ago, and many of the policies dealt with under the heading of Justice and Home Affairs had only very limited Community involvement before the Maastricht treaty. The extent to which the adoption of the concept of subsidiarity (see p104-105) involves any reversal of this broad trend has yet to become fully apparent, although so far few issues which have been within the competence of Brussels in recent years have ceased to be so.

The picture is a patchy one, with the nature and extent of EU involvement in policy-making differing from issue to issue. In some areas, national governments have been more willing to relinquish some of their capacity to determine policy than in others. The representatives of any country inevitably have to ask themselves what benefits are to be derived from a common approach, and to balance possible gains for Europe as a whole against pressing national considerations. They also have to bear in mind what public opinion at home will stand.

The Level of Union Involvement in Policy Areas; Some Examples

	Much involvement	Joint involvement	Little or none
Agriculture	*		
Fishing	*		
Trade	*		
Drugs		*	
Environmental		*	
Regional		*	
Working Conditions		*	
Defence			*
Education			*
Health			*
Housing			*
Welfare			*

Eurobarometer has regularly polled people across the Union about their views on which policies are best decided in Brussels, and which ones are better handled by national governments. The findings usually indicate that they prefer European-wide decision-making in those areas where the problems cross or go beyond national boundaries (the fight against drugs, the environment and overseas aid), and national action on issues where the decisions impact upon them more directly (education and health).

Broadly, their wishes are in line with existing practice, for the emphasis upon subsidiarity (as affirmed at Maastricht) stresses that decisions are best taken at the most appropriate level. Those which require a cooperative approach tend to derive from Brussels, those which can be taken closer to the citizen are made by national or in some cases regional governments.

A Eurobarometer poll in 1994 found that 74% of those interviewed felt that aid and development issues should be tackled by the EU, 66% thought the same about environmental matters. Only 31% felt that health and social security were better handled by the Union, and, perhaps surprisingly, only 46% thought this about unemployment.

The Varying Effectiveness of Union Action

Even where there is a substantial degree of Brussels involvement, it does not follow that a coherent common policy results from a common approach for it can be difficult to reconcile conflicting national interests and preferences. Member states have their own traditions, and the fight to preserve national interests in particular policy areas can make it difficult to achieve a genuinely coordinated and consistent EU approach.

This is true of industrial policy, an area in which the Union is bound to be interested because of its importance to the future prosperity of the fifteen nations. Any action or inaction is relevant to the employment prospects of many people who work within the sector. Yet, as **Nugent** has observed; 'In practice a fully developed, comprehensive and coherent industrial policy does not exist. What do exist are a large number of policies, themselves usually only partially developed, which affect industry, but which do not in any sense constitute an integrated industrial framework with clear and consistent goals'.

The Sources of Community Policy

Many Union policies derive directly from the treaties. For instance, the way in which matters affecting coal and steel are handled dates back to the formation of the ECSC. But because a topic has been trailed in a treaty agreement does not necessarily mean that there will be significant progress in fulfilling the aspirations of those who negotiated the original document. The peaceful development of atomic energy under the Euratom treaty and the growth of a Common Transport Policy have not been subjected to the same attention accorded to some other policy areas.

By comparison, other issues not dealt with in the treaties have sometimes been tackled more energetically. Before the passage of the Single European Act, there was no mention in any treaty of either environmental or foreign policy, yet in the last two decades a considerable amount of time and effort has been spent in producing agreement in both fields.

Changes are often introduced outside the framework of the treaties, as happened in foreign policy. Back in the 1970s, cooperation began to develop via the initiative known as European Political Cooperation (EPC). It evolved eventually into the Common Foreign and Security Policy which became one of the intergovernmental pillars of the Maastricht Treaty.

Such considerations led Nugent to conclude that 'the treaties are facilitators and enablers of policy development, but they are not always the main causes'. Of the key factors determining the pace and manner of advance in any particular area, he discerned three;

i   'The leadership given by the Commission', which has varied according to the holder of the Presidency. Some figures who occupied the role imparted their own enthusiasms and imposed their own style on the Commission, notably Walter Hallstein (1958-66), Roy Jenkins (1977-80) and Jacques Delors (1985-94). These were creative eras in which new initiatives were taken up and often acted upon.

ii   'The perceptions of the member states of what is desirable'. Representatives of national governments have to be convinced that there are significant gains to be made from acting together, gains not just for the Union as a whole but ones which also coincide with a measure of national self-interest. With the introduction and increasing use of majority voting it is not necessary for all states to perceive these advantages.

iii   'The individual and collective capacities of the member states to translate their perceptions into practice'. Even if there is a sympathetic response for a particular initiative in a national government, the ministers of that country may feel unenthusiastic about supporting it in the Council of Ministers.

Domestic political pressures can create difficulties, and any French or German government is going to think twice before it supports measures which could lessen the prosperity of its farmers, just as British ministers have, in recent years, been under pressure from trawlermen to provide better protection for the domestic fishing industry. Sometimes it may be necessary to concede, but negotiators need to show that they have earned some trophies in the

negotiations before they yield to the pressure of other Council
members.

Here, we are concerned with specific issues and the way in which the
Union handles them. Some are the subject of policy decisions made many
years ago, some have been the result of more recent initiatives and some
are still evolving. We are not concerned to cover every policy area with
which the Union is currently involved, but to spotlight particular ones on
the grounds of their importance, the recent controversy surrounding them
and also because of the way they impact upon the United Kingdom.

It is convenient to divide issues into three broad categories, those
concerned with **financial and economic policy,** those which deal with
social policy and those which are concerned with the **external relations** of
the fifteen member states.

Financial and Econ. Policy	Social Policy	External Relations
EMU and the Single Currency	The Soc. Chapter	For. & Def. Policy
The Common Agricultural Policy	Immigration	Overseas Aid
The Common Fisheries Policy		
Regional Policy		
Environmental Policy		

Before we consider any of these, however, it is timely to take a look at the
Union Budget, to see where it gets its money from and the changing
priorities in spending over recent years.

?

Why are there common policies in some areas, but not in others?

What sort of issues are best decided at European level, and
which by national governments?

The Budget and Associated Issues

> *The Union budget differs fundamentally from the national budgets, both by its scale and by the structure of expenditure. If expenditure on the common agricultural policy and external action is ignored, the Union budget is mainly an investment budget, designed to strengthen the Union's economic potential. As the Union develops and assumes new tasks, so does the budget'*
> *Peter Schmidhuber, a member of the European Commission.*

In the words of a Commission document; 'The budget of the European Union is the financial image of the Union's policy'. However, although the range and extent of Union policy is growing in scale, its budget is relatively small-fry in comparison with that of the national budgets of the larger member states. The contributions of each state to EU finances are also small in relation to their budgetary figures and gross national product.

Yet the budget of the Union is a cause of much controversy, and in Britain the Euro-sceptics and Euro-phobes often point to the costs of British membership. This is because Britain is a net contributor to the EU, and is always likely to remain so. Inevitably, some states get more out of the Union than they put it, whilst others pay in more than they take out. Britain has always been a paymaster, rather than a beneficiary.

Before we discuss the controversies surrounding it, we need to find out how the EU budget is decided, and what type of payments are made into and out of the funds.

The Union Budget (Based on 1994 Figures)

The annual budget of the EU is around ECU 72b (one ecu = 0.82p), approximately 1.20% in 1994 (1.27 in 1999) of the gross national product of the Fifteen member states.

Income is derived from four main sources

- 20.9%

i Customs duties on products imported from outside the EU

ii Agricultural levies charged at the external frontiers of the EU to bring the price of imported foodstuffs from the rest of the world up to the levels of the Union (about one seventh of the total for 1&2)

- 51.3%

iii A proportion of the VAT collected in the member states, calculated according to a uniform assessment procedure. For countries such as the Greece, Ireland, Portugal and the UK, where private consumption is a larger share of national wealth, a limit is set of 55% of the total VAT base.

- 27.0%

iv A new, fourth resource created in 1988 and based on the GNP of the member states. As each state contributes according to its GNP, the figure can be said to be in accordance with its ability to pay.

NB. The figures are rounded to the first decimal point. The third and fourth items are calculated on the basis of the total income received by the Exchequer in each member country, so that the individual states have an obvious interest in the scale of the Union budget.

Expenditure goes primarily on;

- Support for farm prices, including reduction of stocks
- Structural funds
- Joint action in research, energy, industry, the environment and transport
- Cooperation with Third World countries
- Cooperation with the Countries of Central and Eastern Europe
- Administrative expenditure, salaries, buildings etc.

The pattern of expenditure has changed considerably in recent years. For a long while, agriculture was the overwhelming element in EC spending, but Europe is now developing in such a way that money is being redirected to other areas such as the funding of the regional and social programmes. This is seen by comparing the expenditure on items in the EU budget over many years.

In 1973, 80.6% of the money went on agriculture and fisheries, 61.3% in 1992. There was no Regional Fund in 1973, but by 1992 it used up 14.5% of EU spending. On the Social Fund, the figures were 5.5% and 9.3%, respectively. An attempt has been made to contain spending on the EAGGF programme. The CAP now absorbs fractionally less than half of EU funding.(see p 321)

The Budgetary Process

The process begins with estimates of expenditure being sent to Directorate-General X1X of the Commission which has responsibility for formulating the budget. These estimates arrive in the summer of the year prior to which the budget will apply. The likely revenue for the coming year is then calculated. The budget is then drafted in a preliminary form by the Commission before the first day of September, and submitted to the Council. The Council considers this document, and sends its own revised version to the European Parliament by the fifth of October. Parliament debates the amended budget and proposes its own amendments, before returning it to the Council.

The proposals go back and forth between the Council and the Parliament, the two institutions which together form the budget authority. In the case of 'compulsory' expenditure, (just over 50% of the budget, mainly spent on the CAP), the Council has the final word. In the case of other 'non-compulsory' expenditure (eg, on the size of the Social Fund), Parliament has the final say and can modify expenditure according to conditions laid down in the Treaties. It must not increase the overall budgetary expenditure beyond the ceiling devised by the Council.

There can be much conflict between the Council and the Parliament who experience what **Nicoll and Salmon** call an 'uneasy partnership'. The procedure can be slow, so that on occasions there is no settlement by the end of the year. In this case, the Union is allowed to spend each month one-twelfth of the provision made in the previous year's budget, so that the machinery of the EU may continue to function.

After difficulties over the budget in 1980, an attempt was made in the following year to improve the machinery. A Trilogue was created, comprising the President of the Budget Council, the President of the Commission (maybe with the relevant Commissioner) and the President of the Parliament (maybe with the President of the Committee on Budgets). In 1988, it managed to bring about an agreement after a period in which deadlock had been reached.

Another feature of the process designed to make a settlement more likely is that, in December, it has become the pattern for the Council to assemble in Strasbourg so that it is on hand for any last-minute negotiations with the representatives of the Parliament, before the whole body takes its final vote on the budget package.

It is Parliament which ultimately adopts the budget, and it has used its budgetary powers to the full in order to influence Union policies. This determination, together with the long-running threat that the Union budget might be stifled by a ceiling on 'own resources', explains why the budget procedure has often sparked off disputes between Parliament and the Council.

Developments at Maastricht

The budgetary arrangements were not amended at Maastricht, although the three institutions have signed two separate political agreements (1993 and 1995) designed to modify and improve the procedure. Among other things, these allow for more consultation on compulsory expenditure, the amount of which is fixed by the Council.

What the Treaty did do was to raise the matter of budgetary discipline and sound financial management to the status of principles. The Commission must now be sure that resources are available in the budget to pay for whatever measures it proposes or carries out. In addition, it tests all of its proposals and activities against the main parameters of sound financial management, namely clear objectives, cost-effectiveness, and before and after evaluation (Its financial management is subject to the internal control of the the Financial Controller).

The Treaty also strengthened the role and powers of the Court of Auditors, an independent organ of the Union responsible for auditing payments and funding received by EU institutions. The Court has to ensure that appropriate financial procedures have been employed, and to see that money was spent for the purpose for which it was originally allocated. This is part of an attempt to clamp down on fraud within the Union.

Criticism of the EU Budget. A British Perspective

As we have seen, the bulk of the Union's expenditure is skewed towards agriculture, even if the pattern of expenditure is now changing. This is bound to work to Britain's disadvantage, for it has a relataively small agricultural base. In addition, it takes in substantial imports from countries outside the EU, on which levies have to be paid.

Waste in the Union

In his report on the 1993 budget, the President of the Court of Auditors accused the Commission of incompetent management of Union funds.

An estimate of £6b was given for the total costs of 'fraud' across the Union. Much of this was due to administrative errors, failure to comply with complex financial regulations, and questionable policy decisions rather than blatant and deliberate misuse of EU money.

Following pressure from the Parliament, the Commission now has an anti-fraud squad. It met with some initial resistance, for some governments were reluctant to allow Brussels-based officials to inspect their books.

Examples of misuse of Union money include such things as;

- Money from the Social Fund being used to finance the training of staff working for large banks or multinational companies, rather than being spent on retraining the unemployed or those threatened with redundancy

- Aid for Eastern Europe benefiting consultants rather than companies on the ground

In the report covering 1994, Britain was singled out for criticism over several matters, including;

- The failure to recover import duties worth £670000 on tuna from Thailand, and duties (also on tuna) from the Seychelles

- Fraud by companies based in Northern Ireland and depressed Southern seaside towns

In 1992 and 1993 respectively, Britain was responsible for 131/1028 and 180/1297 cases of fraud and irregularity.

The growth in funding of the Regional and Social programmes is good for the UK as a whole, and some areas have benefited generously from assistance given. Nonetheless, the UK is a net contributor to the EU, and pays in to the Union far more than it receives back in the form of financial benefits. In the early 1980s, the Prime Minister, Margaret Thatcher, argued forcefully that Britain was paying too much into the budget and getting too little back. Because agricultural spending was such a predominant feature of spending, the net positions did not reflect a country's ability to pay.

At the Fontainebleau conference in 1984, an agreement was reached which allowed for an 'abatement' or refund, by which Britain received back 66% of the difference between its VAT contributions and what it obtained back in benefits. Over the next five years, these 'abatements' were worth, in total, £4.5b. By 1992, the annual value of the rebate was running at around £1.4b, and in the European Council meeting at Edinburgh there was much criticism by some member states of the payment.

Portugal and Spain now argue that they were not a party to the Fontainebleau agreement in the first place, but as net beneficiaries of the EU budget their comments are unlikely to carry much conviction with British representatives. However, there is still pressure to end the rebate from other countries also, for they question whether a rebate which was appropriate when agriculture used up 80% of the budget is still appropriate when it consumes under half of all EU spending. They also point out that per capita contributions by the British are now among the lowest in the Union, at 88 ecu per person.

The Contribution of Member states to the 1994 Budget (as a %)

Luxembourg	0.2	Italy	14.1
Denmark	2.0	Belgium	3.9
France	19.2	Netherlands	6.3
Germany	30.1	Portugal	1.6
Greece	1.5	Spain	8.1
Ireland	0.8	United Kingdom	11.6

The Commission and some member governments see the rebate as an item for further examinition at the IGC in 1996. But as unanimity would be required before it could be terminated, this is likely to be an issue involved in the overall bargaining process at the conference.

Net Beneficiaries of, and Contributors to, the EU

It is difficult to obtain information about the net position of each member country, for the Commission does not view membership in terms of what countries pay in and what they get out. It argues that there is more to membership than a cost-benefit analysis, and that any figures are therefore misleading. Nonetheless, the Court of Auditors did some calculations in 1987, which gave an indication of the prevailing picture. At that time, before the changes introduced by the Delors 11 package, there were seven net beneficiaries out of the twelve states in the European Community. The five net contributors were Belgium, France, West Germany, Luxembourg and the United Kingdom.

Nicoll and Salmon quote some figures for 1992 (post Cohesion) from a contemporary newspaper, and as these were not disowned by the Foreign Office the information they give was likely to have been broadly accurate. In an adapted form, the figures give the following picture of the balance-sheet of 'winners' and 'losers'. The amounts shown are in billion ecu;

Net Beneficiaries		Net Contributors	
Belgium	1.7	France	0.9
Denmark	0.5	Germany	8.5
Greece	3.9	United Kingdom	5.0
Ireland	2.4		
Italy	1.1		
Luxembourg	0.7		
Portugal	1.2		
Spain	3.2		

The Netherlands broke even on a paid-in/received back basis.

There are some anomalies in the outcome as shown by the table. The Danes and Luxembourgers were net gainers, despite the fact that they had the highest standard of living in the EU, whereas Britain, eleventh in the prosperity league, was - despite the rebate - the second most sizeable contributor. By 1994, there were (according to the German Financial Institute) 3 more countries which suffered a net loss to the Union budget, Belgium, Italy and the Netherlands.

Not surprisingly, Britain and Germany have been the strongest of those voices calling for a curbing of overall expenditure. Some other nations are also alarmed at the size of the EU budget, and this is one reason why they wish to end the British abatement. In particular, it is the cost of Cohesion (much favoured by the southern countries) which threatens to escalate Union spending, and further enlargement to the East is likely to mean the addition of more net beneficiaries. The EFTA enlargement of 1995 actually brought into the Union three more wealthy countries, and for this reason was especially welcomed.

?

Have Britain's budgetary problems been solved?

If Germany and other nations pay more into the EU than they get back out of it, what is the point of their membership?

Economic and
Monetary Union

Economic and Monetary Union (EMU) was first adopted as Community policy at The Hague summit in 1969. It was to be achieved in stages over a period of ten years. However, nothing happened of any significance over the next few years, and there was little political will to press ahead with the idea in the early seventies when the oil crisis was of more immediate concern. There was some confusion over what the policy actually involved, but in 1972 a new exchange-rate system, the snake, was established, by which currencies were kept broadly in line with each other.

The Tindemans Report on European Union (1976) discussed EMU, even though it did not spell out what it meant and set definite target dates for its fulfilment. It portrayed EMU as one of a number of policies which were fundamental to the achievement of a Union, but it stressed the importance of a balanced development of the Community of which EMU, like regional and social policy, was but one aspect. It recognised that 'there is no agreement on how to achieve a common economic and monetary policy...In the present state of affairs, no real progress can be expected'.

As President of the Commission from January 1977, Roy Jenkins (a former British Chancellor of the Exchequer) took up the theme of economic and monetary union, and made the achievement of a new advance in that area a priority of his Presidency. In 1978, it was agreed to establish a **European Monetary System** (EMS), and this came into effect a year later. The idea was to create a zone of monetary stability as free of currency fluctuations as could be achieved. Such instability was a problem for businessmen whose firms were wary of making the long term investments which would enable the common market to function well.

Many of the European currencies were linked via the system which was supposed to maintain parity between currencies and promote economic convergence or. The EMS had three elements;

i **The European Monetary Cooperation Fund (EMFC).** 20% of the gold and dollar deposits of member states were to be placed in this fund which used the deposits to achieve currency stability by buying and selling EC currencies.

ii **The ECU,** a weighted basket of currency values, in which the more important ones such as the franc and the deutschmark inevitably carried more significance than the lira or punt. Many EC transactions began to be calculated in ECU, and this unit was used in setting amounts to spend in, for instance, the Regional Fund.

iii **The Exchange Rate Mechanism (ERM).** This was a system of fixed exchange rates, with each currency having an exchange rate linked to the ECU. Rates between countries were allowed to fluctuate by only 2.25% (or up to 6% in certain cases) from their stated value.

Britain did not join the EMS when it was founded, though it participated in the ECU and EMCF arrangements. Along with Greece, Portugal and Spain, it not join the ERM, though in principle the Single European Act passed a few years later committed countries to so doing.

The EMS brought about some benefits, for it produced a greater degree of monetary stability in the Community, and helped to bring about greater convergence between the policies of the member states. But with some countries outside the system, and others failing to operate within the narrow band of the ERM, it was never as effective as it was designed to be.

The Delors Plan, 1989

In the late 1980s, enthusiasts for economic and monetary union wanted to see a new move forwards as part of the programme to complete the workings of a single market. They argued that whilst a single market would end many barriers to trade, it would not by itself have any impact on the economic and monetary policies which governments pursue. Yet these policies, concerned as they are with such areas of economic activity as growth, employment and investment will have an impact on the market, for after 1992 the national economies would become more closely tied to each other. In other words, there was a need for greater harmonisation of economic policy to make a single market really effective.

The idea of a new push on EMU also had political implications, as its advocates well understood. They were looking for a drive towards closer integration, and a single currency would be a significant step on the way. On the one hand, closer political cooperation would make it easier to achieve the harmonisation of economic and monetary policies involved. On the other hand, the achievement of EMU would itself be a highly significant step towards political union. The two areas were clearly associated.

In April 1989, a report on EMU was presented by Jacques Delors to the Council of Ministers. It envisaged a three-stage progression to its ultimate goal of full monetary union, though it did not lay down a timetable for its implementation;

Stage One

This involved the removal of all barriers to a free market, as laid down in the 1986 Act, and improved monetary cooperation with all countries participating in the European Monetary System. The fulfilment of Stage One would help to bring about a convergence of economic policies and performance among the member states. Before there could be progress to the next stage there would need to be a new treaty setting out the way in which EMU would operate and be brought about.

Stage Two

This involved the creation of a Central European Bank, which would be independent of national governments. It would coordinate the national banks of member countries (eg, the German Bundesbank and the Bank of England).

Stage Three

This involved 'irrevocably locked exchange rates' between the European currencies, and the use of a single currency, the ECU. The Italian lira and British pounds would disappear.

The Delors Report was accepted as the basis for future action by Community leaders. It was envisaged that once the process had started, all involved would work towards its completion. When the three stages had been accomplished, there would be full monetary union, with all key monetary decisions being taken at European level. The role of the Central Bank would be at the heart of EMU, for it would manage the money supply of the European currency, and - like the national central banks today - be responsible for currency stability. It would be able to impose constraints on national budgets.

To move towards the goal of EMU, it was accepted that there would first need to be a linking of all the currencies in The Twelve, but four of them were still not in the ERM (Greece, Portugal, Spain and the UK). Spain entered in mid 1989, and the British Government did the same just over a year later (see box, p227).

However, the British Government was sceptical about the value of the Delors Report from the start. The Conservative manifesto for the 1989 Euro-elections referred to what ministers saw as a serious problem;

> *...as the recent report of the Delors Committee makes clear, full economic and monetary union would involve a fundamental transfer of sovereignty...The Report...implies nothing less than the creation of a federal Europe. Such ideas go way beyond what is realistic or desirable in the foreseeable future.*

British Experience in the Exchange Rate Mechanism (The ERM)

The Exchange Rate Mechanism operated successfully for several years after its introduction in 1980. In the early-mid 1980s, there was some flexibility in its workings, and occasional devaluations occurred whenever a country could not maintain the value of its currency. It became more rigid after the passing of the Single European Act, amid talk of the need to bring about convergence of the European economies to prepare for EMU.

Britain's reasons for not joining had differed from the other countries. They were concerned about the weakness of their economies, whereas in Britain the objections were more doctrinal. Spain decided to join in 1989, as did its neighbour Portugal three years later.

In 1989-90 there was pressure on the British Government to enter the ERM, and those in favour of membership included many voices in industry, the City and at Westminster. Labour, the party formerly so cool on Europe, had also come out in favour, and the more pro-European members of the Cabinet saw it as the inevitable and desirable next step.

Those in favour felt that it would provide greater stability for the pound, and that in the future there would be no need to have high interest rates to prop it up when it was under pressure. There would be less temptation for currency speculators to buy or sell sterling if it was not subject to fluctuations in value. It would also make it easier for businessmen to plan ahead if they knew that the value of the exchange rate would not fluctuate so wildly. Supporters believed that it would also help in the battle against inflation, for membership would impose a straightjacket on the British economy, and force governments to adopt policies of fiscal rectitude.

Opponents lamented precisely this constraint, and felt that Britain would lose much of its freedom of manoeuvre by a surrender of its economic sovereignty. They argued that it was essential that member states should have the ability to determine their own currency value. They were also alarmed that the straightjacket meant to control inflation could also be so tight that it would drive up interest rates and unemployment because of the deflationary policies involved.

Eventually, despite Mrs Thatcher's gut instincts, the Government joined the Mechanism, in October 1990. Many would say that this was done at an inopportune moment, when sterling was at too high a level. At the time of entry, it stood at 2.95 deutschmarks, and it was allowed to fluctuate in the wider band.

At such a level, membership helped keep imports and inflation down, but made the task of exporters difficult because British goods were made relatively dear in other countries. Some people wanted a realignment of currency values within the ERM, whilst others thought that to demonstrate confidence in the pound and in British membership we should seek an early opportunity to join a narrower band.

In the summer of 1992, the pound was towards the lower end of its allowed range within the mechanism, and in September it touched bottom. Fears of a very close result in the French referendum and anxiety about the chances of Britain getting out of recession given its high interest rates, put sterling in difficulty. On September 16, Black Wednesday, the Bank of England was unable to defend the pound against speculators, and Britain withdrew from the ERM. Membership may have helped control inflation, but it was held by many to have impeded a wider economic recovery.

In the aftermath of the October crisis, there was some talk of rejoining, but few saw this as a likely probability. Britain was not the only country to experience currency difficulties that Autumn, for at the same time Ireland, Portugal and Spain came under pressure, and the punt, escudo and peseta were all devalued. Italy left the ERM. France too experienced difficulties, but in the French case the Bundesbank was quick to come to the resuce and provide heavier support for the franc. Such speculation continued in 1993, and further devaluations occurred, with Portugal and Spain being forced to do so again. With the franc again under pressure, the ERM had to move to a 15% rather than the tight 2.25% fluctuation band.

Membership of the old ERM was a truly demanding criterion for eventual membership of a single currency. Keeping within a margin of 15% posed no such problems, and even the Italian Government was tempted by the prospect of a return to the fold.

The outcome of the currency crises of 1992-93 was a serious blow to the workings of the ERM which has operated on the less rigid basis ever since. In effect, in its original form it had collapsed and could only continue on the basis of a much looser and more flexible mechanism. Its breakdown was really the culmination of a long period of doubt and tension for the members involved.

The official view was that the new flexibility had saved the mechanism and the EMS, and French and German politicians were keen to paper over the cracks which had been revealed. Nonetheless, the failure of the ERM dealt a blow to the hopes of many who wanted to see EMU accomplished in line with the Maastricht timetable, and the prospect of convergence being achieved by more than a handful of governments began to seem remote. Supporters still wanted to see it come about, but many came to accept that this could not happen at the earlier date.

Maastricht and After

At Maastricht, following discussion in the Intergovernmental Conference, the cause of EMU was linked to the furtherance of political union for the Treaty itself was meant to achieve ever closer cooperation among member states. It was viewed by eleven states as an important step on the road to a united Europe.

The TEU made progress towards a single currency irreversible, and set out the details as to how EMU would come about. Stage Two, a transitional phase, was to involve the creation of a European Monetary Institute (EMI) to strengthen the coordination of monetary policies in the member states and pave the way for the creation of the Central Bank. Stage Three which could begin at the earliest in 1997, otherwise in 1999, was to be the decisive one, for this would see the establishment of the Bank and the introduction of the single currency in at least some of the states.

In 1996, the Finance Ministers of The Twelve were to meet to decide which countries fulfilled the convergence criteria for the adoption of the single currency, as set out in the box. If seven or more met these criteria, then they could proceed to Stage Three. Otherwise, 1999 was the key date, when all countries meeting the requirements would go ahead, no matter how many were involved. Those outside the currency union would join as soon as they were able to do so.

The British Government reserved the right to opt out of a single currency even if it fulfilled the criteria (see p284), and during the ratification debates in Denmark ministers made it clear that their country would only participate following the verdict of the people in a referendum.

The Arguments Concerning EMU and a Single Currency

The merits of monetary union and a single currency have been hotly debated. Once EMU was in operation, the currencies of all member states would be irrevocably locked to one another at the same exchange rate; devaluations and revaluations of individual currencies would be a thing of the past. The Euro (the new name for the single currency following a rejection of the term ECU) would be the currency in use for all transactions. After a 'honeymoon' period of months or years in which national currencies and the Euro might exist alongside each other, there would then be a switch to a true single currency.

The case for a Single Currency

A single currency seems to be the logical corollary of a single market. The argument goes as follows. If in a single market nations can lower their costs by 'competitive devaluation' of their currencies, they will. Other states will counter this by restoring the non-tariff barriers and outright tariffs that the 1992 process swept away. In other words, the single market would be eroded, if not eliminated. Use of the Euro would make such currency tactics impossible, and hence keep trade free and open.

There are more particular benefits. For private individuals and companies, there are advantages in a single currency and monetary policy. No longer would it be necessary for travellers or businessmen to change money from one currency into another, which means that transactions could be eased and that losses on currency dealings would be ended. It is also hoped that a single currency would stabilise inflation and give the Union the financial clout needed to turn it into a major global economic power.

The French have been particularly committed, for they fear that without a single currency then Germany will effectively be able to set European monetary policy on its own.

The Case Against

Opponents of a single currency are concerned about the loss of their national coinage. In Britain, they wish to cling to the pound as an emblem of national sovereignty, and say that a country which has lost control of its currency has lot its independence. They realise that key decisions on interest rates would pass out of British hands. Neither do they wish to see economic policy dictated by a Central Bank, with British ministers having only a marginal impact on its conduct.

In Germany too there is a growing revolt over the single currency. Many Germans also see the Euro as an alien and unwelcome creation. They are similarly loath to forfeit their mark, which they regard as the most concrete expression of their country's postwar success. It has become a national symbol of their prosperity.

There are also serious practical difficulties. Some consider that Europe's economies are too diverse for EMU to work satisfactorily. If the economies are not successfully brought into step with each other, then EMU could well end up dividing rather than uniting the EU. Monetary union, far from advancing the cause of integration, could actually break it, with a more catastrophic version of the collapse of the Exchange Rate Mechanism.

If it is to be achieved, there is a need for convergence, and it is in the meeting of the criteria that many of the difficulties arise. It requires the economic performance of all countries to be broadly comparable, which is why the Cohesion Fund was established. Some countries (see table on page 285) are inevitably going to find the criteria difficult to fulfil, and with unemployment currently at around 20m within the Union some governments are more concerned to combat the recession. The measures they wish to take could make it more difficult for them to defeat inflation, one of the four criteria. In other words, the policies needed to create a single currency would promote higher unemployment at least in the short term.

Problems in Achieving EMU

Britain will not join a single currency in 1996-97, and I increasingly doubt whether anyone will be ready to do so.
John Major, 1995.

It is quite possible to have monetary union without political union. It is a mistake to believe that monetary union need be a huge step on the path to a federal Europe. The Austrian schilling has been fixed against the deutschmark for thirteen years... yet nobody would deny that Austria [is a] sovereign state.
Kenneth Clarke, February 1995.

Monetary union and the single currency it involves is an ambitious goal. It has far-reaching implications, and some governments are reluctant to commit their countries to this aspect of the Maastricht process. Britain is not the only country in the EU with problems regarding such a step. In France, the Government of Mr Chirac has had to cut spending in its bid to qualify for EMU by 1997, obliging him almost to halve his budget deficit from 5.6%. The presence of France, like that of Germany, is widely seen as basic to the success of EMU, but the monetary discipline needed to qualify has already provoked enormous hostility at home.

Many Germans are alarmed that in order to allow more nations to qualify the convergence criteria might be relaxed. They regard the criteria as more important than the actual timetable, and fear that a dilution might weaken the future viability and success of the EMU venture.

The British Government is very attached to the idea of the nation state, and the fear of some senior Conservatives is that to join a single currency would be to lock the country into an irrevocable movement towards political union. A previous Chancellor, Norman Lamont, believes that 'the intent and purpose of the Maastricht Treaty is clear. It is to bind the members so tightly to deepen European political integration'.

A single currency need not necessarily mean political union, but a decision to join would be a crucial step, what John Major has called 'the single most important economic decision this country has faced this century'. Hence his unwillingness to decide on British membership until all of the facts were available; the option is being kept open.

The Labour Party, whilst broadly supportive of EMU as an objective, has stressed the importance of ensuring that not only are the convergence criteria met, but that there should be additional factors taken into decision, employment, and perhaps investment and productivity.

As it happens, Britain would seem to be one of the relatively few countries which could qualify at the time when the decision has to be made. At best, unless there is a relaxation of the criteria planned at Maastricht, then there could be only six or seven countries ready to press ahead. Such a relaxation would make the whole exercise more hazardous as the Germans are only too well aware.

?

Is economic and monetary union a. desirable and b. feasible?

What benefits would a common currency offer to the people of the EU?

Implementing Maastricht

The Maastricht Timetable

It was planned that full attainment of EMU should be reached in three stages;

i Fulfilment of the Single Market.

ii 1994-7 (though the deadline could be extended to 1999)

> *A European Monetary Institute was to be set up in Germany with limited authority on matters of financial and monetary management: its role was to be primarily consultative and advisory.*

In Stages i and ii, states were to prepare for full EMU by progressively bringing the performance of their economies into line with the best performing states.

iii If the Convergence Criteria have been fulfilled by a majority of states then in 1996 (Dec) the European Council will set a date for the implementation of EMU, and set up a European Central Bank to replace EMI and set in motion procedures for introducing the Single Currency. If they have not met the criteria, Stage iii begins on Jan 1 1999 for all states who have done so.

The Convergence Criteria

The Criteria to indicate the necessary economic and monetary stability are: low inflation, low long term interest rates, a budget deficit under 3% of the naional GDP and two years of currency stability in the narrow band of the ERM. (The first three are now considered the most important given the dilution of the original ERM).

Institutions of EMU

i **European Council** - Responsible for major EMU decisions, acting unaminously or by qualified majority.

ii **Council of Ministers** - Normally Economic and Finance Ministers; will report to European Council on key isssues.

iii   **European Commission** - Responsible for proposing policies on EMU to Council of Ministers and monitoring their implementation.

iv   **European Monetary Institute** - Responsible for developing EMU through stage ii.

v   **European System of Central Banks** - Responsible for managing EMU from beginning of Stage iii; comprises European Central Bank and national central banks.

vi   **European Parliament** - To be informed and consulted on numerous aspects of monetary policy; must approve certain changes.

Meeting the Convergence Criteria

	Inflation	Lending	Debt
Austria	2.5	-5.5	68.0
Belgium	1.6	-4.5	134.4
Denmark	2.1	-2.0	73.6
Finland	1.3	-5.4	63.2
France	1.7	-5.0	51.5
Germany	2.1	-2.9	58.8
Greece	9.9	-9.3	114.4
Ireland	2.5	2.7	85.9
Italy	4.9	-7.4	124.9
Luxembourg	2.1	0.4	6.3
Netherlands	2.2	-3.1	78.4
Portugal	4.2	-5.4	70.5
Spain	4.7	-5.9	64.8
Sweden	2.8	-7.0	81.4
UK	2.7	-5.1	52.5
TARGET	Within 1.5% of average of 3 best performing countries	3% of GDP (- = borrowing)	60% of GDP (Gross debt)

Based on figures provided by European Monetary Institute in November 1995. Only Germany, Ireland and Luxembourg were already on target at that time. The UK appeared to be on target to meet the criteria in 1997.

The

Environment

There was no awareness of the need for an environmental policy when the Treaty of Rome was signed in 1957, and so the subject received no attention from those who devised its contents. When knowledge of environmental issues increased in the 1970s, the Community began to adopt a range of initiatives, although the topic was not initially seen as a priority in its thinking.

The Impact of the Single European Act

In the early days any measures taken had to be justified as relevant to the achievement of a common market, so that they came under the orbit of economic policy. It was only with the passage of the Single European Act that the EC officially recognised that this was an area within its competence, and obtained formal authority to legislate on the environment in its own right. The process of harmonisation required action to ensure that common standards were established across the Community.

Environmental policy is not a subject which can be considered in isolation, for environmental considerations need to be taken on board in the development of several aspects of EU thinking. This has happened more in the last few years, for article 130R.1 of the SEA made it clear that policy could not be compartmentalisd but was 'a component of the Community's other policies'. Preventive action has been recognised as the guiding theme of any environmental policy, and the principle that 'the polluter pays' for damage done is one that the Commission has followed.

Between 1973 and 1992, the Community initiated five Action Programmes on a wide range of topics, and it is the fifth one which covers the period through until the turn of the century. The approach employed in all of the Programmes was not to introduce legally-binding regulations but rather to issue directives which gave individual countries more freedom to devise policies in tune with their national circumstances. The SEA accepted that Community action was only desirable on those issues where the objectives it embraced could be better fulfilled at the EC level rather than by member states acting on their own.

As a result, the standards of implementation have varied among member states, and some countries have managed to avoid the obligations laid upon them. Domestic pressure from manufacturers and financial constraints have often limited the extent to which directives have been adopted. It can be very costly to comply with the standards laid down by the Commission, which is one reason why the 1975 directive on the quality of bathing water has been so half-heartedly implemented in several countries.

In the past, it has always been easy for those who wish to evade their responsibilities to argue that the Treaty did not establish environmental goals and that therefore there was no clear point of reference against which policies could be tested. This has enabled the laggard countries to comply only half-heartedly or not at all with EC initiatives. But the SEA made it clear that environmental policy was a legitimate area for Community concern, and it laid down minimum standards in several fields.

The Impact of Maastricht

The Maastricht summit confirmed the new status of environmental policy. Agreement was reached on four goals, the first three of which had already been recognised;

   i   To preserve, protect and improve the quality of the environment

ii To protect human health

iii To make prudent and rational use of natural resources

iv To promote international measures to tackle problems which have implications over an areas wider than the Union itself.

The objectives are very vague and this enables them to command general agreement, but their inclusion in the Treaty was a further sign that the environment is now recognised as an area of growing significance. Among indications of the new importance attached to protecting our surroundings, encouragement has been given to those firms which launch products which are environmentally-friendly. They can be rewarded with the EU eco-label. In addition, a European Environment Agency has been developed (1994) in Copenhagen to accumulate statistical data on many features of policy, and this resource bank will be able to share technical information and good practice.

The environment is an area likely to grow in importance, for increasingly problems are seen to be international rather than purely national. They require a common response, for the problems of pollution and other forms of environmental damage do not follow national boundaries. Action is often necessary on a larger scale. The Chernobyl disaster is an indication of the way in which the internal problems of one state impinge seriously on many more. So too are the difficulties associated with acid rain and the threat to the ozone layer.

Environmental Issues and How They Have Been Tackled

Amongst the issues on which the European Union legislates are water pollution, including setting standards for drinking-water as well as for bathing-water quality on beaches, air pollution from factories and cars, noise pollution, the packaging of chemicals and other products, plus the transport and disposal of waste.

The Fifth Action Programme, **Towards Sustainability**, is the boldest to date. It stresses the causes of pollution, and identifies five areas where a strong EU approach is essential (agriculture, energy, industry, tourism and transport). The focus is on the way in which all EU policies must be made to conform to the needs of environmental policy, and on the differing responsibilities of all tiers of government, from local to European, in ensuring that appropriate action is taken.

The EU, covering as it does some three million or more square kilometres, is well-placed to tackle some of the most pressing environmental problems. It has given a lead in raising standards in areas such as water pollution and the use of lead-free petrol which Britain has been slower than some other countries to follow.

Scandinavia has long been in the forefront of attempts to tackle acid rain and other issues, and Denmark, a member for more than twenty years, has shown that action by national government can be effective. Some of the environmental groups in Denmark and Sweden have shown concern that in the drive towards the single market - with its emphasis on free competition - their high standards might be jeopardised.

Environmental policy still lacks the priority attached to achieving free competition, and in any conflict between protecting the environment and the needs of the market it is often the wishes of the producers which carry the heavier weight. The Italians originally had an energy-efficient approach to the use of petrol, for the high cost of oil (all of which was imported) made it desirable to encourage the use of smaller cars. Yet pressure from the Commission, itself under the influence of the motor manufacturers, has led to a dilution of the original standards.

The Problems of the North Sea

Pollution of the seas has been an area of considerable concern for environmentalists. Many dolphins and seals have died because of viral disease and bio-accumulative pollutants, and half of the turtles examined in the Caribbean and Pacific reveal tumours, with many incidents of shellfish poisoning and toxic damage.

The state of the North Sea poses a particularly serious problem, and the International Council for the Exploration of the Sea (ICES), the official scientific advisers, foresees a catastrophic crash in some fish stocks without a serious attempt to tackle the linked problems of sea and air pollution. To protect species, action is needed on heavy metal, chemical and sewage pollution, and nutrient inputs, mostly fertilser from farmland and nitrates and phosphates from sewage works. 400 oil and gas installations and toxics spilled from oil tankers have added to the severity of the difficulties. The North Sea's problems are a microcosm of a looming global crisis of pollution and overfishing.

Whereas according to the UN Food and Agriculture Organisation all the world's major fishing grounds are now at or beyond their biological limits, the EU countries have over the years increased their subsidies to fishing fleets, with much of the money going into building larger boats. The Union has a policy of buying for scrap 20% of Europe's fishing fleet to attack overfishing, yet it has provided hundreds of millions of pounds to aid poorer countries build bigger boats.

If Europe cannot save the North Sea there is little hope for other seas, for the EU has the most sophisticated regulation of trade and waste. In theory, it has a mechanism for controlling quotas and the size of fishing fleets (see p327-328). It has technical expertise, less corruption, and more control in its fishing and waste industries than almost anywhere else in the world.

British Environmental Policy; the Impact of Parties and Pressure Groups

Interest in environmental matters in Britain has waxed and waned. To some extent these fluctuations have occurred in response to the fortunes of the economy, but they have also reflected international concern. At times when there has been a major controversy abroad (such as the nuclear disaster at Chernobyl and the French nuclear tests in the Pacific) or when there has been a matter of concern at home (the decommissioning of the Brent Spar oil rigg or the consumption of beef affected by 'mad cow disease'), green groups and their activists have been able to command widespread attention for their concern with the 'quality of life'.

British membership of the EC coincided with the era in which environmental politics began to interest the Community's policy-makers. As the Community became more active in establishing environmental standards, British ministers found themselves forced to respond to initiatives from the Commission. Hence 'the most striking feature of the Government's policy on pollution is the extent to which it is dictated by EC directives' (**Milton**).

It is EC directives which have forced the British Government to tackle issues such as motor vehicle emissions, lead poisoning, and other forms of air pollution resulting from, amongst other things, the dangers to the atmosphere presented by smoke and sulphur dioxide. Similarly, it is EC law which has placed questions of water quality and acid pollution on the political agenda.

The same concern for high standards meant that in 1991 the Commission insisted that seven major construction projects were halted because there had been no assessment of their environmental impact. This failing was in direct contravention of a 1985 directive, and led the Commissioner, Carlo Ripa di Meana, to take legal action through the EC machinery over two of them.

Blackpool fails bathing test

Blackpool may be noted for fresh air and fun but the bathing water along its beaches still fails European Union quality standards, statistics revealed yesterday.

The Golden Mile is tarnished by black marks for Blackpool south, central, and north in a list of tourist resorts which do not make the grade.

Cleethorpes, on Humberside, Bognor Regis, West Sussex, and Sandwich Bay in Kent are also below the exacting cleanliness standards insisted on by Brussels.

But the latest report on bathing water quality, for 1995, says UK standards continue to improve. The Government has notified the Commission of 464 beach resort areas which qualify for monitoring around the UK coast. And the latest figures show that 413 now comply after regular testing.

The Guardian, 15.5.1996

The Quality of Water in Britain

For years, it was common for British people to mock continental countries over the allegedly poor quality of their drinking water and the lack of hygiene in their sanitation arrangements. Yet as comparisons were increasingly made between British procedures and those of other member states in the Community, it became apparent that several of them had tighter standards of control than those operating in Britain.

The EU has introduced nearly thirty directives on the quality of water, affecting matters ranging from the low standards of sea-bathing water and the lack of cleanliness of beaches, to the impurities to be found in water for human consumption. British ministers responsible for water privatisation in the mid 1980s found it necessary to establish the National Rivers Authority as a watchdog with powers to check pollution levels in lakes and rivers. As **McCormick** notes;

> In short, EC law was able to achieve what many years of domestic and foreign pressure on the British Government had failed to achieve. This created an interesting irony; while the water industry was privatised (and thus freed of direct government control), it was also made subject to considerably stronger environmental regulation.

The issue of beach hygiene has long been a contentious one, for in regular reports the Commission has commented unfavourably on the pollution of the British coastline, even in resorts often considered fashionable and in areas such as Cornwall where people might not expect to find untreated sewage and other effluents. In 1975, the Bathing Water Directive laid down certain minimum standards but British governments have been reluctant to enforce them. Because of this, Lancashire County Council applied pressure on the Commission in a bid to persuade it to prosecute ministers for their failure to take action over the raw sewage said to foul Blackpool beach (See extract opposite).

For many years, British parties ignored environmental issues, and when they did give them attention the policies which resulted often lacked coherence. What changed the situation was the outcome of the 1989

European elections when the Greens won 14.9% of the popular vote and pushed the Liberal Democrats into third place. For a year or two, the environment suddenly featured strongly in political discussion, and other parties sought to establish their 'green' credentials.

The Liberal Democrats had a longer history of concern for environmental issues than did the other parties, and several of their spokespersons enthusiastically embraced the cause. Labour was anxious to show that red and green could mix, and even some Conservatives began to speak of the threat to the ozone layer, acid rain and other matters of contemporary interest. Indeed, Mrs Thatcher described the task of protecting the balance of nature as one of the 'great challenges of the late twentieth century'.

Yet the new-found interest did not long survive in the minds and priorities of many politicians, and environmental politics began to fade into the background in the early 1990s. This was partly because of the impact of recession. 'Deep Greens' had portrayed their preoccupations as being at variance with the demand for economic growth, and at a time when there was some growth this did not seem so unreasonable. When the country's industries were hard-hit by a downturn in the economic cycle, the resulting problems of business closures and unemployment placed a new emphasis on policies directed at restoring growth. As **McCormick** has observed; '...when the economy is troubled, people attend to more immediate bread-and-butter issues such as jobs and the cost of living'.

However, the diminished interest in discussion of the environment also reflected the fact that to some extent the Greens had won the argument. All parties had in some degree responded to their agenda, and some 'greening' had occurred, particularly on the Left; this did not disappear when the matter was no longer centre-stage. As we have seen, pressure from the the European Community was another factor in this process, for the Conservative Government found itself pressed by Brussels to comply with EC laws.

Pressure Groups

Like other pressure groups, those which operate in the environmental arena have increasingly turned their attention to Brussels, for an increasing amount of legislation derives from the European Union. Some groups have direct representation at the Community level, whereas in the case of many of the smaller ones they have officers who spend much of their time on scrutiny of the detail of the latest directives. Greenpeace and Friends of the Earth have been the most well-known of the environmental lobbyists, but groups such as the World Wide Fund for Nature and many of those involved in the area of animal rights (the RSPCA and the Federation of Veterinarians among them) have liaison officers active on matters of EU policy.

In many ways other European countries are ahead of Britain in the standards applied in environmental matters. Because of this, on a number of issues there is little point in British pressure groups lobbying Europe unless it is with the purpose of persuading the Commission to apply pressure on the national government. Thus the Campaign for Lead-Free Petrol has continued to place most of the emphasis of its campaigning on Whitehall and Westminster, rather than machinery in Brussels or Strasbourg.

Yet on some occasions, European pressure has helped to raise British standards. Friends of the Earth and other groups lobbied the Commission over Britain's exemptions from a Water Quality Directive governing the nitrate content of water. The Commission then sought to ensure compliance with the directive from the British Government, and in 1988, faced with the prospect of a challenge in the European Court, ministers agreed to abide by the European standard in the future.

On other issues, the Commission has shown itself susceptible to influence from British companies. The firm which manufactures tetrapak cartons for fruit juice was alarmed by a Community directive on packaging waste, and was successful in persuading representatives of the Commission that their packaging was not an environmental hazard. The directive was later amended to allow for the representations made in Brussels.

The Way Ahead

If ever there was a topic on which it is necessary for governments to cooperate with each other, it is on matters concerned with the environment. No aspect of the quality of life is more fundamental than the purity of the air we breath and the water we drink. Many of the problems are not national but international, and require a coordinated response. Pollution respects no national boundaries, and no state can preserve its environment by a strategy of isolationism.

There are new policies which could be adopted. They go beyond simply setting minimum standards, and include the development of a comprehensive strategy to link environmental concerns with economic and industrial policy. In particular, help for the countries of Central and Eastern Europe is necessary to assist them in overcoming the toxic legacy of the Soviet era and in improving their overall environmental standards.

The European Union, given its size, location and composition, is in many ways an appropriate body to take action and urge the adoption of new policies. It provides the political forum within which the member countries can agree on common action to protect our shared environment. It has the potential to take the lead in the formulation and implementation of a global strategy to confront the ecological threat to the planet.

However, success depends on the political will to act, and this in turn depends upon the attitudes of fifteen governments. Policy on the environment is one of those areas affected by the subsidiarity debate, and since the Edinburgh Council there has been pressure from some states to scale down EU involvement in national decision-making. Britain is not the only country to regard any reversal of previous trends with some relief, for the record of some of the Mediterranean states in environmental matters leaves much to be desired.

'The 'European Union' is a particularly suitable organisation to tackle environmental policy'. Do you agree?

Dilemmas of Environmental Policy; a Summary

1   National pressures can undermine policy. Environmental considerations take second place to the promotion of economic development. The uneven levels of prosperity in the EU affect national attitudes.

2   Promotion of the single market can affect environmental standards. The search for high standards is not allowed to be used as an excuse for protectionism within the EU. Some states may attempt to impose strict regulations (eg, on food labelling) as a means of keeping out goods from other countries which do not employ the same standards. In the chemical and packaging industries, some states have introduced tough rules as a means of protecting home industries.

3   Promoting economic growth and environmental protection at the same time can be difficult. Many companies are more aware of the costs of compliance with EU legislation, than with any benefits derived from controls. This casts doubt on the efficacy of voluntary means of environmental protection.

4   Even the most environmentally conscious in the EU (the Nordic states and Austria) are subject to pressures to adjust their priorities, for reasons of economic necessity. They are still a potential force for good in the Union, although as less populous states their influence on decisions is relatively small-scale, and this will reduce their ability to raise overall standards. Moreover, Norway, one of the pacesetters in environmental regulation voted to stay outside the EU.

5   The inclusion of Central and Eastern states in the future will require additional resources to help them clean up their environment. The emphasis in the past has been on intensive production whatever the cost. Some states (eg, Poland and Slovakia) used brown coal as the main energy supply, and this is a heavy pollutant. Also, existing legislation is often inadequately enforced.

Regional Policy

One of the original objectives of the Community was to ensure that there was balanced economic and social development across the territories of the member states. They vary in size from Luxembourg to Germany, and in per capita income from Luxembourg to Greece. Those who inhabit the regions within member nations also vary dramatically in their living standards. Some areas are ones of industrial decline and heavy unemployment, and others have not experienced much industrialisation, whereas parts of the EU are affluent or relatively so.

It was recognised from the beginning that unequal development between member states was a barrier to closer integration, so that it was always acknowledged that there should be some redistribution of wealth within the EC. The Preamble to the Treaty of Rome called on them to 'strengthen the unity of their economies and to ensure their harmonious development by reducing the differences existing between the various regions and the backwardness of the less favoured regions'.

Yet despite this original goal, little progress was at first made towards correcting economic imbalances. In the early days, Community policies favoured the strongest regions, the areas best situated for marketing, selling and transporting their products. Those which were conveniently located had the best chance of flourishing, for they had the shortest links between producer and consumer. More distant regions were at a disadvantage, hence the demand for greater recognition of the problems of peripheral and other ailing regions.

The History of Regional Policy

The European Regional Development Fund (ERDF), the primary agency through which assistance was given to the less prosperous areas, was originally created in 1975. At first, it was not an important priority in spending, but one which became more significant with enlargement and with the creation of the single currency and moves towards EMU.

It was the pressure of enlargement that provided the original spur to tackle regional differences. Some of the states which joined the Community in the 1970s and 1980s had particular problems. They were poor by European standards, and with their entry regional disparities increased. Holland points out that 'prior to the southern enlargement the per capita income disparity between the richest and poorest areas was at a ratio of 5:1; after the Iberian accession, this leaped to a ratio of 10:1'.

In Greece, Ireland, Portugal and Spain the weakness of the economy meant that in a single market they would be vulnerable, for they could never compete with their more successful partners. They needed funding to raise their overall level, in the hope that improved infrastructure (eg, a good road network) would increase overall prosperity.

Because of these developments, members agreed in 1988 to reform the structure of those funds which seek to tackle the problems of the ailing regions - notably the European Regional Development Fund (ERDF), the European Social Fund (ESF) and the Guidance Section of the Agricultural Fund. They also decided that over a five year period twice as much money should be made available to this area of policy, with the intention that the structural funds would account for a quarter of all Community spending by 1993.

At the same time, agreement was reached on common propositions to underpin the funds alluded to above. They were to be concentrated on areas of greatest need, to be based on medium term programmes for regional development rather than one-off projects, to be organised on the basis of partnership between the Community and the recipient body and finally to be financed on the principle that money should be additional to rather than in place of funding from the appropriate national body. In other words, the key terms were **concentration, programming, partnership and additionality.**

Forms of Assistance

The Regional Fund. This lends money in addition to the governments' domestic regional policy spending and to that of public authorities. It aims to help reduce the most obvious regional imbalances by means of investment subsidies to the disadvantaged areas

Coal and Steel Community. Loans have aided large scale mining and power projects, and have primed new business initiatives in former coal and steel areas, with grants to ease redundancy and other payments to workers.

European Investment Bank. Lending has assisted large-scale capital and infrastructure projects, mainly by public authorities; indirect lending through agencies has helped small businesses.

The Social Fund. This has assisted national programmes of training and retraining, and numerous small projects put forward by private and public bodies.

The Cohesion Fund. Set up at Maastricht to help reduce the gap in economic standards between the member countries, with a view to paving the way for economic and monetary union.

Maastricht and Cohesion

Two thirds of EU spending on the ERDF now goes now goes to four Mediterranean states, Greece, Italy, Portugal and Spain.

At Maastricht it was agreed that there should be further change and the subsequent Council at Edinburgh set out plans for a new initiative, the establishment of a Cohesion Fund. By then, the Community was spending

£11.5b on its structural funds, a proportion of which was going to the United Kingdom. It was felt that the programme of regional development had been a broad success, and so an increase in its scale and funding was arranged. A new European Investment Fund was created for the purpose of guaranteeing loans intended to finance projects of common European interest, and this was due to operate from 1994, as an independent agency within the EIB.

The purpose of the Cohesion Fund was to address the problems caused by the adoption of the single market. At an early stage there were 'fears that the opening up of markets might increase disparities between countries, either by making the poor poorer or by degenerating into very uneven distribution of the gains from the opening up of markets'. These problems had become more apparent during enlargement, but the creation of the single market and the prospect of Economic and Monetary Union provided additional challenges and made further policy adjustments necessary. Cohesion was a necessary precondition of expecting nations to meet the Maastricht convergence criteria.

A further indication of the new importance attached to regional policy was the establishment of a Committee of the Regions (see p172-173). It consists of representatives of regional and local bodies who act in an advisory capacity. COR would normally be consulted and asked for an opinion by the Council or Commission on matters with strong regional implications, and it has the power to issue an opinion on its own initiative where this is considered appropriate and/or necessary.

The Objectives of Regional Policy

The purposes of regional policy were set out in 1975, when the ERDF was established;

i   To promote the development and structural adjustment of underdeveloped regions whose per capita GDP is less than 75% of the Union average

ii   To redevelop regions or areas seriously affected by the decline of industry

iii   To combat unemployment, and in particular to assist young people into employment

iv   To adapt the workforce to industrial and technological change

v   a. To adapt production, processing and marketing structures in agriculture and forestry, and b. To promote the development and structural adjustment of rural areas.

The Regional Fund (ERDF)

The Regional Fund has no basis in the Treaty of Rome, but was established after the first enlargement of the Community. Grant aid from the ERDF is intended to help finance initiatives in both private and public sectors which encourage problem areas, with special help being given to small and medium-sized enterprises in industry and tourism. They are not for use on social infrastructure programmes, nor for projects which are purely the financial responsibility of local councils or boards.

The contribution for individual projects and progammes is normally 50% of the total investment, and the EU insists on the principle of additionality. This means that any aid granted should be additional to that of member states, not a substitute for it.

It was as a result of the Single European Act and the moves towards a common market free of all barriers to trade that a new emphasis was placed on what was called 'Economic and Social Cohesion'. The purpose was to enable the Community to 'aim at reducing disparities between the various regions and the backwardness of the least-favoured regions'.

The Investment Bank (EIB)

The EIB was created by article 130 of the Treaty of Rome. It comprises representatives of the fifteen countries, and it is located in Luxembourg. It raises money on the capital markets of the Community and elsewhere, and makes money available to assist in the balanced development of the Union. It makes grants to public authorities, private enterprises and financial institutions for such things as;

i Projects which contribute to the economic development of regions in difficulty, and thus further cohesion - eg, capital spending on energy installations and infrastructure

ii Projects of common interest to several member countries or to the Community as a whole such as improving transport structure or reducing energy consumption; environmental policy is important here, with funding for schemes to tackle the treatment of water supplies and to help combat atmospheric and other forms of pollution

iii Projects in certain cases involving modernisation or conversion of undertakings by the use of more advanced technology, or the creation of fresh activities

(It also can provide for operations in developing countries).

Because it is a non-profit making undertaking and has an impressive credit-rating, it can borrow at favourable rates. Interest rates charged to clients are therefore competitive, and related to the Bank's own borrowing costs, rather than to the status of the institution wanting to borrow the money. It makes direct loans for up to half of the capital cost of each project, subject to a maximum figure. It is the largest provider of loan finance in the Union.

Although some of its money goes to environmental and energy schemes, regional development has always been its prime target. From 1987-91, it lent nearly 32b ecu, and since the changes in 1992 the amount has continued to rise.

Which Areas Benefit?

The UK regions which are judged to lack indigenous wealth and which benefit from Union cohesion policies are Merseyside, the Highlands and Islands of Scotland, and Northern Ireland. They qualify under Objective I of the 1988 agreement, 'the promotion of structural adjustment in regions whose development is lagging behind'. Many of these are rural, and they include the whole of Greece, Ireland and Portugal, along with Southern

Italy and parts of Spain. This absorbs the greater part of regional spending, 36.2b ecu in the first four year period after the restructuring.

Objective 5b, concerning the development of rural regions, caters generally for smaller areas (57 at present) which have particular problems of agricultural income, environmental difficulties, and remoteness, among other considerations. There are none in the UK.

The subsidies given under the Regional Development Fund are designed, among other things, to create new jobs, and one Commission estimate has put the number created by regional policy at 60000 a year since 1975. But the effects of assistance can be wide-ranging, for help in the construction of a power station to improve electrical supply in a particular region can powerfully assist in overall economic development.

There have been some impressive examples of regeneration deriving from projects backed by EC/EU funding. They range from sea water purification in the Bay of Naples to the transformation of a derelict industrial zone of Southern Belgium into a modern industrial estate. Closer to home, in Northern Ireland much benefit has been derived from programmes of urban renewal in Belfast, with money being made available to improve waterworks, roadworks and airport facilities, as well as for the promotion of industry and trade in general.

The combination of enlargement (to include less developed countries such as Greece, Portugal and Spain) and the creation of the single market have provided the spur to develop regional policies. The new article 130a of the Treaty of Rome commits the fifteen nations to 'reducing disparities between the various regions and the backwardness of the least-favoured regions'.

There is inevitably a conflict of interest between the northern countries which pay most heavily into the Union budget and the southern ones which are the greatest recipients of aid. But those less developed states together have considerable significance in the Council (see p00). In the bargaining process over the direction of EU policies in general they have been able to ensure that their needs are given due recognition.

Two British Regions; Case Studies

Each region of the Union has its own particularities, and is affected by the policies collectively pursued. Many policies are of special benefit to the regions, ranging from competition policy (ensuring that firms everywhere can compete on a level playing field), the deregulation of transport policy (allowing cheaper movement of goods between regions) and measures to promote liaison and contacts between small and medium-sized businesses in the fifteen countries.

The Union now allocates 25% of its budget to promote the harmonious development of the regions. Nearly two thirds of this money goes to disadvantaged priority regions, under Objective One. The two examples chosen illustrate the different ways in which regions can benefit from Union assistance;

Northern Ireland

Although Northern Ireland has a level of GDP slightly above the criterion set by the EU, it was granted Objective One status.

It has suffered seriously from a decline in manufacturing employment, and has jobless totals well above the UK and Union average. Moreover, it has special problems, deriving from its negative image brought about by hostility between the Catholic and Protestant communities.

For the five years 1989-1993, it was granted £550m as part of a Community Support Framework, in addition to money deriving from other EC initiatives. A new Northern Ireland Plan covers the period from 1994-99.

Money has been spent on a vast variety of projects, including the development of the inner city area in Belfast alongside the River Lagan, help to improve integrated education facilities and support for the Belfast Action Teams which work in some of the most deprived areas of the city to encourage local economic growth and community involvement.

The West Midlands

The problems of the region were brought about largely by industrial decline in key sectors such as coalmining, engineering, ceramics and manufacturing. Twenty years ago, more than $^3/_4$m were employed in the major industries. Ten years later, the number was about a half million, and the decline continued into the early nineties. Across the region, jobless levels were usually above the UK and EC average, as were the numbers of long term unemployed. With inner city decline and a rise in the population of areas away from traditional urban centres, diversification of industry was needed, with enhanced training provision.

In 1988, the EC granted several parts of the West Midlands Objective Two status, triggering aid from the ERDF and allowing funding to help revitalise affected communities. Since then, more than £300m has been given via the Regional and Social Funds, some of it going to combat long term youth unemployment and to integrate young people into the job market. Under Objective Five B, help has gone to rural areas where agricultural incomes are low.

Schemes include money to regenerate the infrastructure, such as the that in the derelict Heartlands Area of Birmingham, and that spent on reclaiming disused industrial sites in the Black Country. Most famously, assistance has been granted for the development of the airport, the improvement of the inner city road network in Birmingham and the extension of the NEC.

For what sort of regions is EU policy particularly effective?

Why is cohesion a necessary feature of EU policy?

The Common Agricultural Policy

> *I remember the terrible days of hunger and even starvation at the end of the war, above all in my own country. For years after, fear of food shortages remained all too real and we had to act so Europe could feed its own people,*
> *Pierre Lardinois, European Farm Commissioner, defending CAP in 1970s.*

In the wartime people were accustomed to shortages and understood the reasons for them. In the years which followed, a guiding theme of agricultural policy was to ensure that food was plentiful and available at reasonable prices. It was also important to see that the farming community received an appropriate reward for its efforts, but in some areas the harsh geogaphical and climatic conditions made it difficult to ensure farm profitability.

Today the idea of shortages may seem ridiculous, but for a generation after the war it was an important factor in the thinking of those responsible. When Lardinois spoke, the Community was beginning to bring demand and production of food into reasonable balance. The CAP had obvious attractions; it appeared to solve the problem of insufficient output and at the same time ensure a reasonable return to farmers and keep consumer food prices reasonably under control.

The Importance of Agriculture

Agriculture is unlike other sectors of the economy. It is very price-sensitive. People spend much of their money on food, and prices can rise or fall sharply depending on seasonal and climatic conditions. If they go too high, the consumer suffers; if they fall too low, some farmers might suffer and be driven off the land. The availability of plenty of food - at the right price - matters to everyone.

When a policy for agriculture was devised, it was recognised that this was politically sensitive issue for three other reasons;

i   The agricultural work-force in a number of member states represented a significant electoral bloc. The survival of any government which alienated the farming lobby was precarious. In France, it now accounts for only 3.6% of GDP, and 6% of employment - but it still accounts for 17% of votes.

ii   More than any other section of the economy, agriculture was heavily protected by national subsidies and tariffs. Almost every country - from the Japan to the USA, from Denmark to Switzerland - subsidised its farmers after the war, and it made good sense to do so.

iii Agriculture was more than a commodity; it reflected individual social and cultural values that were of great significance, especially (as we have just seen) in France.

The costs of the policy rocketed in the late 1970s, and huge surpluses of food products began to accumulate. The main reason for the massive and unexpected boost in output on European farms was the unpredicted scientific and technological revolution in agriculture. In spite of regular attempts to curtail price support, farmers have been able to compensate by constantly boosting output per acre.

However, the importance of agriculture in the Union is more than just a matter of facts and figures about prices and production. It is about maintaining a rural way of life, and preserving the income of those who live in agricultural regions. Rural protection is an issue which arouses strong feelings, for those who live in areas such as the Massif Central can only afford to stay there because the agricultural policy of the EC for years gave them guaranteed prices.

In parts of the Community there has been a population move from rural to urban areas, and if farm incomes were to be significantly reduced then more depopulation is likely to occur. There would be no point in staying in a hostile environment. This could have alarming consequences on the countryside as well as on local levels of unemployment. It would be the more serious because small farmers are likely to use their land in an environmentally friendly way. Whereas in Britain much agriculture is intensive and dedicated to high yields, in France there is significantly more organic farming. Many of the allegedly 'inefficient' French farmers are much more sympathetic to 'natural' methods of production.

This is the background to the controversies surrounding the debate about the Common Agricultural Policy (CAP) which was introduced in 1962. The Treaty of Rome committed The Six to a common policy, and the scheme which emerged was the result of strong bargaining from France and Germany, both of which were determined to uphold the rights of the agricultural community in their respective countries.

The Bavarian farmers supported the idea of a protective agricultural policy from the beginning. Other Germans wanted to see a common market for industrial goods, and the French were looking for a policy which created a common market in agriculture but one which ensured that the large farming interest in France would benefit. The negotiations between the two countries gave each side enough to satisfy the wishes of many of their citizens.

The Treaty of Rome

Article 39 set out the main objectives of agricultural policy;

- To increase agricultural productivity
- To ensure a fair standard of living for the agricultural community
- To stablise markets and to ensure that supplies are available to the consumer at reasonable prices

The purpose was to provide guaranteed prices for farm produce along with loans and grants for modernising farm procedures. The CAP aimed to give farmers a decent income and to guarantee consumers a steady supply of produce at reasonable prices. The objectives were geared to the needs of producer and consumer, as they were then conceived.

The debate in the early sixties was not simply a technocratic or strategic one as it was in the negotiations leading to the formation of Euratom. It had to accommodate various political concessions. The final package placated national concerns by safeguarding the position of Europe's rural population, whilst at the same time providing German industry with the prospect of a customs union of goods, services and capital.

The broad lines of CAP policy were based on three fundamental principles;

i   The Community was concerned to create a common market which meant that there were no internal barriers to trade, and an external tariff against imported goods. This was to apply to agriculture, and thereby help to safeguard the interests of EC farmers who otherwise might have given up the struggle to make a decent livelihood. Any imported goods would be charged a 'levy' so that they would become more expensive than goods produced within The Six.

ii   There must be a common market covering the whole Community and the whole range of produce to replace a situation in which each member state had its own market arrangements to protect agriculture. Otherwise, farmers in some areas and specialising in certain products would be at a competitive disadvantage.

iii To ensure that the costs of the policy were equitably borne, some special financial arrangement was necessary. The European Agricultural Guidance and Guarantee Fund (EAGGF) was established, and this had two aspects; firstly, it had the Guidance Section which financed structural measures, and secondly, a Guarantee Section which covered the much more expensive area of price support.

Decline in the number of farms

The number of farms has declined in all countries of the Community.

Thanks to harmonized statistics this trend is clearest in the six original Member States, some of which have lost up to 50% of their farms.

Number of farms

	1970	1980	1987
Belgium	184	115	93
Denmark	–	123	87
Germany	1075	850	705
Greece	–	–	953
France	1588	1255	982
Ireland	–	224	217
Italy	2850	2634	2784
Luxembourg	8	5	4
Netherlands	185	149	132
Portugal	–	–	635
Spain	–	–	1792
United Kingdom	–	269	260

[1] Excluding the new German Länder, post unification.

Information adapted from 'Our Farming Future', European Commission, 1992

Many of the objectives planned at the time when the CAP was devised have been fulfilled. Consumers have been able to obtain secure supplies at stable prices, and have not been a prey to the fluctuations in world markets. The farming community has maintained a fair standard of living, and many of its practices and much of its equipment have been modernised. The result is an agrarian community which is much smaller (down from around 20% of the Community's workforce to around 7% today), and an agricultural industry which is more competitive.

How the CAP Operates

The CAP is managed by the Commission (Directorate-General VI), which has a close and effective relationship with various management committees dealing with particular produce. On these committees, sit officials drawn from each of the fifteen member states. The precise arrangement by which production of each crop or product and the markets for them are managed varies from one case to another, but broadly it is as explained in the box below.

The Mechanism of Intervention

An annual target price for any particular produce is fixed in April or May. This is the price at which the farmer may expect to sell the product. If this happens, then the system is in balance, and no further action is necessary. If the market price is below the one which he or she can expect to obtain, then instead of offloading the goods onto the market, the farmer can sell to an agency of the CAP for an intervention price.

The intervention agency will then pay most of the costs involved in transport and storage of the goods. It will either sell them in the export market (most notoriously in the past, often at cheap, subsidised rates to the communist East European countries), or to the Union itself to use as food aid for developing countries. Occasionally, food is 'denatured' - destroyed.

The system of farm price support is obviously good for the farmers who get guaranteed prices for their goods. It is easy to mock the extravagance and waste to which it leads (see next section), but two points should be borne in mind;

i Most countries, such as Japan and the United States, still subsidise their agriculture, although the scale of EU assistance has admittedly been very substantial. The EU as a body is doing what otherwise individual states may continue to do on a national basis.

ii Many products other than agricultural ones have long received governmental subsidies from their national governments, not least some of the nationalised industries of postwar Britain. Until recent years, when there has been a much greater emphasis upon free markets, subsidies were considered normal rather than an inefficient extravagance to be condemned.

The Role of Pressure Groups in Operating the CAP

Pressure groups such as the National Farmers Union are inevitably interested in the way in which policy is carried out. They have their own links with the Commission which handles most technical considerations, but as most strategic decisions are taken by the Council then it is worth recognising the importance of consultation and negotiations between their organisation and Whitehall officials.

The agricultural lobby has made much use of umbrella organisations, in addition to recognising the importance of lobbying national governments. Activity began in the early days of the CAP, and the shape of that policy owes much to the input of many farming groups such as COPA. They have maintained a careful watch over the development and implementation of the CAP ever since.

COPA is a high-profile group, though it is easy to confuse activity with influence. It has often succeeded in reaching internal agreement on significant and controversial subjects such as agricultural prices, and though deviating positions do occur this is not a common feature. It realises that a united front is likely to strengthen its case. Where differences do occur, members tend to forward their views more positively through their national government.

Problems With the CAP Today

The theory behind the CAP seemed to be appropriate for the time, and there were good reasons for developing the CAP in the way that it was set up in a community of six nations in which agriculture loomed large in the national economies. In practice, there have been substantial difficulties, and in the last two decades the problems of the policy have been increasingly apparent.

Today, the situation is different from 1962 in several respects. The disadvantages of encouraging over-production have become more evident, and the nature of the Union has changed. Agriculture has become less significant in the economies of most states than it once was, and the impact of enlargement has altered the balance of production in the EU.

Overproduction

Sometimes the target prices set for particular goods were well out of line with market conditions. Because they could be sure that their goods would be purchased, the temptation was for farmers in the EC to produce more than was needed, and this led to the creation of lakes and mountains in such produce as milk, wine, butter and vegetables. Between the First Enlargement (when Britain joined) and the late 1980s, production rose at a rate of 2% a year, whereas demand from consumers rose by only 0.5%. The surplus was a drain on Community funds.

The Position of Consumers

As a result of the guaranteed prices, some produce became more expensive for the consumer. In the early 1990s, estimates suggested that the cost of the CAP to Europe's citizens was some $130b a year, a sum reached by adding the cost of subsidies to the additional amount paid by consumers in inflated prices. Food was available, in plentiful supply and much more cheaply, on the world markets.

Enlargement

Enlargement has inevitably had an important impact on the Community. The accession of the Southern countries, Greece, Portugal and Spain, brought about a new interest in exotic fruit products, and this meant a change of emphasis from the former preoccupation with dairy farming and grain. Their entry also added to the costs of the agricultural budget.

The prospect of further enlargement to the East will also have an impact, for Poland has a large agricultural sector. Under the present workings of the CAP, it would qualify for extensive support, adding greatly to the costs involved.

The Position of Britain

Before Britain belonged to the EC, it had a 'cheap food' policy. Its system of agricultural price support generally produced a satisfactory balance between the demand for and supply of food. On joining, Britain soon found itself at odds with a policy which had long been roundly condemned on this side of the Channel. It relied on artificially high food prices to encourage production and protect farmers' incomes and way of life.

Although the CAP was popular with many British farmers who stood to benefit from it, it met with much opposition from other quarters. Politicians and people objected to the amount which they paid into the Community budget to support 'inefficient French farmers'. The attack has continued ever since, and by the time of the 1992 election it was being suggested that the CAP was costing British familites an extra£17 a week for food. Purchases on the world market could be made much more cheaply, and critics were unconvinced by the argument that at least the CAP offered the prospect of a more stable supply of food than was often available on the world markets. Four years later, the figure is around £20 a week for a family of four.

This is a deceptive argument. World prices only exist as a price of last resort, as most commodities are traded at higher contract prices. Moreover, if support schemes like the CAP were to end farmers would grow less in a free market and the world price would tend to rise. The ending of support schemes could also mean that some small farms are sold to large agribusiness conglomerates which use more crop chemicals to increase yields and profits - and this would fly in the face of another common British objection to the CAP.

European Community budgetary arrangements were never devised in the interests of a country such as Britain, so that it is not surprising that the issue of the CAP which uses much of EC money is so contentious. The bulk of EC spending on agriculture was always on agricultural support. This policy was never likely to be so beneficial to Britain whose agricultural base was much smaller than that of most continental countries. Also British farming, relatively efficient, needed the protection of guaranteed prices less than parts of France and elsewhere.

Party Viewpoints

In agriculture, the lesson is clear. A country far from self-sufficient in food has no interest in paying high EU prices for what is available more cheaply elsewhere, particularly from Australia, New Zealand, Canada, the West Indies and the developing world. The CAP cap doesn't fit, and few want to wear it, yet it will not change in fundamentals.
Austin Mitchell, a Labour 'anti-EU' MP

In Britain, criticism is particularly strong on the Tory Right and from elements within the Labour Party. Labour officially supports fundamental reform for it sees the CAP as wasteful and inefficient, whereas the Right think that a policy which is fundamentally flawed is incapable of reform; it wants the CAP to be abolished. Many Conservatives particularly dislike the highly interventionist nature of the policy, and would prefer a policy which is more market-oriented.

Critics in all parties feel that the CAP represents a bad deal for consumers and taxpayers. Many would point out that it damages the countryside, for a system that automatically rewards increased output has intensified production and encouraged the use of ntirates and pesticides. Some might add that much of the detected fraud in the Union is to be found in the distribution of money assigned for agricultural spending.

Reform of the CAP

By the middle of the decade, the CAP was widely seen as becoming unmanageable and in serious need of reform. The high prices paid to farmers for food placed a considerable burden on the Community budget which also had to subsidise sales of surplus food to countries outside the European Community.

It was hard to reform the CAP because the policy was demonstrably good for so many continental farmers, notably the French ones. What helped the Commission to resist the pressures of the farm lobby was the mounting cost, £23b in 1992. Also a reduction of subsidies would help to bring about a settlement in the Uruguay Round of the GATT talks, for the farmers in countries which did not subsidise their agriculture as much (especially in the US, Australia and New Zealand) were becoming resentful of the favourable conditions accorded to their European counterparts.

The 1992 Reforms

The aims of the reform have been effectively summarised by Pascal Fontaine; 'to break the link between subsidies and quantities produced and shift the emphasis to quality, to bring production more into line with demand, and to discourage intensive production which is so damaging to the environment'.

In 1992, agreement was finally reached on a package of measures including;

- A sharp reduction in the prices paid to farmers of nearly 30% for wheat, 15% for beef and 5% for dairy products
- A percentage of land to be 'set aside', ie not used for production
- Direct compensation payments (grants) to farmers to compensate for their loss of income.

319

This package was intended to bring food prices within the European Community closer to the levels in the rest of the world, reduce costs to the Community budget and reduce prices in the shops. At the same time, farmers were compensated for their loss of income, but such grants are less expensive in the long run than subsidising excess food production.

Most European farmers were critical of the changes, and opposition was strong in scattered communities from the Lake District to Sardinia. The set aside scheme made the French farmers feel more belligerent about the proposed Gatt settlement which followed soon after, for by the agreement they were being asked to leave even more land uncultivated.

Many sceptics have cast doubt on the effectiveness of the set-aside scheme, wherby farmers get paid more than £100 an acre to grow nothing on 15% of their land. Farmers are being tempted to take their least fertile land out of production and use fertilisers more intensively on the rest.

However, more of arable farmers' subsidies come in the form of area payments paid on crops which they do grow. In 1993-94, there was, among other examples, a 33.5% subsidy on cereal crops, a 43.4% one on sugar beet and a 63.8% one on oilseeds.

The General Agreement on Tariffs and Trade (GATT) Talks

Negotiators had begun talks in Uruguay back in 1986 to liberalise world trade, and from the beginning a reason for the delay in getting a settlement was disagreement about agricultural support. Although agriculture accounts for only a small proportion of world trade, it has traditionally been fiercely protected.

The sort of deal which many countries wished to see was that the West would cut its farm subsidies, and thereby open its markets to non-subsidised but efficient agricultural nations such as Argentina and Australia. In return, the West could benefit from a chance to expand its efficient service sectors into a larger world market.

Final agreement was reached in December 1993, and a part of the final detail concerned agriculture. Subsidies were to be cut by 20% over six years. French farmers remained sceptical of the outcome, but were assured that concessions on cereals and promises of Community help if things worked out adversely, would ensure that they did not suffer.

Further Reform

The trend in recent years has been to attempt to bring agricultural spending under control, and this will be the more necessary if Poland and some other Eastern European countries are granted entry to the Union (There, as many as one in four of the workforce still labour on the land, compared to an EU average of 6-7%). The EU budgets of recent years have seen a decline in the proportion of money going into the farming community, and other sectors have proportionally benefited.

The Percentages of EU Spending on Agriculture and Fisheries				
1973	1989	1991	1993	1997 Projection
80.6	67.0	57.2	49.3	45.0

The 1992 package was a start in the right direction, but further changes will be needed. The move away from high guaranteed prices for key products is likely to continue, and in future there may be more emphasis upon subsidising the income of the farming community via direct payments rather than providing them with artificially high prices.

More land is likely to be taken out of production in return for set-aside premiums. The trend to put spare land to non-agricultural uses such as extending woodland areas and creating golf courses is likely to continue. Older farmers with small holdings may well be encouraged to retire early, with the prospect of financial incentives if the family gives up its traditional way of life.

Finally, there might be incentives for landowners to grow alternative crops which are in short supply within the Union. More afforestation is another possibility, to develop the timber industry.

The Strength of the National Farming Lobbies in Member States

In France and Germany, governments have to be very attentive to their farming lobbies. French ministers are particularly wary, for their farmers have often taken to the streets to demonstrate against any possible inroad into the CAP. Farmers have recently had to cope with increased competition from produce deriving from Eastern Europe and from outside the continent, and at the same time accept cuts in agricultural prices and land taken out of production.

French farmers were strongly opposed to the GATT settlement, and the further package of reductions provoked seething resentment in rural France. Ministers had to be escorted by riot police, and were liable to be pelted with eggs, potatoes or even manure! It was felt that cuts in production would undermine rural communities, and ultimately impact on schools, transport and community life.

By contrast, the interests which are opposed to the undue emphasis on agriculture in the EU budget are less well organised. Consumers and environmentalists are less easy to mobilise, and do not have the 'insider' status accorded to the agrarian lobby.

Originally it was the Germans who had the most protected agriculture among The Six. The CAP was devised with the interests of their farmers in mind, and the language of the objectives laid out in article 39 of the Rome Treaty bears a striking rememblance to that of the German Agricultural Act of 1955, with its talk of increased production to provide a reasonable standard of life for the farming community.

As part of the original bargaining, German representatives were determined to obtain a policy that preserved the privileged position of the Bavarian farmers. The effect was to guarantee high prices, so that overnight when the CAP was implemented in 1964 French farmers saw their prices rise by more than 20%. The sixties and seventies were a golden age for those who worked the land, who later became trapped in an artificial system of price support.

The votes of German farmers matter. There are 600000 farms in Germany, affecting some 3m voters, and no German government is going to antagonise a group which has long-standing roots in their local community often going back over many generations. Any German Minister of Agriculture sees it as a duty to protect the farmers' livelihoods; he or she could not afford to ignore their voice. It is calculated that around 80% of German farmers vote for one of the present coalition partners. With less than 70% from them at the support at the polls, their chance of electoral success would be much reduced.

The Importance of Agriculture Today

In any assessment of the merits and weaknesses of the CAP, it is important to remember that without it there would probably have been no Community; it is part of the tape which bound The Six together. When it was established there were still memories of wartime shortages and farmers in some areas wrestled with primitive facilities and unproductive land.

The importance of farming varies significantly across the Union. It matters much less in some countries than in others, and whereas it produces approximately 17% of the national income in Greece and 16% in Ireland, it accounts for only for 5% in the UK.

Agriculture is still highly significant in the economy of the EU. Its contribution to the Union's GDP is very small compared to manufacturing industry and services, but it is important to the EU in several ways. It contributes to the wealth of the Union, and ensures that there is enough food to make it self-sufficient. Moreover, it is still an important source of employment, for 9m work in agriculture on farms as farm workers or processors of agricultural produce of some kind or other.

There remains much to be done to make the Common Agricultural Policy more efficient and market-oriented, and a further overhaul of its workings is almost inevitable - however difficult it is to achieve because of the strength of the agricultural lobby. The huge costs of the CAP and excess production in some areas need to be curbed, whilst at the same time the needs of the farming community and the protection of rural interests have to be constantly safeguarded.

Attitudes to Reform of the CAP

	In favour	Against
Britain Denmark Netherlands }	Generally efficient agricultural systems and food-processing industry	
Irish Republic	Increasingly successful agricultural sector, plus development of food processing	
Greece Italy Portugal Spain France }		Specific products concerns. In Greece and Italy, some benefit from abuses of CAP Strong pressures from farmers, be they large or small producers.

The issue is made more urgent by demands for admission by East European states. Enlargement may force radical reform because it will prove impossible for Brussels to subsidise Poland, Hungary, the Czech Republic, and other countries at the level enjoyed by Western farmers.

More priority needs to be given to devising a package which places emphasis upon investing to boost employment and prosperity in rural communities, rather then subsidising unwanted production. Farm support needs to be uncoupled from output, and targeted more at those regions and communities which need assistance most.

'A success for Europe, a disaster for Britain.' Is this an appropriate summary of the impact of the CAP?

Can the CAP be reformed?

The Common Fisheries Policy

It took many years for the Community to develop a policy on fishing, for there was much disagreement between member states over the way in which each country's interests should best be protected. The Common Fisheries Policy (CFP) is related to the Common Agricultural Policy, but it was not until 1973 that a policy was finally agreed. Enlargement produced a momentum for change, for with the accession of Britain and Denmark the Community acquired two members with key fishing industries.

The fishing industry began to experience problems in the 1970s. For one thing, costs rose because of the energy crisis and the rising price of oil. However, more serious was the realisation that the Western European waters could no longer sustain the intensive fishing effort carried out in them.

Until then, fishing in the North Sea had been a free-for-all, with scant respect for any conservation measures, but in 1977, with the new CFP, restrictions were imposed. The fishery limits of all member countries were extended to 200 miles, and boats from Eastern European countries and the USSR which had been over-fishing were thereby excluded (Some countries outside the EU, ranging from Iceland to the Soviet Union, also extended their own limits by way of response).

The policy adopted lays down regulations on fishermen's access to EU waters, quotas, measures for the conservation and management of resources of stocks of fish which swim in waters of member states, programmes to improve production and the conclusion of fishing agreements with non-EU countries, plus long term security for the fishermen who depend on the EU for protection.

At the heart of the common policy was the principle that fish stocks should be managed on the basis of scientific advice, so that viable stocks can be maintained and stocks that have been seriously reduced can be replenished. Hence the need for a total allowable catch (TAC). Each year a decision is made on the total catch which may be taken of each species without damaging the future of the stock. This total is then broken down by fishing areas, and divided into quotas for each state, and in some cases for non-member states such as Norway with whom the EU has reciprocal fishing agreements.

In 1992, the earlier agreement was amended and extended, the main point of the revision being to provide for the Council 'to set...objectives and detailed rules for restructuring the Community fisheries sector with a view to achieving a balance on a sustainable basis between resources and their exploitation, taking account of possible economic and social consequences and of the special characteristics of the various fishing regions'.

Why a Common Fishing Policy?

The root of the problem in the fishing industry concerns declining resources, for more than half of the world's main fishing grounds are heavily overfished and falling in productivity, and the rest are fully exploited. According to the United Nations Food and Agriculture Organisation, the ecological limit of the annual catch from the world's oceans is about 100m tonnes a year - a figure already being exceeded.

This then is the general justification for careful control of the world's fishing industry. Fishing grounds are seldom allowed to recover, and there is a need for better management of stocks. Europe attempts to do this via the Common Fisheries Policy. In a situation where there are too many fishermen and too few fish in the Union, it is important to ensure that stocks are managed in a responsible way, and that the livelihoods of those who work in the industry and those who consume its produce are adequately protected.

One of the problems of regulating the fishing industry is that stocks caught in the waters of one country may well have been spawned and matured in the waters of other states. Cod are a migratory fish, moving into UK waters as they mature. Thus, according to one survey, of the fish caught in the British area of the North Sea, there were few one year old cod, rather more two year olds and very many three years olds; many of these cod would have been born in Danish waters. The same is true of herring, which spawns off the Scottish and North of England coasts. The young larvae drift eastwards to nursery areas of the Danish and other continental coasts, to return to British waters in the third and fourth years when they are mature enough to breed.

It may be necessary to impose strict disciplines in the waters of one state to rebuild and maintain stocks important to fishermen in another country, another argument for a common policy. Fish conservation cannot be managed in a purely national context. It needs a Union policy to ensure that everyone respects the rules of conservation and has fair access to the stocks available.

The Impact on Britain; The Fishermens' Objections

Britain has the largest stocks of fish in the European Union, so that the opportunity to fish in British waters was a definite benefit for other member states, but not for British trawlermen.

The consequences of the policy for Britain have been serious, and the number of larger vessels still fishing from British ports has sharply declined as has the number of smaller deep-sea boats. Fishing towns such as Grimsby and Hull, Aberdeen and Fleetwood, have been seriously affected. The story is a similar one for some continental cities as well. The trend has been for fishermen to sail from smaller ports in shorter but more efficient vessels.

Recent Disputes

British fishermen, especially in Cornwall which has been hard-hit by restrictions, have faced a future of serious competition and shrinking fish resources. They believe that the fishing practices of other nations are damaging stock in British waters. The decline in the catch of other species has inspired the British to fish more extensively for tuna on which there is no quota. They use the drift-netting technique, and the length of these is a cause of controversy. The standard European Union link is 2.5 kilometres, but many British nets are longer overall though the actual length of netting does not exceed the requirement.

The British have been allowed to use them on the grounds that they allow substantial gaps between the netting sufficient to allow dolphins and other large fish to escape. They use a large mesh size which only enables them to catch large 14-18lb tuna, and they object to the use by Spanish trawlermen of smaller mesh which allows them to catch smaller and often younger fish, stocks of which are threatened.

It is with the Spanish, and to a lesser extent the Portuguese, that the British have had particular difficulty. In the eyes of British trawlermen, a mini-armada of nearly 100 Spanish trawlers invade their traditional grounds. Because they are UK registered, they are able to trawl in British territorial waters, even though they only have to report to the UK port of registration twice a year to claim their recognised status. This is the 'quota-hopping' of which critics of the CFP so disapprove. It enables foreign-owned vessels (usually Spanish, but some Dutch and Portugese) to claim a share of the fish catch allocated to the British fleet.

Among particular disputes, three have been especially contentious;

1 The Irish Box

Events came to a head in December 1994 when William Waldegrave, representing Britain in the Council of Ministers, agreed that Spanish vessels were entitled to access to the waters off South West England (This is the so-called Irish Box, a protection zone of 92000 sq miles around the island of Ireland). The Spanish representatives were in a strong negotiating position because when the country joined the Community in 1986 trawlermen were allowed access to the Box from 1996.

In the debate in the Council of Ministers, Britain abstained rather than vote against the agreement, on the grounds that last-minute concessions ensured that the Spanish vessels did not use their newly-won rights to exceed their quotas. As long as they kept out of the Irish Sea and the Bristol Channel, they could fish in the Box, provided that no more than 40 Spanish trawlers were present at a given time, as opposed to the 70 or so originally claimed by the Spanish.

British fishermen were outraged that the influx of Spanish vessels could decimate stocks in already over-fished waters. They wanted the Spaniards kept out of the fish-rich western approaches completely.

2 The North West Atlantic, 1995

Another aspect of controversy concerns the practices of Spanish fishermen in the contested waters of the North West Atlantic. Five weeks of tension in the Grand Banks fisheries off Newfoundland culminated in an arrest by the Canadian authorities of a Spanish trawler accused of illegal fishing in international waters; the Spanish Government sent a gunboat to protect the vessel. The Spaniards accused the Canadians of piracy on the high seas, and Britain was in an awkward position - caught between a Commonwealth allegiance and adherence to EU policy. The dispute became heated, with the Canadians resorting to gunboat conservation to protect their stocks, and the Spanish vowing only to accept at gunpoint.

When the issue was eventually settled, a blind eye was turned to what had already been netted in 1995. Under a peace plan, The Fifteen agreed that Europe and Canada should have equal shares of the lucrative halibut catch in future years, with strong enough enforcement measures to prevent over-fishing by Spanish trawlermen. Provision was made for independent inspectors on trawling vessels, a satellite monitoring system, and also for strict mesh-size regulations to protect immature fish.

3 The Scottish Salmon Industry

Scottish MEPs have been concerned about the threat to the salmon sector caused by unfair competition from Norwegian fishermen said to be flooding EU markets with low priced salmon. Norway generously subsidises its salmon fishermen by writing off their bank debts, and this enables them to 'dump' their produce at unrealistically cheap prices. Hence the disturbances which have taken place in several EU ports, from Scotland to Brittany.

The Importance of the Fishing Issue to Britain

> *British fishermen and British people and our elected officials in Parliament are not going to lie belly up like a dead cod while Brussels takes over fish resources and creates a European fishing fleet which inevitably would be Spanish in the south-west and Dutch in the North Sea.*
> *Spokesman for Cornish Fish Producers' Organisation*

Some critics, including the trawlermen, want Britain to withdraw from the CFP altogether, for they feel beset by problems which have arisen since their country joined the Community. Fishing stocks are a sensitive issue for them, for already North Sea pollution poses a threat to cod and haddock supplies (the staple of the UK fish and chip shop), and mackerel already are almost commercially extinct.

Imports pose a further problem. They now account for some 40% of the EU fishing market, for fishermen face the increasing influence of supermarket seeking cheap fish, competition from farmed fish, and from other agricultural products of which fish is only an element.

But it is the threat posed by the Spanish fishermen which really upsets them, and threatens their livelihood. British trawlermen are upset by the presence on the UK register (see p 330) of Spanish vessels which are allowed to trawl in British territorial waters. They also feel growing resentment at European restrictions on their catch, for they believe that whereas Britain is enforcing them they are being widely ignored on the continent. They claim that Spain has two fishing fleets, a legal and an illegal one. (See box)

Compliance with the Common Fisheries Policy

A Report of the European Commission, published in March 1996, claimed that policing of the CFP was woefully inadequate. It suggested that whilst the quality of British inspectors was impressive, Britain's monotoring was unsatisfactory because of the lack of sufficient staff to do the work.

The Commission argued that several states were tempted to exploit fishing possibilities beyond the limits laid down in the CFP. It found that British boats were the main culprits in illegal fishing. Of 371 infringements brought to its attention in 1994, the British were responsible for 119, the French for 73, the Irish for 62 and the Spanish (much criticised in Britain) for only 22.

The Fisheries Commissioner, Emma Bonino, has also accused Britain of increasing the tonnage of its fishing fleet when it should have been reducing it. This meant that the Government had sacrificed £12m in EU aid for the fleet modernisation which several countries had achieved.

NB Eurostat figures show that the composition of the European fishing fleet is as follows (The figures in Column 1 are for boats over 30 metres, those in brackets for the overall number of fishing boats).

Spain	557	(20072)	Denmark	159	(4452)
Netherlands	346	(993)	France	134	(6828)
United Kingdom	243	(10251)	Portugal	100	(12641)
Italy	172	(16460)			

Greece has the largest number of boats (20377), but only 48 exceed 30 metres in length.

For politicians, especially those representing constituencies with fishing ports, there is a need for a change of policy. The Labour Opposition has portrayed British policy as feeble acquiescence, but among anxious Conservatives the issue has been but one more matter on which the disadvantages of British membership of the Union are becoming daily more apparent. They see this as one more problem deriving from Brussels interference, and some talk of British withdrawal from the CFP unless substantial changes can be agreed in Brussels.

Critics seeking reform of the CFP want to see radical change designed to place a much greater emphasis upon conservation of fish stocks, and protection for the long term interests of communities heavily dependent on fishing.

What impact has the membership of a.Britain and b. Spain had on EU fishing policy?

? Why is the Common Fisheries Policy so controversial in Britain?

Immigration Policy

Immigration refers to the arrival of nationals from outside the European Union at its frontiers, rather than to the movement within the EU of citizens of member countries. There was a time when those countries were keen to encourage such immigration because of a labour shortage in the Community, but for two decades a more restrictive policy has been applied. At a time of high unemployment, there is a desire to protect EU workers from competition for jobs.

Methods of control have long varied among the fifteen countries, with some imposing more restrictions and others adopting a more lenient approach. The trend has been towards the use of more rigid checks on entry, and this is achieved by visas, the exchange of information between states and the establishment of agreed procedures for handling different types of cases.

In 1991, the Commission put forward plans to curb the ever-swelling influx of economic migrants trying to secure political asylum in the European Community. It stressed the need for a fast-track procedure for the refusal of applications which were manifestly unfounded, along with tougher fines on airlines bringing in passengers without appropriate documents and stricter interpretation of humanitarian principles for admitting people who could not prove a fear of persecution. The proposals were not unlike the measures favoured by the British Government.

335

Yet the Government was fiercely opposed to the Commission's conclusion that policies of this sort should be determined within the framework of EC institutions. Ministers would not tolerate arrangements for telling them to implement what they were perfectly willing to do anyway. This approach was typical of the attitude on a range of issues within the sphere of the Home Office, including the wider questions of immigration, visa control and measures to combat drug trafficking, international fraud and terrorism.

The question of British sovereignty was a key issue in the difference of outlook. It was similarly apparent in the British view of the need to retain frontier checks at borders, in the belief that an island can best defend itself against drug imports and terrorism by maintaining port controls.

Most member states believed that since the free movement of people within the Community was an agreed objective of the single market, the EC should control this aspect of immigration, as well as policy on visas for short-stay visitors from non-Commonwealth countries. Britain opposed any dilution of national control over visas or other aspects of immigration policy.

The Impact of Maastricht on Immigration Policy

At Maastricht, the agreement was that legal, immigration and policing policy should be decided by intergovernmental cooperation, and thus form a separate decision-making pillar like that for foreign and security policy. This was the third pillar of the TEU. Policy therefore still actually remains in the hands of the member states.

Yet at the Summit it was accepted that there was a 'common interest' in several areas including immigration. Control is exercised via cooperation between the relevant interior ministers in the different countries, and along with relevant officials they meet in a sub-committee of the semi-secret K4 committee, the intergovernmental body which runs policy on justice and home affairs. This procedure allows ministers to operate outside the normal Brussels machinery.

The third pillar of 'Justice and Home Affairs' includes many controversial areas, and among these immigration is one of the most sensitive. It is the more contentious because agreement was also reached at Maastricht that there should be a common visa policy (outside the third pillar), and this requirement was built into the Treaty as a new article 100c (EC). From 1996, decisions on this are to be taken by qualified majority voting.

Fortress Europe and the Issue of Border Controls

In 1995, EU ministers were keen to further tighten control over immigration policy to secure the rapid expulsion of unwanted aliens to their countries of origin in Eastern Europe and the Third World. The expulsions policy was part of the strengthening of the EU's external frontier controls, a programme which was advanced to compensate for the lifting of passport checks at the Union's internal borders.

The Commission was equally keen to ensure that in imposing a tight 'Fortress Europe' policy, it should press ahead with plans to eliminate internal border controls and to allow freedom to travel for third country nationals. Under present rules many immigrants who are legal residents but not citizens of a member state need visas to travel to other parts of the EU. The Commission was willing to give 10m of them a guaranteed right to travel freely throughout the Union without visas. It planned directives to apply these measures throughout the EU - something to which the British Government was firmly opposed. If the Government tried to block the directive, it would then be open to challenge in the European Court of Justice for failing to honour its commitment to the 'free movement of people'.

The Commission recognised the declaration in the Single European Act which allows member states to 'take such measures as they consider necessary for the purpose of controlling immigration'. However, its lawyers argued that the weakening of internal border controls was more than compensated for by the toughening of the external frontier.

Who Might Want to Come to Britain?

> *I have always been in favour of a Europe in which we can compete and*
> *trade without hindrance, but I cannot stand by while our quality of life is*
> *jeopardised by a provision in the treaty which we have failed to tackle.*
> *Charles Wardle, Letter to PM, 12.2 95*
>
> *We believe this [maintaining immigration controls] is an essential*
> *safeguard, not only against illegal immigration but also to combat*
> *transnational crime and terrorism. Entry control makes sense for Britain*
> *as an island state, and we have no intention of giving it up.*
> *Reply by John Major.*

The episode of border controls goes to the heart of the issue about the extent to which the EU can impose policy on the British Government. It was highlighted in February 1995 when a junior minister, Charles Wardle, suddenly resigned because he was alarmed about the implication of EU immigration policy and the way in which Britain was reacting to it.

He asserted that 15m 'foreigners' were legally resident in the Union, and that if there were no passport controls Britain could be open to mass immigration. The figure was misleading, for actually a third of these people who were registered as living in the (then 12) EU states were citizens of another EU country. The removal of passport checks would have no impact on them, or on the much larger total of around 355m EU citizens living in their own countries, for all of these people have unrestricted rights of movement across the Union anyway.

Research at the Migration Research Unit at University College, London, suggests that the 15m included 1.2m people from outside the EU who were already resident in the UK. Therefore, out of the total of 15m Wardle quoted less than 9m fell into the category of people originating from outside the EU, who were living in another EU country and who did not yet have EU citizenship. Under the SEA, they would have the right to visit the UK without any hindrance, but they would not have rights to settle or seek work. The removal of passport controls should not make much difference to the numbers of these people coming to the UK, for most of them would have no trouble getting in for a visit.

Mr Wardle and those who support his viewpoint fear that many of them might visit Britain and stay on illegally. Yet he was less clear on exactly why the number of people who stay illegally under the present arrangments should increase dramatically if the requirement to show a passport on entry is lifted. The Channel forms a natural barrier which is likely to discourage substantial immigration from the continent. Moreover, it is questionable how many of them would want to come and settle in Britain, a country whose standard of living is 11th out of the current 15 member states.

It is a myth that everyone in the EU desperately wants to come to Britain. Mostly they want to go to Germany, which by virtue of its economic strength, its geographical position bordering the improverished ex-Soviet satellites and its sense of humane responsibility as defined in its post 1945 constitution, has accepted far more of the world's dispossessed than other European countries.

EU figures only cover those legal immigrants who have registered as residents in one of the member states. There may well be another $3^1/_2$-$5^1/_2$m 'illegals' in Europe, though according to the International Centre for Migration Policy Development in Vienna the flow has peaked, following the adoption of stricter rules across Europe for the fast-track removal of those classed as economic migrants.

Immigrants In the European Union, 1992. Where They Came From

Other EU countries	4907200
Elsewhere in Europe	3304400
Africa	2762700
Asia	1565200
America	798500
Central/Eastern Europe	747300
EFTA	408500
Australia/Oceania	88700
Unknown	113200
Total	14695700

Figures from Eurostat

Immigration into the EU continued to rise until 1993, but has been falling ever since. There was an increase in migrants as a result of the conflict in former Yugolslavia, but these refugees were not granted asylum, only provisional rights to stay. Governments around Europe have already started sending people back to safe areas, and the assumed mass emigration from the East has not materialised.

The Position of the British Parties

The British Government is intent on vetoing any attempt to remove its border controls at the 1996 Conference. It takes the view that as Prime Minister Mrs Thatcher had received from other EU states a 'solemn declaration' which gave it an 'opt-out' on border controls, and that this accepted the right of Britain to retain its existing arrangements. It stated that any member state could maintain border controls 'for the purpose of controlling immigration from third countries'.

There are differences within the Labour movement on the issue of immigration. The Front Bench at Westminster supports the Government's insistence on continued passport controls. It fears that the removal of border controls could force Britain towards Continental-style internal checks, including the introduction of identity cards. The leader of the European socialists, a Labour MEP, has accepted that in the long run the abolition of all internal border controls is likely, and sees fears of a flood of immigrants as 'a complete travesty'.

The Schengen Group

> *Partly because of our island geography and historical patterns of migration and border controls, and partly because of its secretive nature, Labour does not believe that Britain should participate in the Schengen Agreement... Decision-making on issues covered by the third pillar should be intergovernmental and subject to unanimity.*
> *Party Conference booklet on Europe, 1995.*

Nine members have already established themselves as the Schengen Group, and Austria is expected to join them. But the three northern states do not wish to abandon the twenty year old Nordic free travel area which also includes a non-EU country, Norway. If this is sorted out, Britain and Ireland will be left exposed as the only countries unwilling to abandon passport controls at the internal borders. Ireland has no objection in principle, but is reluctant to abandon its traditional common travel arrangements with the UK, unless Britain should follow the European lead.

From March 1995, people travelling from Britain to the continent have been subjected to full passport controls, just at the time when most other states have been dismantling controls. The nine members of Schengen, the countries on a fast track towards harmonising immigration policy, have established a free-movement zone eliminating the need for travellers of any nationality to show passports as they pass between those countries.

The Importance of Immigration Policy for Britain

Race has for several years been a difficult issue for British politicians to handle, but apart from the attitudes of more extreme parties and of politicians who are willing to whip up racial feeling by one community against another, there is a broad consensus on policy. This involves strict control over numbers entering the country, economic and social assistance to areas affected by substantial immigration and the use of legislation to outlaw racial discrimination.

Implicit in the attitude of the British Government to the European initiatives described above is the feeling that other countries are more lax on immigration control than Britain, and that this lack of vigilance will result in large numbers entering Britain in spite of the fact that we have imposed our own tough policy. Yet, the evidence across Europe is that governments and opposition parties in several countries are using the issue, in tandem with policies on law and order, to gain favour with voters, and there is little support in Europe for liberal immigration laws.

Beyond those fears about numbers, however, there is the more general concern of some politicians about increasing European interference in the

British way of life. The Tory Right see the issue of immigration as a classic example of meddling by the Commission into matters which are better resolved within the British political system.

For instance, ministers are very sensitive about European intervention into Britain's race laws. A 1995 EU plan to outlaw racism was a wide-ranging one, including proposals to ban the distribution of racist or xenophobic literature, public incitement to race hatred, and participation in organisations which imply racial discrimination. In November, the Home Secretary, Michael Howard, blocked the proposal, claiming that more time was needed to consider the implications for British law - a decision he later reversed.

His original view was that we already have the laws which are necessary, and he spelt out a nationalist position on the issue;

> *It would have meant changing our laws in a very significant way for reasons that dont'really have very much to do with the circumstances we encounter. We have a longer history of laws affecting race relations than almost any other country in the European Union, more comprehensive legislation and better race relations. I believe our laws should reflect conditions in our country. Circumstances in other countries differ. They are perfectly free to have laws that meet those circumstances.*

Because immigration is a matter for intergovernmental cooperation, policy is controlled by member states acting in agreement. If there is no agreement, they cannot act at all unless there is an issue in which the policy of one country conflicts with treaty obligations, as over the free movement of labour. Yet topics such as a common immigration policy and a common visa policy are ones in which some countries feel that they have a strong national interest, and they arouse particular controversy in Britain. The Maastricht Treaty extended European responsibilities in these areas. In as much as greater harmonisation of policy can be achieved, then this makes a contribution to the process of integration in Europe. It also poses a threat to ideas of national sovereignty.

Are internal security and the 'free movement of peoples' compatible?

Why is immigration such a sensitive issue for Britain?

Social Policy;
The Social Chapter

The Treaty of Rome had little to say about social policy, and the emphasis in this area was left clearly in the hands of the member countries. It did propose that there should be a Social Fund with the task of 'rendering the employment of workers easier and increasing their geographical and occupational mobility'.

There was a concern to see that equal pay, as demanded by article 119, was widely accepted and enforced. Topics such as health and safety at work and the entitlement of migrant workers to social security provisions, were also viewed as important. The Social Fund was duly established, and its objectives have been subsequently widened to allow for measures to act against unemployment and to extend the rights of particular groups in the Community, most notably women.

A controversial area has been that of workers' rights. Back in the late 1970s the Vredeling draft directive was concerned to provide workers with clearly-defined rights, especially the right to be consulted by their employers - some of which were multinationals with employees in more than one member state. However, it was the passage of the Single European Act which transformed thinking in this area.

Jacques Delors, the Single Market and the Social Charter

Jacques Delors and others argued that it was necessary to protect ordinary people who might suffer from the ravages of an unregulated free market after 1992. For him, the EC was more than a common market, but rather 'an organised space governed by commonly agreed rules that (will) ensure economic and social cohesion, and equality of opportunity'. In other words, there was a social dimension to the market, which involved the protection of individual rights so that the Community worked for the benefit of all its citizens.

The Social Charter

The Commission asked the Economic and Social Committee to produce a document which set out the social rights to which Europeans were entitled. In May 1989, the Commission drew upon its findings and produced a draft 'Charter of Fundamental Social Rights'. It was a bold document, but one which soon ran into opposition from the United Kingdom.

Mrs Thatcher denounced it as 'more like a socialist charter...full of unnecessary controls and regulations which will tie up industry, which will put many, many more costs on industry, which will make it uncompetitive, which would therefore increase unemployment and mean that we could not compete in the rest of the world for the trade we so sorely need'.

Labour was enthusiastic from an early stage, for many of its MPs felt that the single market required detailed and harmonised social legislation. To them and to many trade unionists, it was seen as an essential element in the arrangements for 1992. It was largely the visit of 'Frère Jacques' to the TUC Conference in 1989 (and his assurances about the social dimension) that helped to wean the Labour Movement away from its previous anti-Europeanism.

It was all the more attractive to Labour because a European programme along these lines might enforce on the British Government just the sort of

344

worker protection legislation which the Prime Minister had been abandoning throughout the decade. This was precisely why she disliked it. She saw it as 'socialism by the back-door', a piece of discredited social engineering which 'smacked of the era of Karl Marx and the class struggle'. Other Tories spoke of 'creeping Marxism'.

The Social Charter; Mark Two

Largely as a result of pressure from the British Government, the original draft was much watered down in its next version. The rights secured were more limited in scope, so that proposals concerning a minimum wage, pensions for the elderly and worker-participation in company decision-making were dropped, and other items diluted. Even the revised form was unacceptable to the British who alone refused to go along with the proposals.

The document as agreed laid down the major principles relating to the following rights;

The right to freedom of movement
The right to employment and remuneration
The right to improved living and working conditions
The right to social protection
The right to freedom of association and collective bargaining
The right to vocational training
The right of men and women to equal treatment
The right to worker information, consultation and participation
The right to health and safety protection at the workplace
The right to protection of children and adolescents
The rights of elderly persons
The rights of disabled persons

The adoption of the amended version of the Social Charter in December 1989 was the key step forward for those who believed that the Community should have a social role. Although the British and Danes were unenthusiastic, this was not the general view. In the Commission and in the Parliament there was strong support for a Social Europe to balance the proposed Business Europe.

The Commissioner responsible for policy relating to the Social Charter was a Greek, Mrs Papandreou, who had formerly been active in this field as a member of her own government. For her, 'higher standards, whether they have to do with training, health and safety, working conditions or workers' rights, pay off. It is not only a question of solidarity and social justice. It is also a question of common sense from an economic point of view'.

The Commission was asked to devise an action programme, and a series of Community legal instruments governing the implementation of these social rights. In this way, it would impart coherence to the various initiatives taken at national and regional level. Implementation was left mainly in the hands of the member states, with emphasis being placed on the need for the two sides of industry to conclude collective agreements at national, regional, sectoral or company level.

Yet progress was slow, and two years later (in the run-up to Maastricht) not one of the more controversial proposals had been put into effect. This was partly because the British government liberally used its veto, behind which some other governments were happy to hide.

The Charter itself was a non-binding agreement, essentially a list of aspirations. Controversy centred on the **Social Action Programme**, about 50 proposals put forward by the Commission to make the Charter a reality. On these there was little progress, and the measures which did emerge under the Charter were mainly modest advances on health and safety which required only a qualified majority vote. Other benefits included improved travel conditions for the disabled, and better protection for young persons and pregnant women at their place of work.

The really contentious issues to be debated in the Social Action Programme involved workers' information and consultation through Works' Councils, limits on working time and rights for part-time workers. These were topics regarded by the British Government (and to a lesser extent by the European employers' organisations such as UNICE), as imposing a potentially 'crippling' cost on business and manufacturing.

Significantly, there was pressure for such measures from a number of the more affluent countries in the Community. Germany and Denmark, among others, were keen to avoid being undercut on social costs as well as wages by poorer EC states such as Greece, Ireland, Portugal and Spain. These less-well-off countries had reservations about the costs of implementing the Social Action Programme, but never joined in the ideological crusade of Mrs. Thatcher and John Major.

Maastricht, 1991

In the run-up to the Maastricht summit, there was much opposition in Britain to the Social Charter on the political Right. It was feared that Britain would be forced to sign up for its provisions, and that it would become binding upon the country. Eleven states were willing, and in some cases enthusiastic, to include the document within the orbit of the actual Treaty.

The issue proved very contentious, for John Major was unwilling to concede. The compromise was that the other eleven states would sign a separate contract, the Protocol and Agreement on Social Policy, known popularly as the Social Chapter. This meant that, although in the first instance there would be an attempt to reach agreement by The Twelve on matters of social policy, if this proved impossible then the signatories of the protocol could between themselves decide on the policy they wished to pursue. To take and implement their decisions, they would use the machinery of the Community.

Among the eleven committed nations, decisions could be taken on a majority basis if the issue concerned working conditions, information and consultation of workers, equal opportunities and equal treatment, and the integration of persons excluded from the labour market. Matters such as social security, redundancy, workers representation and the employment of third country nationals, needed a unanimous decision.

Excluding the Social Chapter was seen as a triumph by John Major, and enabled him to claim that Britain had won 'game, set and match' during the negotiating process. The 'success' was politically useful, and it enabled him to divert attention from those aspects of the Treaty which were less palatable to his fellow MPs. Fellow-European statesmen were surprised by the claims which were made by British spokesmen, for several of them saw the Chapter as something altogether more innocuous. Some of its content was a codification of existing practice in the more advanced members of the EC, and other sections were little more than an aspiration to be worked towards over an unspecified period of time.

The Argument Over the Social Chapter in Britain

During the ratification process, the Major Government suffered its only defeat on the exclusion of Britain from the Social Chapter. Some dissident Conservatives who hoped to derail the whole Maastricht process chose to align themselves with the opposition parties to bring about this parliamenta*ʲ* setback, but the effect of their actions was short-lived. The Government put down a motion of confidence, and in the ensuing debate the Tory rebels were brought to heel.

John Major was proud of his 'opt out' which meant that Britain escaped from the provisions of the Social Chapter. He claimed that it did not allow for significant differences in working practices among the member states and that it would undermine competitiveness. He noted that the Japanese did not shackle their companies with restrictions. He further claimed that Europe suffered from its high labour costs, and that measures of social protection could mean that manufacturers were priced out of world markets. This would imperil prospects for employment in Britain.

Labour argued that British workers should be able to enjoy the same conditions experienced by workers elsewhere (see box opposite), and noted that in several respects they were at a disadvantage compared to their European counterparts. It spoke of 'Euro-Luddites', politicians who feared social progress and were indifferent to workers' rights.

Progress in Implementing the Social Chapter

The Social Action Programme has continued since the signing of the Social Chapter, and the Commission has now put forward its detailed recommendations on all of the items it originally contained. Several of those which required legislative action have been controversial, especially the Directive on the Organisation of Working Time. This was approved by the Council of Ministers in late 1993, a decision on which Britain abstained. As a result, British workers are exempted from the benefits it confers, including provisions such as those for maximum working hours, daily breaks and annual paid leave.

In other spheres also, the provisions of the Social Chapter have been put into effect in the fourteen member states which adhere to the Protocol. These include;

Works Councils;	The first directive under the Protocol (due to be established by 1999). See box on p352-354
Maternity and Paternity Leave;	Statutory rights entitling women to maternity leave and men to have nine weeks off in the first year of a child's life

Worker protection for part-time and young workers

Better opportunities for women

Health and safety legislation

Conditions in Britain and Abroad

Labour, several Liberal MPs and many trade unionists like the minimum standards represented in the Social Chapter, for among other things it offers extended maternity rights, better provision for child-care and fairer treatment for part-time workers.

In several respects, EU nations are in advance of Britain in their worker protection. Nine already have a maximun of 48 working hours a week, several have provisions for a minimum wage and minimum annual holidays.

British workers currently put in longer hours than workers in any other member state. It is the only country apart from Ireland where the length of the working week has actually increased over the last decade, as the Eurostat figures indicate;

	1983	1993
United Kingdom	42.3	43.4
Portugal	41.3	41.0
Greece	41.0	40.8
Spain	40.6	40.2
Ireland	40.2	40.4
Germany	40.9	39.7
France	39.7	39.7
Luxembourg	40.0	39.7
Netherlands	41.0	39.4
Denmark	40.6	38.8
Italy	39.2	38.5
Belgium	38.6	38.2

The figures are calculated on the basis that an average working week includes all the hours normally worked, including overtime. They do not include travel to and from work, nor rest periods and meal breaks. Britain comes out badly, partly because it has a much higher rate of overtime than other countries. There has also been a recent trend to increase hours (often unpaid ones) in many companies and professions. Employees dare not resist the demands made of them for fear of jeopardising their career development. To critics, such figures mean that the United Kingdom has become 'the sweatshop of Europe'

When the Social Protocol was approved, Britain was one of two countries which did not have a maximum 48 hour week. It opposed the idea on the grounds that it would cost an extra £5b which employers would have to find. Since then, it has been introduced by an EU directive.

A Brussels View of the British Opt-out

Other nations do not like Britain's opt-out, for they believe that Britain is gaining a competitive advantage by allowing low wages and imposing few regulations. The Commission has devised a white paper (July 1994) on future social policy which envisages full British participation in the programme at some future date, although the British Conservatives take the view that as long as they are in office they will regard their opt-out as a permanent feature.

The white paper did note that when it comes to implementing social policy directives into national law the British have a better record than many other nations such as Italy and Luxembourg, but it could not accept the proposition that the Union can only create more jobs if the labour market is deregulated; 'The pursuit of high social standards should not be seen only as a cost, but also as a key element in the competitive formula'

According to other Europeans, a two-speed social Europe is unworkable and politically damaging, for it enables Britain to adopt lower standards of protection or 'social dumping'.

British Firms and the Social Chapter

British firms are in theory exempt from any provisions of the Social Chapter, but yet in practice a number of them feel obliged to abide by its guidance. Some British-based multinationals are already preparing to introduce works councils for UK employees in spite of the opt-out (see box on p354). They see structured dialogue with employees as a matter of good business practice.

Conclusion

The argument about the 'social dimension' has assumed an importance in British reactions to the Union which is almost out of proportion to its contents. To Conservatives, they have been saved from 'creeping socialism'. For Labour, Britain has been left semi-detached from Europe, and doomed to be the most backward nation in the Community in its social provision.

Why does the Social Chapter arouse such opposition on the British Right and so much enthusiasm on the British Left?

Is the Social Chapter anything more than a meaningless collection of well-meaning platitudes?

Works Councils; A Case Study

The Works Council Directive was the first piece of legislation enacted under the Social Protocol. It required large multinational firms to establish mechanisms for consultation with their employees, so-called European Works Councils (EWCs). Despite the UK's 'opt out', there was much speculation that British based multinationals would extend the application of the Directive to their UK operations.

What the EU Works Council Directive Actually Says

The Directive (COM 94/95/EC) put into effect the principle that companies operating across national frontiers should have uniform standards in their approach to employee consultation and participation; 'Workers therefore will have equality of access to information about decisions (eg, the location of future investment, the impact of technological change and large scale redundancies) through the mechanisms for European level consultation'. The Directive was adopted in September 1994 by the eleven member states who had signed up for the provisions of the Protocol on Social Policy annexed to the Maastricht Treaty. They were required to pass legislation to enact the Directive by 22 September 1996.

As a result of the 'opt out, British multinational companies (MNCs) are now placed in exactly the same position as multinationals based outside the EU. This does not exempt those companies from the Directive, but does exclude their UK operations from its scope.

A British MNC is covered by the Directive if it has 1000 or more employees in the 14 states of the Union, and at least 150 employees in two different states. Like other multinationals of the requisite size, it has to initiate negotiations towards the establishment of an EWC only if 100 employees spread across two states request it. **If the management declines to enter into negotiations within six months of being obliged to do so, or if the negotiations fail to result in an agreement, then a model form is imposed on the undertaking.**

Research of the Institute of Directors (February 1995)

The Institute reckoned that between 150-300 companies based in the UK are covered by the Directive. In total, it successfully contacted 44 of them, 29 of which were IoD members. As many were involved in delicate negotiations, none were prepared at that stage to be named.

They were asked four questions;

i   Have you set up a European Works Council in those countries covered by the Directive?

ii   Do you intend to include UK operations in the European Works Council?

iii What costs do you anticipate being involved in compliance with the Directive?

iv   What are your views on Works Councils?

The response to the survey was as follows;

i   At the time of the survey, only one company already had established a Works Council, but 90% were at varying stages of their response to the Directive. The overwhelming view was that it was better to negotiate an agreement rather than have one imposed. Some respondents were alarmed at the inherent advantage enjoyed by trade union representatives, for they only had to do nothing in the negotiations or fail to move their position to end up with the Commission's EWC.

ii   Many MNCs were strongly opposed to the Directive, and the survey found that the handful of companies which had been given prominence in the media for their willingness to provide a Works Council for their British employees were unrepresentative. 30 of the 44 spokespersons did not wish to include the UK..

iii More than 90% of the companies feared the increased regulatory costs which implementation of the Directive would incur. Estimates ranged from £219000 to £405000, with others speculating that the figure would greatly exceed this sort of amount.

iv   As to their general views on Works Councils, the response was negative. Only one company enthused over the idea. Others were either hostile, or took the view that whilst consultation with employees is a good thing this kind of imposed form of dialogue was at best an irritant, at worst a serious burden. It would conflict with established methods of participation and consultation.

Many companies were worried that the 'opt out' would not be a sufficient protection for them. If it were to remain, they feared pressure on them to conform. If it was ended (as a result of a change of government in Britain), then they would have no right to resist implementation of this Directive or any other the Commission decided to initiate.

Considerations to Bear in Mind

The Institute of Directors is a particularly Rightwing interest group, its attitudes being more in line with those of the Thatcher era than were those of the Confederation of British Industry.

The survey did cover some companies not in the organisation, and therefore may seem to be fair and broadly-based. Yet many did not respond. The questions were asked some eighteen months before the deadline, and some may have reconsidered their view by then - especially if they see other companies falling into line with continental practice. Whatever their initial reluctance, they may come to see advantages in compliance.

Since that survey, there has been some additional evidence of the reactions of British firms. After one year, the Commission found in early 1996 that the Protocol had been applied in 60 cases across the Union with the expectation that this number would increase to 1500. In Britain, opposition from 'big business' had been toned down, with some large companies deciding to participate - BP and United Biscuits, among others.

Aid and Development

The European Union has a relatively good record in its relationships with what was once known as the Third World. It is the largest world importer of developing country produce as well as being the largest donor of aid. Yet such aid and that given by other organisations and states has not been sufficient, for whilst a number of the developing countries have 'taken off', many have at best stagnated, at worst deteriorated. The gap between the prosperity of the advanced rich countries and the most backward poor ones has continued to increase.

When Europe or North America is hit by recession or when falling world prices affect basic commodities, the situation in the poorest countries is aggravated. But this only indicates that a fundamental problem is the inability of many of them to feed themselves. In their attempt to industrialise, they often neglect rural development and food production.

Because of this, EU policy in the second half of the 1980s concentrated heavily on food strategies as part of a comprehensive strategy for rural development. This included food security, development of local resources and preservation of the ecological balance. More generally, it was part of the aim of encouraging self-reliance rather than dependence on external aid. In some developing countries, this priority was considered to be questionable, for they wished to see more rapid industrialisation to enable them to advance more quickly.

Britain's Position

When Britain entered the Community, the relationship between the developing countries of the Commonwealth and the EC was a contentious issue in the negotiations. Since 1973, the traditional links between Britain's older colonies and the UK have been transformed into broader trade and aid agreements with the Community as a whole, although bilateral agreements still persist. Where trade is concerned, the existence of the Union offers wider opportunities for developing countries' exports than the British market alone could sustain.

Some countries, including Britain in particular, have in the past expressed concern that in a period of stringent control of national spending and a limited aid budget, too great a share is going into Union and international aid rather than to bilateral schemes. Its record of bilateral aid compares unfavourably with countries such as Denmark, France and the Netherlands. Aware of this it showed some reluctance to allow more funding to be made available through the European Development Fund, and stressed the importance of national efforts.

In the Council, representatives of other national governments also have been less willing to dovetail their own aid programme into a common Union strategy than the Commission would have wished. They are jealous of their national bilateral ties.

In 1992-93, Britain gave £2245m on overseas development, of which £1278m was in the form of bilateral aid, and £903m was channelled through other organisations. Among these was the European Union, via which Britain gave £412m.

Forms of EU Assistance to Developing Countries

i **Generalised preferences.** Developing countries can export their industrial goods, and certain agricultural produce, to the Union free of duty.

ii **Food Aid.** Surplus food is sent to countries suffering from acute shortages.

iii **Emergency Aid.** In times of natural disasters and other crises, appropriate aid is made available.

iv **Aid to non-governmental organisations.** Aid to projects sponsored by NGOs in several Third World countries.

Additional assistance and aid is given to countries into which the EU has entered into a special relationship. Many of these relationships cover matters such as trade, and financial, industrial and technical cooperation.

The Lome Conventions

The most important and wide-ranging form of agreement on aid is the Lome Convention. Four of these have been signed in Lome, the capital of Togo in West Africa, in 1975, 1979, 1984 and 1989. They link the EU and African, Caribbean and Pacific states, the so-called ACP group which now includes 71 countries, many of them among the poorest in the world. Many of these ACP countries have long-standing links with some of the member states, because of their colonial past. More than half of them are members of the British Commonwealth. The group includes all of sub-Saharan Africa, except South Africa. The Caribbean element has been increased with the recent involvement of the Dominican Republic and Haiti.

The details and conditions of these agreements are regularly modified and updated. The first agreement dealt primarily with aid and trade. Almost all ACP agricultural exports were allowed to enter the EC duty free, and a scheme to stabilise export earnings (STABEX) of such produce was agreed to help developing countries cope with price fluctuations. In Lome 2, many of the provisions were extended, and SYSMIN (a similar scheme to STABEX) was established to safeguard exports of mineral products. Lome 3 sharply increased the aid budget and tackled dissatisfaction with the inadequacy and inefficiency of the funding arrangements for the export schemes. It also placed a new emphasis on sectors (especially food) rather than individual capital projects.

The fourth Lome Agreement came into force in March 1990, and this one is due to run for ten years to the end of the millennium. It addresses exports, financial aid and a framework for technical cooperation. Under the trade provisions, the Union grants are made available without any requirement for reciprocity. In other words, they offer preferential access for ACP exports to EU markets so that almost every product comes in to the Union free of Customs duty or the equivalent taxes.

It provides for aid of over £7700m for the first five years, alongside loans from the European Investment Bank of £850m, an increase of approximately one fifth upon the previous arrangement. The terms have been improved, as a recognition that one of the major problems faced by receipient countries is their burden of indebtedness. The loans are not repayable, other than those which come from the EIB.

Lome was originally designed as a partnership between the Community and the developing countries to cover both aid and trade. It developed out of the earlier Yaounde Conventions which were primarily concerned with the links between France, Belgium and their former colonies. When Britain joined the Community, Lome extended the scope of the earlier arrangement to cover most former British colonies in Africa, the Caribbean and the Pacific. However, the exclusion of former Asian colonies such as Bangladesh and India was a source of some criticism, and while these countries have benefited in other ways from Community assistance, they have not received the same preferential treatment as ACP states.

Apart from aid and trade, there is a third aspect to the Lome agreement, cooperation. The Union makes no distinction between countries on the grounds of their political affiliation, and Lome represents a force for political neutrality. As such, it enables many countries an opportunity to meet regularly and exchange views, as part of a continuous dialogue. It also enhances cultural and social links, and requires all signatories to respect human rights and democratic principles.

The Lome Convention is the largest aid package in the world, and is the main instrument of EU policy on overseas development.

Aid and Trade With Non-ACP Countries

The Mediterranean Countries

The Union has links with other developing countries but those with the ACP countries are more developed. Nonetheless, special arrangements are offered by the EU with Mediterranean countries not themselves part of the Union. It is in the interest of the EU to promote prosperity, for this contributes to the overall stability of the Mediterranean region. More specifically, some of the countries in the area have long-established links with EU states, in the way that Britain does with Cyprus and Malta, France with Algeria, Morocco and Tunisia, and Italy with Tunisia, among other examples.

The EU has cooperation or association agreements with several states, and only Libya is as yet not involved in such ties. With Cyprus, Malta and Turkey there are association agreements which provide for the establishment of customs unions with the Union, and in all cases it is likely to lead at some point to their full membership.

With the so-called Maghreb countries (Algeria, Morocco and Tunisia), the Mashreq countries (Egypt, Jordon, Lebanon and Syria), and with Israel and Yugoslavia, there are cooperation agreements on trade and various forms of financial, industrial and technical cooperation.

Despite the range and detail of the Mediterranean agreements, they all have certain uniform features, including the provision of duty-free access for industrial goods into the Union, with other concessions for agricultural produce - although the pattern varies according to the produce in question. In some cases, the arrangements are reciprocal ones, so that Cyprus, Israel,

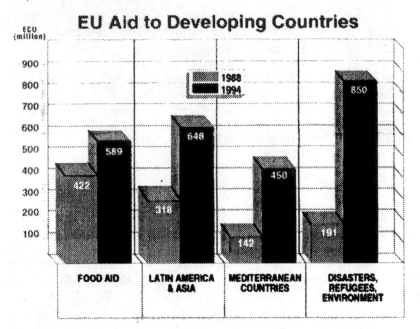

EU Aid to Developing Countries

ECU (million)

Legend: 1988, 1994

Category	1988	1994
FOOD AID	422	589
LATIN AMERICA & ASIA	318	648
MEDITERRANEAN COUNTRIES	142	450
DISASTERS, REFUGEES, ENVIRONMENT	191	850

EP News, 7-11 March 1994

Malta and Turkey allow certain Union exports to enter without duty. All of the countries covered by such agreements are also eligible for grants and loans from the EIB.

Asia and Latin America

With Asian and Latin America countries, agreements with the Union are bilateral ones, more limited in scope. They do not include rights of preferential access to the Union. However, under the Generalised System of Preferences (GSP), there is provision for some preferential treatment for their exports. They qualify for aid from the EU budget which is to be directed to the diversification of their economies, and particularly to the encouragement of industrialisation and the development of exports.

In some cases, these countries lack the close historic and cultural ties which influence relationships with the other ones involved in development assistance. But since 1976, a number of them have benefited from aid programmes, and in recent years the GSP policy has been modified and liberalised to allow for more access to the Union for the produce of the world's 40 or so least developed countries. The EU currently offers more than 300m ECU per annum, to help development in rural regions and promote improved standards of life for the most needy peoples of the world.

Furthermore, like the ACP countries, they qualify for the EU food aid programme, whereby food is given directly by the Union or via non-governmental agencies. Funds are available to help in times of natural disaster and to finance programmes for recovery.

Eastern Europe

Of course, the real growth area in Union financial assistance has been with the countries of Eastern Europe ever since the map of the continent was changed by the fall of the Berlin Wall in 1989. As many of the countries of the former Soviet bloc have been transformed into new democracies, they have sought closer ties with the Union. In several cases association arrangements are in hand to prepare them for full membership of the EU (see p441-442).

The problems of states in Central and Eastern Europe are of a different order to those in Africa whose needs are likely to be with us for many years to come. In some developing countries, such as war-ravaged Ethiopia with its endless cycle of drought and famine, the situation looks bleak. In Europe, the need is for shorter term help, to ease the often painful transition from a Communist to a market economy. In addition to short term relief, they require technical assistance, private investment, trade concessions and expert advice from those who have run such a free economy; then, it is hoped, they can stand on their own feet. Their problems are less daunting and their eventual prospects are much more encouraging, if they get the generous supply of help they need now.

Under the so-called Europe Agreements, the promotion of free trade is the cardinal feature, with the Union reducing its tariff barriers more quickly than the partner countries. However, the needs of these countries vary according to their state of development and the speed with which they are being prepared for admission to the Union, so the principle of specificity is applicable, treating each country on the basis of its individual situation. The Czech Republic, Hungary, Poland and Slovenia are probably the countries most advanced in their preparations for early entry to the EU, whereas with some of the others the long term relationship is as yet less clear.

Famine Relief

The widespread famine in Africa has prompted a response from the EU. Apart from the fact that hunger and suffering demand action on humanitarian grounds alone, spokesmen have also recognised that such conditions are a threat to the growth of democracy on the continent. The EU offers aid to Sudan, but favours this being made available through charities rather than the Government because of human rights violations. Similarly, 200,000 tons of food aid and 15m ecu were sent to Somalia in the Autumn of 1992. The problem there was not so much the provision of relief but the distribution of it against a background of violence, anarchy and attacks on convoys.

Problems of, and Attitudes to, Aid Today

Asked about humanitarian aid to non-European countries, respondents to a Eurobarometer survey in December 1994 were generally aware of, and sympathetic to, EU assistance. Amost half of them thought that it should be increased, and there was little support for a reduction or cessation of help. The Greeks and Portuguese were especially well-disposed to humanitarian assistance, the British, Danes and the Dutch less so; the Belgians were the peoples most disposed to cut or stop aid.

With deep recession in the major industrial countries, it is easy for the more advanced nations to neglect overseas aid. The assistance required by the new democracies of Eastern and Central Europe makes a further demand on the already hard-pressed budgets, so that the severe problems faced by the poorest nations can be overlooked or inadequately tackled. Yet, apart from the moral imperative of helping one's neighbour, there is also an element of self-interest in so doing - peoples who regularly endure poverty and live in constant despair are more likely to turn to political extremism which can be a further cause of instability in the world.

By its own aid programme and through the multilateral agencies, Britain has a chance to help alleviate the problems and shape the direction of aid packages. There are real problems about how the multilateral bodies currently operate, and British influence could be used to resolve the difficult issues concerning trade and debt.

Third World Debt

Such is the burden of indebtedness on developing countries that they attempt to repay in capital and interest more than they receive gross in aid. It has been estimated that they now transfer money to the industrialised world at around $40-50b a year! The IMF and the World Bank are actually in the position of draining resources from developing countries.

The debt issue is a crucial one. Britain has cancelled £1000m worth of old loans and gives new money in the form of grants which do not have to be repaid. At the 1990 Commonwealth Finance Ministers Conference, Britain proposed that the debts of the poorest nations should be sharply reduced and phased over a generation. In total, the developing countries owe some $1300b to banks, international financial institutions and governments, and the costs of meeting interest repayments are beyond their ability to pay and cripple chances of economic reform and sustainable development.

Aid and Trade

Trade and aid are closely linked, and in some cases, especially the new European democracies, an easing of trade barriers would be of inestimable benefit. Protectionism in the form of restrictions on agricultural and other products is very costly to the developing countries. Progress towards a major liberalisation of trade in the GATT talks was a boost to the less developed world. As John Major stated at the Harare Commonwealth Conference in 1991,

> *There is little point in the developed countries providing aid for economic development if the developed countries then deny access to our markets for those very same countries. Failure (in the Uruguay Round) would be an absolute hammer-blow for the developing countries.*

Trade is considered particularly important by the developing countries, and they continue to press for wider concessions for their imports of textiles and agricultural produce. The Union has been in a difficult position, for while asserting the principles of trade liberalisation, internal economic and political pressures have forced it to fall back on certain protectionist measures - though compared with Japan and the USA the EU still offers generous access.

Furthermore, some of the aid projects started a few years ago are now seen to have failed in their main purposes, and others have actually caused environmental damage or ruined local enterprises. Ensuring that programmes are well-targeted, well-run, attuned to local needs and in harmony with the environment is a priority if available resources are to achieve their maximum benefit.

Increasing burden of debt

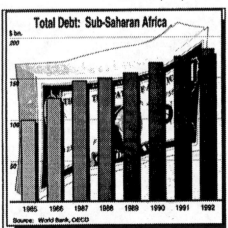

FOR most ACP countries, the number one priority is to tackle the burden of debt which for sub-Saharan African countries has soared from $3bn in 1962 to $183bn in 1992. Total ACP debt is now estimated at $270bn, although the amount owed to the EC is only $1.4bn.

In fact, the scale of the problem was pointedly summarised by the Kenyan delegate, Henry Kosgey: "ACP countries continue to pay more in interest to developed countries than they receive in aid."

Commodities

Many people wonder why it was allowed to rise to such disproportionate levels but one of the causes was the sharp fall in commodity prices which halved the annual value of ACP export earnings from $62bn in 1980 to just $30bn in 1990. The rise in interest rates during the Eighties only made matters worse, while lax lending on the part of some international organisations financed large scale projects such as hotels, conference centres and buildings not only of doubtful viability but hardly reflecting African priorities. One ACP delegate complained that 80 per cent of aid actually benefited Western companies and consultants. Political priorities of the time in the Cold War era also led to some Western donors backing dictators who did not have the interest of the people at heart.

But any action to write off the debt will have to be taken by the donor countries in conjunction with the World Bank, which is insisting on strict new conditions and structural adjustment before approving further loans.

While many ACP delegates are looking for action from the EC, development Commissioner Manuel Marin was firmly wrapped on the knuckles when he tried to take an initiative to deal with a problem the member states see as a national responsibility.

Cases where money has been siphoned off for use by corrupt officials to line their own pockets and not for the good of the peoples in genuine need, bring bad publicity to aid programmes. So does the fighting of factions involved in civil strife whose attitudes prevent aid from reaching its destination.

The record of aid over the years has been mixed. Countries which carry a heavy burden of indebtedness such as Mozambique have a major struggle, and many of the poorest such as the Cape Verde Islands are more or less totally dependent on outside help. Yet if the African scene has looked depressing in recent years, the story of South East Asia has been more encouraging. Singapore, Taiwan and others were early beneficiaries of overseas aid, and have gone on to become the fast developing 'Asian Tigers' of today.

Official Development Aid from OECD Members; (Top Ten Countries)

	Amount in $millions	% of GNP
Norway	988	1.12
Netherlands	2231	.98
Denmark	922	.89
Sweden	1534	.87
France	6959	.73
Canada	2340	.50
Australia	1091	.46
Germany	4700	.39
United Kingdom	2615	.32
United States	12170	.25

Figs. taken from 'World Development Report' of World Bank, 1993.

? Should Britain spend more on its aid programme?

? How effective are the policies of the European Union in promoting aid and development a. within and b. outside Europe?

The Common Foreign and Security Policy

From the earliest days of postwar cooperation, there was always interest in the idea of developing Western security along the lines of the closest possible integration. As we have seen (see p47), the Preamble of the Treaty of Paris dwells less on the issues surrounding coal and steel, and talks in more grandiose tones of setting aside the rivalries of the past and safeguarding peace in the future, by a merging of national interests.

The states of Europe were aware of their military weakness, and keen to put the situation right. Cooperation with the United States through NATO was the route chosen, for The Six were all signatories of the North Atlantic Treaty Organisation. But the Americans were keen to see Europe strengthen its military capability, so that it would be a strong partner of the Atlantic Alliance. They were keen to see Germany play a part in the process, but the Europeans were more anxious about German rearmament for they had been on the receiving end of the aggressive actions of the Hitler era.

In 1950, in a speech to the Council of Europe, Winston Churchill put forward the outline of a plan for a unified European army which would act in concert with Canada and the United States. In the same year, Rene Pleven, the French Prime Minister, put forward his proposals for a

European Defence Community and a European Political Community was then proposed, each with their own institutions (see p53-56).

The EDC involved the creation of a European Army under the control of the political institutions of Europe, whilst the EPC was designed to be a complementary organisation which would add a political dimension to cooperation in defence policy. The EPC was also supposed to coordinate the external policies of the member states. The Pleven proposals were a key move in the attempt to integrate Europe rapidly, and as Monnet realised would have made 'the federation of Europe... an immediate objective'. But the attempt was stillborn.

With the failure of this early attempt at common defence arrangements, Europe had no choice but to act as the junior partner of the NATO alliance. The only further attempt to create a European defence organisation was the development of the Western European Union, which evolved out of the Brussels Treaty Organisation and became a wider body. Britain was a member, and the meetings of the WEU provided an opportunity for British statesmen to meet with those of The Six to discuss common issues.

But the scope of the organisation was quite unlike the Pleven initiative. The French proposal had embraced supranational thinking, whereas the WEU acted on the basis that individual member states should act independently and cooperate on an intergovernmental basis where this was both feasible and desirable.

The Growth of European Political Cooperation

> *The imperative is unchanged. We still need to demonstrate that the Community speaks with one voice, that it is an actor rather than a spectator on the contemporary world stage.*
> *Jacques Delors, 1989.*

From the early 1970s onwards there was more attempt to harmonise foreign policies, such a process being known as European Political Cooperation (EPC). On several issues the attempt was relatively successful, for after the failure to act in concert in response to the oil crisis there was a greater appearance of agreement between the EC nations in dealing with the Iranian hostage crisis, the Soviet invasion of Afghanistan and the Falklands War. Over the handling of apartheid in South Africa, there was a similar wish to act in a consensual way. EC firms were monitored to check the non-discriminatory nature of their employment practices, and economic sanctions were utilised.

Yet despite the outward image of collective thinking and action over these issues, there were underneath many areas of tension and disagreement, and a cooperative approach was only possible on the basis of working on the lowest common denominator. Over South African policy there were many divisions concerning the application of sanctions, just as there were over their use in response to the Soviet violation of human rights in Poland, in 1981. Cooperation in foreign policy was too often slow to get underway once the initial statement of intent had been agreed, and consensus was more often apparent than real.

The Community and the Falklands War, 1982; a Case Study

Over the Falklands War, the attack by the Argentinians on British territory affected the whole Community. There was provision for an economic response but not for a military one, for this was a type of action reserved for national governments. The Ten condemned the invasion, and failing any withdrawal of Argentinian forces suspended trade with the aggressor for an initial one month period. However after that cooperation began to crack, and the Irish and Italian Governments were unwilling to extend the trade embargo.

This outcome was characteristic of many examples of European Political Cooperation. There was initial consultation, followed by enough agreement to produce a modest economic response. But then the fragile unity began to fracture as countries began to think of their national interests - the Italians, in particular, had strong links with the Argentinians. Agreement was, in practice, far short of a common foreign policy, so that the main response was a British one, with some supporting action from the Community.

For several years, EPC had been conducted on an intergovernmental basis outside the formal provisions of the Treaty of Rome. The passage of the Single European Act formalised the process of foreign policy consultation and cooperation between the member nations, and brought it within the EC framework, though not actually into the Treaty itself.

Decision-making was still to be conducted via agreement between all the members acting largely on an intergovernmental basis. But the SEA represented an attempt to take EPC into the Community framework, and its importance was certainly recognised and enhanced. This is why **Holland** could see the Act as 'the first step on the slippery slope to a common foreign policy and a federal Community'.

It was certainly the case that the cooperation in foreign policy received a new impetus. **Ginsberg** has drawn attention to the marked increase in foreign policy initiatives in the five years after the SEA was implemented (188, compared with 121 in the previous five years), and the trend towards developing a common and coherent approach to foreign policy was accelerated. Yet this is not the same as a common foreign policy, for it remained the case - and still does - that most member states intended to carry out their own external policy, with the backing of the Community if this could be obtained.

Foreign policy has continued to test the ability of the Community to act on a common basis, and this was again apparent in the Gulf War. The Middle East had long been an area where a minority of members had conflicting national interests with their partners in the EC. This meant that on any specific matter it was difficult to move beyond the immediate declaration to any practical implementation of the line laid down.

Over the Iraqi invasion of Kuwait in 1990, it was not hard to agree that all EC citizens living in that country needed to be protected, and that sanctions should be imposed against the aggressor, Saddam Hussein. Beyond that, it was more difficult to know how to move forward. There was no EC military machinery which could be used to threaten him, and it was left to the British and French to make their own individual approaches to avoid war breaking out. There was no effective Community approach in the run-up to and duration of the Gulf War.

Maastricht and Beyond

Foreign Policy Issues

Dissatisfaction with Community policy was much discussed in the IGC on Political Union in 1991, and several states wished to replace EPC with a more developed Common Foreign and Security Policy (CFSP). A majority led by Germany felt that there should be a significant list of areas where the EC could take politically-binding decisions. These included many aspects of UN policies, relations with the United States and the Soviet Union, and arms control. More sensitive even than this idea was the suggestion that the practical implementation of some of these policies should be conducted on the basis of qualified majority voting.

Negotiators edged towards a compromise whereby the European Council would lay down, unanimously, the principles of joint action, the general and specific objectives in carrying out such action, and the conditions, means and procedures for the implementation of the general lines of foreign and security policy. Then, this guidance would be translated into detailed but still unanimous decisions by foreign ministers. They might designate certain procedural matters and areas of implementation for subsequent decision by majority. The distinction between policy and implementation was not clearly spelt out.

Defence Policy Issues

In the run-up to Maastricht, the issue of defence arrangements was one of the most arcane but also one of the most hotly-disputed areas of policy. The issues went beyond the substance of European political union, and encompassed relations with the United States and the wider international community.

The British were convinced that the French President, Mitterrand, was using the issue as part of the long-standing Gaullist strategy of separating Europe from American power and influence. By contrast, the French believed that Britain's approach to defence matters reflected the general ambiguity of its attitude to the evolution of Europe, and demonstrated its

371

Atlanticist leanings. Mitterrand also took the view that a common foreign policy for the EC would be meaningless without a common defence policy.

On defence, the representatives were moving towards an agreement that control of defence should remain, at least until 1996, with the Western European Union, a non-EC body including nine of the twelve members, with the prospect of it increasing to ten if Greece was admitted. The European Council would be able to 'request' action by the WEU on military aspects of a peacekeeping operation, but not give instructions. The French and Germans were clearly hoping that over a longer period the WEU with an embryo European army could be integrated into the new European Union.

The status of the WEU has been unclear for a long while. Its membership overlaps with NATO and with the EC, but not all European members of NATO belong to it. It has existed since 1954, but never had a military command or military forces at its disposal. It has a small secretariat in Brussels, and an assembly that meets at regular intervals in Paris. It has been activated in recent years, most notably organising European minesweeping operations in the Gulf during the Iran-Iraq war and then as the European naval presence during the war to free Kuwait.

Britain, backed by the Italians, made a distinction between **security policy** which the EC should be entitled to define (preferably at intergovernmental level), and **defence policy** proper. It rejected the idea that the EC should be responsible for defence in the foreseeable future, claiming that any Community takeover would undermine NATO and prompt a US withdrawal from Europe. Security policy involves a wider network of agreements to make war less likely, whereas defence is primarily a matter of how nations physically defend themselves when under attack.

Britain felt that the Europeans should put more effort into consolidating their defence arrangements. But they insisted that NATO's integrated military command must remain paramount in Europe and that the Europeans were only entitled to organise for independent military operations outside the NATO area.

The Outcome of the Maastricht Summit

At Maastricht, European Political Cooperation was taken a stage further and placed within the wider conception of a Common Foreign and Security Policy'. The CFSP was the second of the 'three pillars' of the new European Union.

At the Summit there was agreement that there should be closer cooperation on foreign and security policies to 'assert the Community's identity on the international scene'. Progress in these areas should build upon and develop existing forms of cooperation. National governments were still to be in the driving seat, though EC institutions such as the Commission and Parliament were able to express a view and have their recommendations take into account.

The Treaty developed the position set out in the Single European Act. In the Act, there was a commitment to 'formulate and implement a European foreign policy', but at Maastricht it was agreed that the new European Union should 'define and implement a common foreign and security policy...covering all areas'. This was to include 'all questions related to the security of the Union, including the eventual framing of a common defence policy, which might in time lead to a common defence'.

The procedure laid down involved regular cooperation between the states on matters of general interest. Where appropriate, the Council would define common positions to which the policies of member countries would have to conform. It could decide unanimously those matters where the implementation decisions should be taken by a qualified majority vote. Majority voting did not extend to defence policy.

The Western European Union was given the role of elaborating and implementing 'decisions and actions of the Union which have defence implications'. It was to be developed 'as the defence component of the European Union and as the means to strengthen the European pillar of the Atlantic Alliance'. Defence was therefore to remain a matter for NATO, but the European arm would be strengthened by an increase in the role and importance of the Western European Union which was to become the bridge between the two other organisations.

The British could take some comfort from the fact that the decision to place foreign affairs on an intergovernmental basis outside of the Treaty of Rome meant that this reduced the British legal obligation to conform to any Community foreign policy. But there are two aspects of the settlement which particularly moved forward the process of developing European Political Cooperation - the possibility of majority voting for some less fundamental issues and the arrival of defence on the scene as a matter for further discussion and cooperation.

The Future

> *We will not allow Brussels to control our defence policy. Britain will not be told when to fight...Britain is blessed with very brave soldiers, sailors and airmen, willing to give their lives - for Britain, not for Brussels.*
> *Michael Portillo, Conservative Conference 1996.*

Matters of defence, security and foreign policy go to the very heart of the debate on political union. Until now there has been only limited scope for joint decision-making on foreign policy matters (see box opposite), but many members would like to see the development of common policies which would include the eventual framing of a common defence policy. In the eyes of many committed Europeans, the eventual goal of a common policy would be the creation of a European Army.

This is an area of contention, particularly within the **Conservative Party**. As Foreign Secretary, the pro-European Douglas Hurd went further than before in envisaging independent European defence structures outside of NATO. He was keen to stress close collaboration on defence between the British and French governments, and in October 1994 he remarked that; 'An effective European defence, and effective institutions to underpin it, require both our countries...to build on the substantial cooperation we already have'.

A Single Voice for Europe?

One of the problems in articulating a coherent foreign policy is the lack of a single voice. No-one 'speaks for Europe'. Back in the 1970s, Henry Kissinger, the American Secretary of State, was said to have asked;'When I want to speak to Europe, whom do I call?'

There is no-one who can speak, let alone act, on Europe's behalf. Europe sometimes seems to speak with different voices, and in response ti issues such as the Gulf War or the fighting in Bosnia there tends to be a lack of clear thinking. Alarmed at the dithering and squabbling in this field, Jacques Delors spoke of 'organised schizophrenia'.

On occasion, the immediate handling of issues has been the responsibility of a troika of the foreign minister whose country holds the Presidency, his predecessor and likely successor. At other times, the President of the Commission and the Prime Minister of the government which holds the Presidency of the Council have acted.

It was because of this lack of an effective procedure that Malcolm Rifkind, the British Foreign Secretary, suggested in early 1996 that Europe's foreign and security policies could be made more efficient. He wanted a policy-formulating unit, extra funds and a high-profile figure to represent the EU's agreed foreign policy to the world. Tory sceptics were worried that such a 'supremo' could easily become the master rather than a servant of the Union.

The Conservatives had previously opposed giving the EU any defence responsibility, in direct opposition to the French and German governments. Yet Maastricht backed the goal of a common European defence. Hurd accepted that this could mean the integration of the WEU and defence as a new fourth pillar of the EU itself.

Membership of Security Organisations; The Situation Today

	UN	NATO	WEU	EU	OSCE
Austria	✓			✓	✓
Belgim	✓	✓	✓	✓	✓
Denmark	✓	✓		✓	✓
Finland	✓			✓	✓
France	✓	✓	✓	✓	✓
Germany	✓	✓	✓	✓	✓
Greece	✓	✓	✓	✓	✓
Iceland	✓				✓
Ireland	✓	✓		✓	✓
Italy	✓	✓	✓	✓	✓
Luxembourg	✓	✓	✓	✓	✓
Netherlands	✓	✓	✓	✓	✓
Norway	✓	✓			✓
Portugal	✓	✓	✓	✓	✓
Spain	✓	✓	✓	✓	✓
Sweden	✓			✓	✓
Turkey	✓	✓			✓
United Kingdom	✓	✓	✓	✓	✓
Canada	✓	✓			✓
USA	✓	✓			✓

The Clinton Administration left no doubt that Washington wants to see changes in the way NATO operates, with the Europeans taking much more responsibility for their own security and defence. Significant military forces are already being designated by NATO for future military operations by the WEU, and they are seen as the foundations of a future European army. Apart from the existing **Eurocorps** - troops of Belgium,

France, Germany, Luxembourg and Spain - the WEU will be able to draw on British units which are part of NATO's multinational Division Central and the Anglo-Dutch naval amphibious force.

Such a role for the WEU would probably involve a concentration on humanitarian, peacekeeping and peacemaking operations carried out on behalf of the United Nations, still having close links with NATO. If there was to be a move towards a European defence union, then France might agree to participate in some NATO defence ministerial meetings which in the past it has boycotted; it is not currently part of the military organisation.

Both Britain and France are thought to be discussing how to coordinate their nuclear forces, and the Chirac Government is more sympathetic to NATO. Whereas his predecessors wanted a European defence identity outside NATO, he wishes to see one develop inside. Both governments are keen to develop the WEU as a European wing of the Atlantic Alliance, capable of operating outside NATO but with US blessing.

President Chirac talks of the possibilities of the WEU becoming a fully fledged EU defence policy. Any move towards a European army, however tentative, is likely to arouse the ire of Tory Euro-sceptics, who are already gearing up to oppose moves towards closer union. For them, talk of any embryo European army suggests a drift towards federalism, and they may not be reassured by the idea that neither the Commission nor Parliament would play any significant role in EU defence decisions.

NATO's eventual role in European security and defence is far from clear. Unlike the WEU, it has the capacity to wage outright war, but some believe NATO may evolve into a framework for collective European security. The idea is that NATO's most important contribution in the post-Communist world is political, focussing on a partnership not only with the countries of Central and Eastern Europe but also with Russia and the other former Soviet republics.

Links with the former Communist countries might also be developed via the former Conference on Security and Cooperation in Europe (CSCE), which has since the end of the Cold War been known as the Organisation for Security and Cooperation in Europe (OSCE). It has also stressed the links between security, economic and environmental issues in the past, but it could be developed as a new peace-keeping body embracing all the countries of Europe. It currently has over fifty members.

Britain concedes that the WEU can have a coordinating role in defence and foreign policy, but insists that a member state must be allowed to pursue a policy more or less energetically than its partners, or indeed to act first, informing its partners, but not necessarily awaiting their endorsement. Labour has also shown no enthusiasm for the EU having any control over defence policy because of the party's allegiance to NATO and its fear that a defence community might lead to nuclear aspirations. Some individual backbenchers have called for a European army. Liberal Democrats want common foreign, security and defence policies to become part of the EU treaty, with the Union gradually becoming the European pillar of NATO.

There are many difficulties which limit the progress of moves towards a cohesive European Foreign and Security Policy, and defence is a particularly sensitive subject. It is not difficult for any one country to determine the areas of policy in which vital national interests have to be protected. In any collection of fifteen states, it is inevitably hard to reach agreement on Union goals. In the case of some of them history, tradition and/or present realities incline them to want to play a more active role in foreign policy and defence issues on their own, rather than in concert with their European partners.

Britain and France are the main military players in Europe and showed over the Gulf and Bosnia (see opposite) that they can work fruitfully together in the security field. They are closer on the defence policy than at any time in the postwar era. But in the longer term the French are willing to move further down the road to a common defence policy, and some other countries want to progress from the present situation. Britain is clearly important to any European defence scenario, but the development of Eurocorps shows that in this area of policy a two-speed Europe is a possibility. Its establishment shows that many Europeans believe that the EU needs its own force if it is to respond effectively to conflicts within the continent.

The Fighting in Former Yugoslavia

The conflict in former Yugoslavia is a good example of the lack of harmony and coordination in EU foreign policy thinking. Substantial differences of approach arose, and there was irritation in some quarters at the way in which the Germans 'stampeded' the Community into premature recognition of the breakaway republics. Britain and some others preferred to wait and work for an overall settlement of the problem, but they agreed on the German preference.

As the blood-letting developed in Bosnia, where the Serbian population was determined to extend its area of control at the expense of the Croats and the Muslims, many Europeans lamented the failure of the EU to sort out such a problem on its own doorstep. The Union was much involved in the attempts to achieve a ceasefire and meaningful peace negotiations, but in the face of the determination of each of the combatants to fight on mercilessly to achieve its goals, the efforts of the joint EU/UN peacemakers were doomed to failure and frustration. Ceasefires were agreed and promptly ignored.

For a considerable time, the US Administration portrayed the civil war as a European problem. It was prepared to give humanitarian aid, but did not wish to become directly involved. As the evidence of 'ethnic cleansing' mounted and attacks on humanitarian relief forces increased, NATO attacks were launched on Serb bases with full American support. When the Bosnians and Croats regained some of the ground lost to the Serbs, all sides were more ready for peace talks which eventually took place at Dayton, Ohio, where a provisional settlement was reached.

The episode revealed American frustration at the lack of EU success in resolving a crisis within its own continent. There were differences between the US Government and the Europeans, and between European governments as well; some member states were fearful of becoming involved in a conflict relatively near their own borders. An effective common approach to such issues is unlikely until mechanisms of political cooperation are in place to allow its development.

Why is Britain likely to be in the slow lane as Europe moves towards closer cooperation in defence and foreign policy?

What are the difficulties in creating a common approach for a. defence policy and b. foreign policy?

'The pursuit of a CFSP within the European Union is potentially the most contentious area of dispute for British Euro-sceptics'. Do you agree?

TEACH YOURSELF

To Recap

The EU Budget generates much contention, although the amounts involved are relatively small in relation to national finances. Union activities are financed from four sources;

- Customs duties
- Agricultural levies
- A proportion of VAT income
- The 'fourth resource', a share of GNP

Expenditure was for many years overwhelmingly dominated by the costs associated with the Common Agricultural Policy. More recently, much money has been used on cohesion, regional development and social policy. The CAP still uses approximately half of the Union budget.

Policies

There are some 'common policies', such as the CAP, the Common Fisheries Policy and the Common Commercial Policy. In a number of areas, the competence of the Union has increased, so that European Political Cooperation has grown into the Common Foreign and Security Policy, and there is increasing coordination in many areas of policy - eg, immigration and control of drug-trafficking.

Of course, the original concept of the pioneers was to establish a 'common market' between The Six. For many years, commerce, trade and the free movement of goods, were the key aspects of EC policy, and the completion of the single market in 1992 was the realisation of an earlier vision. Nearly 300 new laws were introduced to complete the single market, and several regulations on matters ranging from trading standards to food law affect our daily lives.

Many of these policies have an impact on national sovereignty, in that decisions taken in Brussels are binding on member states. On issues such as fishing rights and immigration, Britain increasingly finds itself at odds with several of its Union partners. As the areas of policy which fall within the orbit of the Union machinery increase, so too do opportunities for conflict between states worried at the pace of integration, and those which wish to widen the EU's sphere of influence and thereby deepen the integration process.

Questions to consider

1   Read the extracts below and then answer the questions which follow;

The British rebate

The British rebate has been a long running bone of contention dating back to 1984 when it was negotiated by Mrs Thatcher amidst bitter acrimony. At the time, agriculture accounted for some 80 per cent of the budget and it was accepted that Britain did not receive as much proportionately from the CAP as the other member states, so a refund was negotiated. Since then the situation has changed with agriculture taking up less than 50 per cent. The size of the rebate has grown to Ecu3.5bn, leaving Britons paying, Ecu88 each, as one of the lowest contributors to the budget on a per capita basis. This has led to Parliament calling on the Commission to propose adjusting the rebate when it comes up for review in

1999. However, as John Tomlinson (Birmingham West, PES) said in the debate, the contributions table does not take into account receipts.

France, for example, still receives more than double the amount paid to the UK. Although it is important to remember that the some Ecu9bn spent on aid and administration does not come back to any of the member states directly, Mr Tomlinson maintained that on a per capita basis, Britain was the second or third highest net contributor, even though in the wealth stakes it only ranks tenth out of 15. A future Labour government

would therefore be defending the rebate just as resolutely as the present one.

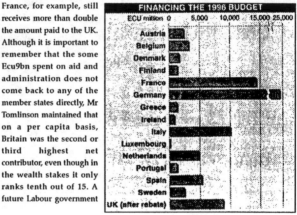

FINANCING THE 1996 BUDGET

EP News, 13-17 November, 1995

John Palmer on why the Euro-sceptics have lost a powerful rallying cry

British membership of the European Union now costs only £16 per head of the population - a dramatic reduction from 10 years ago when it averaged several hundred pounds per head.

Britain is paying a smaller per capita net contribution to the EU budget than seven other member states including France, Germany and Italy.

Figures prepared by the German finance ministry for what was still a 12-nation European Union in 1994 show a British net contribution per head of £16 compared with Belgium (£25), Italy (£36), France (£37), the Netherlands (£96) and Germany (£135). Figures for the current year are confidently expected to show that Austria and Sweden will also make bigger per capita payments than Britain, but net beneficiaries include Spain (+£64), Portugal (+£298) and Ireland (+£393).

For most of the past two decades Britain has been the largest annual net budget contributor after Germany. The 1994 figure is reached after taking gross payments of £5.5 billion, subtracting EU spending programmes in Britain worth about £3 billion and adjusting for an annual budget "rebate" worth over £1.5 billion last year.

The system under which Britain exceptionally benefits from an annual rebate was negotiated in 1984 by Lady Thatcher after a protracted confrontation with the rest of the then European Community. But the remarkable reduction in Britain's relative share of the burden of financing the European Union is also due to factors which British politicians are slower to recognise.

One factor is the change in the pattern of EU spending in the past five years and the smaller share of the budget now taken up by the common agricultural policy. Moreover, because Britain's position in the economic league table has declined it is now regarded as one of the poorest countries in the EU. As a result Britain's less developed regions are now entitled to bigger aid programmes from Brussels. Since each country's transfers to Brussels are in part linked to its GDP per head, Britain's relative impoverishment has helped reduce its budget payments.

The Government does not contest the fact that Britain's per capita contribution is much lower than in past years. But Whitehall officials claim that the 1994 figures were partly influenced by "special factors" which may not be fully reproduced in future years. "We recognise the general trend but feel one should not make too much of one year's figures," one official said yesterday.

On the other hand the accession to the European Union of three new member states - Austria, Finland and Sweden - earlier this year could lead to a further reduction in Britain's net budget contribution. All three countries are richer than the EU average and are expected to pay in substantially more than they will receive back in spending programmes.

The big reduction in Britain's budget payment deprives Euro-sceptics of one of the most potent criticisms of British membership of the EU. The Labour MEP for the Lothians, David Martin, said yesterday: "Bearing in mind the role which the European Union has played in maintaining peace and stability over the past 40 years and its vital importance for our future prosperity, £16 a head can only be regarded as excellent value for money."

As the European Union enlarges to perhaps 30 member states over the next decade or so, the budget system is bound to be drastically overhauled. Given the big gulf in wealth between western and eastern Europe, even the poorest of the existing EU countries may end up as net contributors.

The Guardian, 20.3.96

383

'£3.6bn bonanza' for EU countries

John Palmer in Brussels

A slump in agricultural spending by the European Union is providing an unexpected bonanza which could help to finance a big increase in EU infrastructure investment, and also return cash from Brussels to national government.

A confidential report to be presented to the European Commission today says that underspending in the EU farm budget could total more than £3.6 billion over the next three years.

Last week EU finance ministers rebuffed a proposal by the commission president, Jacques Santer, to switch about £1 billion of expected farm savings to boost investment in trans-European transport and energy networks and other job creating projects. The Chancellor, Kenneth Clarke, and other ministers insisted that any spare cash in the EU budget should be returned to national governments.

But the new report going to the commission predicts much larger potential savings, thanks to a bigger than expected drop in spending on the Common Agricultural Policy. "The estimate of the [£3.6 billion] savings may prove, if anything, to be conservative. The savings between now and 1999 could be even greater," a senior commission source said.

The slump in spending on the CAP is partly due to a faster rise in prices on world food markets than in Europe, and partly to curbs on excess production introduced as part of the reform of the CAP during the past decade. The narrower price differential between international and European markets has enabled the EU to slash food export subsidies.

The EU's agricultural surpluses and its notorious food mountains have all but disappeared in the case of many key products, such as grains and dairy produce. Moreover, the cost of incentives to farmers to co-operate with the CAP reforms and to develop new uses for the countryside has proved less than forecast.

This year the total EU budget is put at about £57.4 billion, of which the CAP accounts for around £28 billion. The prospect of a big underspend in the EU budget should make it easier to win the agreement of all 15 governments for at least part of the savings to be invested in the trans-European networks, in industrial research and development and help for small businesses.

The Guardian, 19.12.95

i   Why has spending on agriculture been sharply reduced in the mid-1990s?

ii   What settlement was Mrs Thatcher able to achieve in 1984 over the 'budget issue'?

iii   In what way has Britain's financial relationship with the Union improved over the last decade?

iv   What are likely to be the main developments in the EU budget over the next decade?

v   'The net contributions of each country should bear more relation to their level of prosperity'. Do you agree?

2   Explain why agriculture has always played such a large role in the development of the European Union, and why it is difficult to achieve effective reform of the original provisions of the Common Agricultural Policy.

3 To what extent is it a/ desirable and b/ possible to bring about a single currency in the European Union. Explain the likely effects of such a move.

4 To what extent do the aid and development policies of the European Union effectively tackle the problems of recipient nations?

5 Why has it not been possible for the Union to achieve more common policies than have yet been developed?

6 'A European security policy, perhaps including a European army, makes good sense in the modern world'. Discuss.

7 Why has it been so difficult to bring about effective cooperation in matters of foreign policy affecting the member states?

8 What is involved in the Social Chapter? Why has the policy been so contentious in British politics and yet so acceptable to most other European governments?

9 Choose any three of the following policy areas, and explain the developments that have already taken place. Explain the reaction of British governments in each case;

Environmental policy   Fishing policy
Immigration policy   Regional policy   Security policy

10 What are the main issues surrounding the European Union budgetary arrangements? Why does Britain qualify for a rebate of some of the monies it pays into the EU?

11 Account for;
a. the influence of the agricultural lobby in European Union affairs
b. the United Kingdom's continuing opposition to the Common Agricultural Policy (ULEAC)

12 'CAP apart, the European Union has experienced considerable difficulty in achieving effective common policies'. Discuss (ULEAC)

13 Does the European Union need its own integrated defence system? (ULEAC)

Chapter Five: Attitudes

Attitudes to Integration in Member States

Belgium

Along with Luxembourg and the Netherlands, Belgium had already had some experience of practical cooperation before it became a founder of the ECSC. The three Benelux countries had been involved in a customs union and this encouraged them to work towards wider economic and political harmonisation. In addition, the governments and peoples of each state knew that they could achieve more by working together than they could by acting on their own, particularly in the economic and political arena.

Belgium has been generally supportive of all moves to closer integration in Europe. Paul-Henri Spaak played a leading role in devising the draft treaties, and since then the country has been responsible for urging the EC forwards in many of its initiatives, not least in the run-up to Maastricht.

Lacking as strong a sense of national identity as some other member states, the Belgians have had no problems with federalist notions, and have seen benefits in advancing more swiftly in that direction. Similarly, they have few fears of EMU, CFSP and majority voting, and see all of them as part of the general move towards closer integration.

Denmark

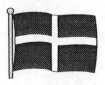

Denmark has traditionally been one of the few countries which stresses national sovereignty in its approach to the EU, and it still displays some resistance to political supranationality. The Danes prefer to work via intergovernmental cooperation, with a built-in right of national veto.

They have had several chances to express themselves on their feelings about the European Community and their country's role within it. In the four direct elections to the Parliament in Strasbourg, turnouts have been low by continental standards (see p248).By contrast, in the four referendums on membership of, and changes within, the Community, interest has been high, for in these there has been a keenly contested election, with a real issue at stake;

Year	Turnout	Issue and Outcome	Degree of Support
1972	90.1%	**Yes** vote to join the Community,	63.3%
1987	74.8	**Yes** vote on Single European Act,	56.2%
1992	82.3	**No** vote on ratification of Maastricht	50.7%
1993	86.2	**Yes** vote on ratification	56.8%

There appears to be no overwhelming popular support for further integration, and the issue of Europe arouses excitement only when the future role of the country is under discussion. Even then, the voting is often finely balanced, suggesting that, like the British, the Danes are not natural Euro-enthusiasts. For them, the considerations have to be weighed on their merits.

The explanation for Danish scepticism may well lie in the country's geographical location, for sandwiched between Scandinavia and Western Europe the Danes have an allegiance to their fellow Nordic peoples as much as to countries in the heart of Europe. They have not sought involvement in international politics, and have not been in the forefront in joining European organisations, unless their interests have been obviously at stake.

Maastricht and Beyond

After the Maastricht negotiations were completed, the Folketing approved the Treaty overwhelmingly (130-25). All but two small parties were in favour, and although there was some unease about the move to a single currency there was also satisfaction that Denmark could already meet the convergence criteria. Yet when members of the public had a chance to express their verdict, it was obvious that the politicians were out of step with popular opinion.

In a referendum in June 1992, they narrowly decided that they did not want to accept the Treaty. Many explanations have been given for the Danish rejection, such as the fear of being run by a European super-state, the lack of democracy in EC decision-making, the fear of having to serve in an eventual European army and also of European citizenship. The opponents were by no means united in their dislike of Maastricht, and much misinformation was spread in the campaign. However, there were two broad strands of hostile opinion;

i   On the Right, many objected to what they saw as the unnecessary move towards political unity, in what was essentially a common market. The far Right also spread alarm about the prospect of the door being opened to greater immigration from Southern Europe.

ii On the Left, critics stressed a threat to Denmark's right to raise its social and environmental standards. They would have preferred to see stronger EC policies in these areas.

For the Treaty to go ahead after this rejection, the Danes needed reassurance on several points, so that they could be taken on board the Union bus after a second referendum. This would involve a declaration that the Danes were not bound to move towards the third stage of EMU, as well as a commitment to greater openness in EC decision-making and a strengthening of the European Parliament. They wanted the right to 'opt out' of the security provisions of Maastricht, and other modifications on social and environmental matters. At Edinburgh, December 1992, Denmark gained the exemptions it wanted from the Maastricht Treaty, so that the way was cleared for the second (and successful) referendum.

The Situation Today

On some issues the Danes are more positive than Britain. Many see political union along more supranational lines as a way of containing the potential might of united Germany. They are more keen on economic and monetary union than many British politicians, and have supported the creation of new supranational institutions such as the Central Bank needed to operate a single currency.

On the Social Chapter the Danes are insistent that the EU should raise its social standards. They are keen to avoid the danger of 'social dumping' by multinational firms keen to exploit the gulf between the more welfare conscious states in the Union and the low wages and poor social conditions of Southern Europe.

They are also sympathetic to enlargement of the Union, and were encouraged by the accession of their Nordic cousins in Finland and Sweden. They also favour the admission of Eastern European states, including the three Baltic ones of Estonia, Latvia and Lithuania.

They are not natural Euro-enthusiasts, and tend to lag behind the pioneers of close integration. Rather, as cool Europeans, with some doubts still about a political as opposed to an economic Europe, they assess matters pragmatically. Years ago, it was said of a Danish Prime Minister, that '(he) does not want to join Europe, but he does want to sell cheese'.

France

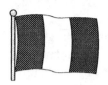

The French commitment to the idea of unity in Europe is a long-standing one, for Frenchmen such as Monnet and Schuman were to a large extent responsible for moves to initiate the whole European project.

Not all leaders have shared Monnet's enthusiasm for a ceding of sovereignty to supranational bodies in Europe, and de Gaulle was particularly determined to preserve his country's independence and freedom of manoeuvre. Since his passing, however, other Presidents from Pompidou to Mitterrand have been more willing to move the process of uniting Europe forward. The reunification of Germany in 1990 gave added urgency to this task, and Mitterrand particularly was convinced of the need to cement ties within the Union to ensure that Germany was firmly anchored in Western Europe.

For Mitterrand, the end goal was some form of federation. His use of the phrase 'a federal finality' when talking of the ultimate objective of the Union clearly suggests that he was in the Monnet school. Yet despite such language, he and many other Frenchmen were and remain committed to the pursuit of national self-interests. Whilst urging the need for the closest cooperation on some topics, they reserve other areas of policy for national solution. At Maastricht, Mitterrand firmly backed the intergovernmentalist approach used to handle the issues of immigration and law and order, and defence and foreign policy.

The present President, Jacques Chirac, has sometimes expressed himself ambiguously on European matters, but after becoming President in 1995 he has been keen to see his country tighten its belt and curb its spending so that it can meet the Maastricht criteria. He has introduced controversial new austerity policies to enable France to pass the EMU fitness test, and this involves him having to halve his budget deficit from 5.6% to be within the 3% limit. For many Frenchmen, there are practical arguments for a single currency - low interest rates, currency stability and an expected boost to trade.

Chirac tends to avoid the rhetorical flourishes of his predecessor, and is less of a Euro-visionary. A United States of Europe is not on his agenda, but his approach differs little in essentials from that of earlier French Presidents. He fights to defend French interests, but at the same time believes in European cooperation and the importance of Union institutions. To his fellow-countrymen, this seems like sensible dualism, an acceptance of the need to divide and share political power in the modern world. History and geography have combined to place France in the forefront of the drive for closer cooperation, and the attempt to achieve this has been backed by members of all parties for much of the postwar era.

The French have somehow managed to sound both nationalist and European, in a way that the British have not been able to do. For many of them, there is no conflict in being both, and subject to reservations about losing control of certain policies they want to be in the forefront of any moves to integration and be seen to maintain their position as Euro-enthusiasts.

Germany

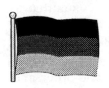

Germany as a united entity has only existed since 1990. Before then, the governments of the Moscow-backed German Democratic Republic ruled in the five Eastern Länder, whereas the bulk of Germans lived in West Germany, which was a founder member of the ECSC and by the seventies a leading Power in the Community. Unification has created a mighty German state of some 80m people.

The Union has been good for Germany. The CAP has been beneficial to the agrarian community which has received substantial subsidies. Although much of this money originally comes from the German economy (Germany is a heavy net contributor to the EU) such a method of reallocating the nation's resources has long found favour with most German people.

The Germans have long prided themselves on being the most European of states, and along with President Mitterrand of France Chancellor Kohl has been a foremost supporter of the idea of moving to ever-closer integration. He has taken the view that whereas all European nations need unification, Germany needs it more than the others, so that his unified and powerful country is firmly locked into Europe. He understands the fears of some other nations about Germany's past record and also their anxiety about the potential strength of the German economy, actual and potential. In his words, 'We need European integration as the other side of the coin of German unity'. Hence his approach of a 'European Germany, not a German Europe'.

Growing Doubts Among the German People

Kohl is also acutely aware of some stirrings of a new national sense of self-awareness, since unification. The growth of strongly nationalist feeling in former Eastern Germany (with some ugly racial behaviour) points to the need to anchor the country firmly in the West European camp. The 16m people in the East have their own preoccupations.

The 62m in the West, denied a national debate on the implications of Maastricht for their political future and above all for their currency, increasingly grumble about the cost. They also fear that their country, as the strongest on the continent, will be forever the milch-cow of a Europe eventually stretching from the Atlantic to the Urals.

Kohl's own credentials as a European statesman are impeccable, but he knows that the Euro-enthusiasm of the past is being reexamined, especially among the younger generation. He feels a sense of mission to bring about greater unity before he departs from the scene. He is committed to the idea of a federal Europe, and has spoken of his

Helmut Kohl

395

ambition to 'put the European train on the track in such a manner that it can only roll forward'. He is prepared to sacrifice the mark to bring about political union, if this is a means to the end of a European federation.

Greece

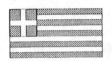

Greek politicians believe that their country needs to show its commitment to integration, for unless it is a fully consenting member the country still faces the prospect of being on the economic and political periphery of the Union. Fear of being marginalised is very strong in Greece. This is why political parties are unanimously in support of the EU, and the public are pro-federalist. According to the opinion pollsters, Greece commonly emerges as the most ardently pro-integrationist state in the Union.

Greek governments have shown recently strong support for the goal of political union, and have wanted to prove that they are 'good Europeans'. They have backed most of the leading initiatives, such as the Delors Plan and a single currency, and although the strict convergence criteria make it unlikely that they could join EMU in its early stages they would like to do so as soon as this is possible. They would prefer to see a delay in implementing the Maastricht agreement rather than be in the second division of a two-tier Europe.

Greek representatives are sympathetic to Germany's drive for more powers for the European Parliament, for as a country which itself gave birth to modern ideas of democracy they are conscious of the 'democratic deficit' in present EU institutions. Pro-European sentiment is particularly strong among the Greek people, who are traditionally critical of their own governments and often claim that if they were run from Brussels they might be better administered.

What has particularly helped the Greeks is the Cohesion Fund of which they were a strong backer. As the poorest member of the Union, living standards are below even those of Portugal. Since membership, subsidies have helped to transform the predominantly agrarian society, and restore the shattered economy. Many Greeks see their membership as the best chance of improving their living standards.

Ireland

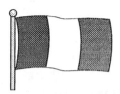

Membership has been good for Ireland, for it has offered something to almost everyone from farmers to feminists, and for many of them it remains a priority in their future thinking and plans. Discerning politicians have recognised that their country is such a beneficiary of the Union, that, in the words of one former Taoiseach, Garret FitzGerald, '...Ireland must seek to compensate for this by playing a positive and constructive role in the present running and future development of the Community'.

The country quickly benefited via the Common Agricultural Policy. Since then, the Regional and other Funds have been generous, and the Irish have been enthusiastic about cohesion as a key element in their membership. Everywhere, there are visible signs of EU money, not least in the motorway programme, for those few which have been constructed have all been paid for with Brussels money.

The Balance of Advantage in Irish Membership

EU Commission figures show how much Ireland has benefited from its membership, receipts far outstripping net contributions;

	Contributions (£m)	Income (£b)
1985	208.7	1.10
1987	249.7	1.07
1989	280.0	1.26
1991	339.5	2.14
1993	443.9	2.18

Ireland supports monetary union for the same reason as the Greeks, in the hope that it will raise living standards. It similary supports all policies which might help to bridge the gap between the richer and poorer nations of Europe, although Ireland is fast growing out of the latter category.

Many Irishmen are sympathetic to Europe for a different reason, seeing it as an alternative to the fervent nationalism which has so much affected their own past history. Their involvement has helped them to replace the inward-looking, old-style national feeling with a new commitment to Europeanism and to the wider world. Irishmen, unlike people in mainland Britain, seem to have no identity crisis about being Europeans.

Italy

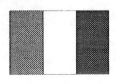

Postwar Italy had no reason to look back on the history of the nation-state with particular pride. In the years before Mussolini's rule the country had been torn apart by internal schism. When he was in power the Italian attachment to democratic government was abandoned, and for several years he was an ally of Hitler. After the hostilities, many Italians felt a need to demonstrate their respectability by showing themselves to be loyal to other West European nations. In so doing, they hoped also to buttress their new democracy at home. Membership of The Six might prove economically and politically beneficial as well as desirable for these other reasons.

Nicoll and Salmon have pointed to the twin approach of Italians to the Community and latterly to the Union, in their reference to the combination of 'pragmatism and idealism' in Italian thinking. They suggest that this accounts for the 'contradiction between the prevalence of pro-integrationist rhetoric in Italian political circles, and their marked inability or unwillingness to translate this into policy action'. They like and support the idea of Europe, but find that applying its rules can be inconvenient or even costly and disadvantageous. This is perhaps why they have a poorer record of implementation than other nations.

The Italians do not carry a heavy punch in Union affairs. Partly this may be because of their failure to show themselves as 'good Europeans' when it comes to carrying out EU policies. It also reflects the postwar weakness and instability of Italian politics and of the national economy. This means that although they do not wish to be in the slow lane when new schemes are planned, they are rarely ready to join them.

Luxembourg

Wedged between Germany, France and Belgium, Luxembourg (with a tiny population and land area smaller than many English counties), has survived as an independent nation by a series of historical accidents. It was a founder member of the Community and retains the privileges of separate national status in the EU. In some circumstancs it can veto measures which command the support of all the other member states, representing nearly 370m Europeans. It seems hard to justify a situation in which it has two seats in the Council to represent under 400000 people, when Germany has only 10 to represent 80m.

Luxembourg clearly has much to gain from membership of the European Union, which accounts for its generally positive attitude to any proposals designed to bring about further integration. Membership has given Luxembourg far more of a say in European affairs than its size and resources would allow it to reasonably expect. Moreover, its former Prime

Minister, Jacques Santer, has become President of the Commission, and a powerful figure on the European stage.

On almost every economic indicator, its people are the best placed in Europe. Income per head is nearly 70% above the EU average, and outstrips that of other prosperous nations such as the Germans and Danes. It carries little public debt, and easily became the first country to meet the Maastricht criteria.

Netherlands

The Dutch have, like the Belgians and Luxembourgers, always been in the forefront of any moves to closer integration in Europe. Like the other Benelux countries, they backed most of the policies discussed among The Twelve in the run-up to Maastricht, for the country has much to gain from its membership of a peaceful and prosperous Community. On their own, the Dutch would play a much less significant role than they can do in a union, for size, geography and recent history have shown that they are vulnerable in times of continental upheaval. As the host country at the 1991 summit, the Dutch representatives played an important role in brokering the agreement.

With the approach of another IGC conference, the Dutch are keen to see the Union move forwards, and for them the priorities are more majority voting, progress on CFSP (as long as it is compatible with NATO's primary role) and democratisation of the European institutions. In particular, they would like to see the 'democratic deficit' tackled by a strengthening of the European Parliament.

Portugal

Most Portuguese consider their country to have benefited from membership, and are fully supportive of the idea of closer union in Europe. Whatever reservations they have about particular issues, they tend to view them in the context of the general drive to unity.

Their support for positive steps to further cooperation is an effective way of demonstrating their standing as a useful member of the Union.

Portugal supports the idea of EMU, but as with Greece and Ireland the high level of government spending, debts and inflation have led it to favour a more cautious approach to the convergence timetable to enable it to prepare. On closer political union, it also tends to be more pragmatic than some nations, and its politicians are more willing to examine the British viewpoint. This was apparent in the memo of November 1990, in which five criteria were listed as being necessary in the move to political union. It must;

i   Be pursued gradually

ii Be based on a pragmatic view of political, economic and social realities in Europe

iii Respect national identities and diversity

iv Preserve the existing institutional balance

v   Ensure the correct application of the dual aspects of subsidiarity and solidarity.

Spain

Spain is, in principle, enthusiastic about union of all kinds, economic, military and political, although it tends to show some concern over the impact of questions of detail. It worries that it might become a net contributor to the Union, having benefited in the past from Union funding. It is also concerned about its economic competitiveness in relation to Northern Europe, and about aspects of the Social Chapter. It similarly wishes to maintain a right of veto in certain areas, notably on environmental policy where high EU standards could penalise Spanish producers.

Spain has generally kept itself to the fore in the evolution of the Union, and has not shown anxiety about an eventual federalist goal. For Spaniards, sovereignty is not an absolute concept which is possessed or abandoned. Rather, it is something which can be shared, and this means that it is possible to pursue Spanish and European objectives at the same time - as long as due regard is paid to the details of what is being agreed as a Union priority.

The New Entrants

It is too early to assess the attitudes to, and benefits of, membership for the new entrants.

Austria was a welcome member of the club, for it was viewed as a country whose strong position as regards budgetary performance would help speed EMU on its way. Moreover, its geographical position in the heart of the new Europe and its ties with Germany made it seem an ideal member. Austrians were initially enthusiastic for membership, and in the referendum vote, 66.4% were in favour, on a turnout of 81.3%.

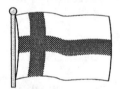

For the peoples of **Finland**, their membership of the EU is one further step away from their former dependence on the USSR. Turning to Europe is an obvious move for a country which fears an imperial revival in Russia, or a chaotic breakdown there. Their physical security is best protected via the Union, and they hope for trade benefits as well. However, they also have a strong wish to strengthen ties with the three Baltic republics.

Finland is not a member whose support can be taken for granted. Finns do not easily fit into any camp, and are not by instinct convinced Europeans. In the referendum vote, 57% were in favour in a high turnout of over 80%. The result indicates that support is not overwhelming, and needs to be backed up by worthwhile gains.

For many years, **Sweden** was conscious of its position as a neutral nation, and as long as the EC was identified in people's minds with a blocking mechanism against the Soviet Union, they were not interested in joining it. Conscious of their national identity, they were reluctant converts, and throughout the 1980s support in opinion polls for entry small. What changed things was the fall of the Berlin Wall, and increasing doubts about that national identity.

By the early nineties there was a strong wave of Europhoria. In the ratification referendum, the vote in favour the vote was a narrow 'yes' (52.2%), after a late surge in which the pro-Europe campaign was backed by most of the political and business establishment. Many industrial companies, notably Volvo, were worried that a 'no' vote might jeopardise future investment in Sweden.

For all those who feared that Sweden was in danger of being isolated on the edge of Europe, there were those who felt that the country might end up losing itself in the continent. Doubts have already surfaced, and the Swedes feel the need to see solid gains before they are convinced that the effort was worthwhile. Some Swedes are already showing deep anxiety about creeping Europeanisation, and in the environmental field they are most concerned to protect their regulations on clean air and water.

The impact of the Nordic states on the future of the Union is important, out of all proportion to their size. They have entered Europe with their traditional commitment to social and sexual equality and to the maintenance of national identity very much intact. The Nordic peoples are in an equivocal state of mind, and will look to Europe to prove itself to Scandinavia, rather than the other way round.

Attitudes to, and benefits from, the Union

Attitudes towards the European Union and the attempt to promote closer integration in Europe are related to popular perceptions of the benefits of membership. Some countries have found membership highly beneficial and recognised that it gives them an influence beyond their means. They are more willing to embrace initiatives such as the single currency.

	Has your country benefited from EU membership?		Opposition to a Single Currency
	Yes	**No**	
Austria	32%	47%	43%
Belgium	45%	35%	26%
Denmark	59%	29%	59%
Finland	39%	42%	53%
Germany	40%	36%	45%
Greece	72%	18%	20%
Spain	39%	41%	18%
France	39%	39%	23%
Ireland	80%	7%	17%
Italy	52%	22%	10%
Luxembourg	66%	19%	21%
Holland	66%	20%	29%
Portugal	66%	21%	21%
Sweden	19%	54%	54%
Britain	40%	43%	56%
EU	44%	35%	33%

Information adapted from a Eurobarometer survey of 15,800 people in December 1995.

Is it true to say that the countries most in favour of integration are those who stand to gain most from it?

Why is German enthusiasm for integration on the wane?

Britain and Europe;
A Review

Britain joined the EEC fifteen years after it began its operations, twenty years after The Six had pioneered the path to unity. Whereas other late entrants seem to have made the adjustments in attitude required to make a success of membership, this has not been the case for many British people, and in particular for some of their elected representatives. The British have found it hard to adjust, hence their reputation on the continent as 'reluctant Europeans'. Perhaps this reflects a national difficulty in coming to terms with Britain's reduced circumstances in the world.

In 1945, Britain seemed to be a major Power, though its strength can be overstressed. Since then, it has become apparent that Britain's declining economic fortunes have meant that it could not sustain the position it once held, and it has been hard to come to terms with that situation. Managing national decline is not a glorious role for politicians, and it is one which invites little popular enthusiasm. Some of them still hanker after the world leadership which was possible in their parents' generation. Many more concede that Britain's capacity to influence events has been much weakened, but are unconvinced that the logic of events should drive the country more closely into the embrace of our continental partners.

A Global Role

> *Britain has lost an empire, but not yet found a role.*
> *Dean Acheson, former American Secretary of State, 1963*

For years, Britain still attempted to preserve its global role. Sir Anthony Eden spoke for many of his countrymen when he gave his reasons for not signing up for membership of the EDC. Speaking with the authority of a Foreign Secretary, he observed;

> *Britain's story and her interests lie far beyond the Continent of Europe. Our thoughts move across the seas to the many communities in which our people play their part, in every corner of the world. These are our family ties. That is our life; without it we should be no more than some millions of people living on an island off the coast of Europe, of which nobody wants to take any particular notice.*

Not surprisingly, the country which 'won the war' felt that with such a worldwide importance it could win the peace. It did not need to tie itself in to any commitments with the countries which it had defeated or which had been overrun in the hostilities of World War Two. Britain felt that it could afford to remain aloof from Europe. It was not ready to recognise or admit its increasing weakness.

Such an attitude had deep roots in the British psyche, and it may be considered understandable in the circumstances of the time. However, it was combined with an inability to appreciate the enthusiasm and dedication of other nations to closer integration in pursuit of 'the European idea'. Consistently, British politicians then and in more recent years have underestimated the strength of this determination, and have assumed that carefully constructed measures of intergovernmental cooperation would be a substitute for their more visionary approach.

A Change of Direction

In the event, as we have seen (see p69-71), Prime Minister Macmillan found it expedient to apply for Britain to join the EEC in 1961, as it became clear that Britain's capacity to influence the outcome of events had been much curtailed. Neither the Commonwealth or the American connection seemed to count for as much as had been assumed a decade or so before. But not until the retirement of General de Gaulle was British membership welcome to the whole Community.

Apart from a committed band of ardent Europeans, it would be hard to detect widespread enthusiasm for the prospect of entry in 1973. However, there was a fairly general feeling that changes on the world scene and the need for access to the large continental market made accession desirable, even necessary.

When the chance came for the British people to express their view (in the referendum of 1975) they showed a strong backing for membership, for once the country had committed itself it was recognised that it might be a cold world outside should it prematurely depart.

But there never was popular excitement in Britain about belonging the Community. It was appreciated that it was probably wise and necessary for Britain to work with our new partners, for the alternatives did not look very promising. The point was well made by **FS Northedge;**

> [The] important thing about British entry into Europe was that it had almost every appearance of being a policy of last resort, adopted, one might almost say, when all other expedients had failed. There was no suggestion of it being hailed as a brilliant success...the impression remained that it was brought about in humiliating circumstances, and when other options in foreign policy had lost their convincingness.

Eurobarometer, the EC's polling organisation, consistently found that the majority of British respondents favoured closer cooperation in Europe in some form, and recognised the inevitability of further steps along the route to unity, on the right terms. This changed after the Maastricht agreement had been signed. The public mood seemed to move in a more Euro-sceptical direction. This may have been a reflection of the outcome of the

Danish referendum and of other signs of growing doubt on the continent. It also reflected the lack of a strong pro-European lead from British ministers. Throughout the period of British membership, public opinion has been very sensitive to the attitudes adopted by political leaders and the media, and also to the turn of events.

It remains the case that whereas Eurobarometer found that in its polls conducted between 1981-83, the number of citizens who believed that EC membership was a 'good thing' for Britain failed to rise beyond 30%, between 1987-92 it never dropped below the 50% level. Particularly among the young, some of whom were beginning to find opportunities for work in the Community, support for the concept of Europe was notably stronger.

Reactions Since 1979

> *My aims for Britain in the Community can be simply stated. I want us to be where we belong - at the very heart of Europe, working with our partners in building the future. That is a challenge we take up with enthusiasm.*
> *John Major, speech in Bonn, 1991.*

Since 1979, during the era of Conservative rule, there has been a developing scepticism in the Governmental approach to relations with Europe, at times a distinct coolness. Whilst British leaders were concerned to stress and expand the role of the Community as a free trade area, their continental partners often had a different long term agenda. Their vision was of a Community in which the degree of union became ever-closer, and this was written into the treaties. For several years, the full implications of membership were not fully realised in Britain. Even those who were involved in the negotiations and signed up for the next stage in the road to unity sometimes had an inadequate grasp of the detail contained therein.

British ministers - especially during Mrs Thatcher's Premiership - sought to fashion the Community along the lines set out in her Bruges speech of September 1988. Rejecting any form of European superstate, she reminded her listeners of Britain's contribution to the liberation of Europe in 1944-45 and offered a description of how the Community might develop in the future.

Her remarks cast her firmly in the Gaullist mould, for she made it clear that it was neither possible nor desirable to 'suppress nationhood and concentrate power at the centre of a European conglomerate'. She favoured 'willing and active coopeation between independent states', and wanted to see Europe speak with a more united voice. But this must be done in such a way that it 'preserves the different traditions, Parliamentary powers and sense of national pride in one's own country'.It was apparent that she had little or no sympathy with talk of a European Idea. She was no utopian, but took the view that Europe could be made to work to Britain's advantage - as long as British leaders made a firm stand against Community interference and regulation, and were determined to concentrate attention on developing a deregulated market in Europe.

John Major

Her successor, John Major, for all of his initial wish to see Britain 'at the heart of Europe' has been forced to recognise that within his party there is little sympathy for extending British commitments within the Union. He has sought to limit its competence, and delay making any decisions which bind Britain more closely to the other member states. For since the Maastricht ratification, enthusiasm among the Conservatives has distinctly cooled on matters European, and several polls indicate that public opinion is similarly lukewarm on closer ties. Indeed, the issue of the single currency and the adequacy of the British opt-out is a matter of continuing debate. Rather than sign up for a closer commitment, there are some people now willing to contemplate a future for Britain outside the Union.

The Present Situation; Ministerial Attitudes

> *Mr Blair has said he would never let Britain be isolated in Europe - an extraordinary statement. Never willing to be isolated means never willing to stand up for our national interests, never to use the veto, never to stand alone,*
> Michael Portillo, Conservative Conference, 1995.

David Butler and Martin Westlake make the point that Euroscepticism has a long history; 'If there is a European "problem", it is not restricted to one British political party, but more generally diffused throughout the British political and administrative establishment'. They make the point that although it might be tempting to think that the Conservative Administration of John Major is particularly prone to difficulties over Europe today, the problem is one that has afflicted all past leaders of governments; 'In truth, virtually every postwar British Prime Minister has been in a similar position and played a similar role, from Attlee to Churchill and Eden, from Macmillan to Wilson, and from Callaghan to Thatcher and Major'.

Their difficulties relate to the problem of leading parties whose composition reflects the ambivalent attitudes of many British people to the postwar position. Britons are caught between the desire to hold on to country's past greatness and traditions (what Douglas Hurd has called 'punching above its weight'), and yet also to keep pace with the modern world. Although most MPs recognise that the country has a European future, a number of them do not enthuse about the prospect. Other countries, lacking the same attachments as Britain, do not experience the same feelings, or at least not to the same extent. As one former Conservative MP, Sir Anthony Meyer, put it; 'For France, Europe offers a chance to extend its influence; for Britain, Europe is a damage-limitation exercise'.

Most people recognise that Britain cannot separate itself from the European fold, but within it ministers seem to find it difficult to find ways of making the Union work to the national advantage. By seeming to resist the initiatives which other nations want in so many areas, it then becomes harder to achieve those goals that really matter to Britain.

British policy often seems to be beset by contradictions. Ministers frequently denounce interference or 'meddling' from Brussels bureaucrats on matters such as the environment or worker protection, and yet would like to see more Union action on matters such as animal welfare. They make Brussels the scapegoat for the failure to achieve effective reform in this area.

The animal transport row of 1995 is a good example of an issue on which Britain needed allies. In seeking measures to improve journey conditions for live cows, sheep and pigs, the British minister was making a good case for some restraint on the operation of the free market system, and many people from all parties would have supported his endeavours. He was also acting as an effective European, in that he tried to gain support for his cause by looking for allies such as the Germans and Scandinavians who shared his concern. But southern states such as Greece, Italy and Spain were worried that new rules would mean higher meat prices. Their opposition was eventually overcome and a compromise agreed. Despite the fact that three other countries wanted more stringent limits a settlement of the issue was possible - because of majority voting.

By resisting further majority voting, the danger is that 'Britain cuts off its nose to spite its face'. The veto, as its name implies, is a negative tactic which is appropriate if policy is about obstructing measures which are unpalatable. But it does also mean that there are problems when you cease to be an opposer and become a proposer; 'Britain has no veto that other nations do not have, and therefore we remain just as vulnerable to the veto over things we want to do as we currently expect the others to be over things we don't...The British veto sounds fine until you realise that it also means a Greek veto' (**Martin Kettle**).

By resisting an extension of powers to the European Parliament, ministers lose potential support from MEPs who consistently vote for the type of policies which Britain often approves. A majority normally support a crackdown on Union waste and fraud, opening up markets to Eastern Europe and reform of the CAP.

411

Britain often seems to be pursuing aims which are contradictory. It wants reform of the agricultural policy, it wants to enlarge the Union to the East which makes such reform ever-more-urgent, but at the same time it is determined to resist an extension of majority voting and instead allow each state to retain its national veto. If the latter course is pursued, the task of achieving fundamental agrarian reform becomes all the more difficult.

This seems like short term thinking, and opponents of the Conservatives would suggest that the country has been left exposed and isolated in the Union by the way in which a series of events have been handled. British interests and those of other European states sometimes coincide, but by failing to work with those nations on several issues we surrender the chance to make progress on those close to British thinking. This isolation was exhibited in the crisis over mad cow disease.

The Beef Crisis and the Issue of Non-co-operation

Mad cow disease, correctly known as Bovine Spongiform Encephalopathy (BSE), was first identified by scientists in 1986, and thereafter it spread rapidly. The practice of feeding cattle with treated carcasses of other animals, including sheep, was thought to be a key factor in its development. The disease resembled Creutzfeldt-Jakob Disease (CJD), a fatal human condition, and some scientists believed that just as cattle contracted BSE from eating infected sheep so humans contracted CJD from eating infected beef.

In March, 1996, the Government broke the news that its advisory committee on BSE-related diseases believed that there might be a link between BSE and CJD, and this provoked much anxiety over the dangers of consuming certain beef products and a collapse in the beef market. The European Commission, on the advice of its veterinary committee, imposed a ban on British exports of all beef and beef products throughout the world; most countries had already banned British beef as a result of previous alarm about the dangers of BSE in British cattle.

The ban faced many farmers with the prospect of a total collapse of the beef market, and the British Government urged a lifting of the embargo. It put forward proposals to the Commission and in the Council for a package of measures designed to eliminate the risk of BSE in British cattle, involving the slaughter of many animals deemed to be at risk. But several member states were less than sympathetic, fearing the spread of BSE to the continent. They were aware of the damage already done to the meat industry in Europe, for in Germany sales of beef had sharply reduced. Cynical British farmers thought that some countries may have seen an opportunity to fend off competition from British producers.

The list of measures proposed by the British Government was thought to be inadequate by some European partners and they were initially unwilling to lift the ban, although eventually the export of some beef products was allowed. A total removal of the ban would take much longer. British frustration at the slow removal of the embargo led the Prime Minister, John Major, to impose a policy of non-cooperation in the transaction of EU business. Britain would not agree to decisions on any matters awaiting resolution in the Council, without there being progress towards a lifting of the ban; this would involve a framework and time-scale for its ending. The policy irritated EU members, even those sympathetic to Britain's BSE problem and they found it odd that the Government was prepared to hold up progress even on measures which it strongly favoured, such as those to tackle national disasters and emergencies, and those on overseas aid and fraud within the EU. Eventually, at the Florence summit (June 1996), a deal was done, by which Britain agreed to the slaughtering of more cattle than it had originally believed to be necessary and a halt in the policy of non-cooperation, in return for the promise that there would be a phased removal of the ban on beef exports over a period of time.

The issue raised many questions about Britain's place in the Union. Pro-Europeans felt that if ministers had approached the Commission about the problems before they went public with their statement on the possible link between BSE and CJD, it might have been possible to 'manage' the problem, in a way in which EU partners would help resolve the difficulties. They pointed out that Europe was not the problem but the solution to the problem, in that the Commission was prepared to make money available to help compensate farmers for the slaughter policy. Eurosceptics saw the opportunity of denouncing the Brussels machinery for its allegedly anti-British stance, and urged a tough policy on the Prime Minister, particularly after the introduction of the policy of non-cooperation. They saw an opportunity to exploit anti-European feeling, and campaign for a more determined defence of British interests which in their view were being damaged by hostile Europeans. In the tabloid press and on the Tory Right, there was considerable xenophobia, and anti-German feeling was strong; Germany was the country most reluctant to remove the embargo, even partially, for its beef market had been gravely harmed by the scare.

The policy of non-cooperation was widely portrayed as Britain being at war with Europe, although ministers claimed that this was a crude exaggeration. In any war there needs to be an identifiable enemy, and this was how the EU was viewed by many in Britain who were hostile to the Union and all its deeds. This seemed, in their eyes, to be one more episode in the long saga in which British wishes were being overridden, and it was time to call to a halt to European domination and stand up for British interests.

When the Government called a halt to the policy of non-co-operation, it seemed like a climb down, another example of the Prime Minister leading his troops to the top of the hill and then marching them back down again. Pro-Europeans thought that nothing had been achieved which could not have been accomplished without the policy, and that Britain had needlessly antagonised our partners. Eurosceptics and Europhobes were disappointed that the Cabinet had backed away from prolonging the conflict. Both sides complained about the quality of leadership, and the issue exacerbated tension on the European issue within the Conservative Party.

The episode was not without its ironies. Britain resorted to the European Court of Justice in an unsuccessful attempt to get the world-wide ban declared illegal, and critics abroad found it surprising that the country which often questioned the role and decisions of the Court was willing to use it when this suited national interests. Others noted that without majority voting, so much disliked by British ministers, the partial lifting of the ban would have been impossible, as would agreement on a staged total removal. Finally, although the Commission is often attacked in Britain as a bureaucratic monster responsible for many of Britain's problems with the EU, on this occasion it was this body and particularly the good offices of Jacques Santer which were instrumental in working for a settlement, whereas it was in the Council that Britain found itself in difficulty with representatives of other countries.

The whole story illustrated how hard it is for many people in Britain, particularly those within the Conservative Party, to come to terms with European membership and its demands. They dislike Union meddling, and were convinced that the worldwide ban was unnecessary, catastrophic in its impact and probably illegal. The failure of the Court of Justice (in its interim ruling) to lift it served only to confirm their belief that ECJ was behaving in an arbitary and unfair manner where Britain was conderned. Continentals saw it differently, and to them the Commission ban was a legitimate measure to protect public health. They were confirmed in their belief that Britain was not a 'good European'. Yet again,when it came to wheeler-dealing with other states, British isolation was all too evident.

Of course, it does require some boldness to accept the extension of majority voting which would make the enlarged Union work more efficiently, and which will become more necessary as the number of member states increases. It also requires a willingness to respect the prevailing view when it goes against you.

Rather than go along with the tide of European opinion, ministers tend to play the nationalist card with bravura and portray Brussels as the enemy whose ploys must be resisted. They like to believe that in the last few years their thinking has had a gradual impact on other member states, and that the tide of opinion is actually going their way.

With President Mitterrand removed from the scene, with rising opposition in Germany to a single currency and several states only too aware that they are unlikely to meet the convergence criteria, it is easy for ministers to interpret a greater caution - some would say realism - about monetary union as indicating that the argument is moving in their direction. They sense a growing consensus that the time is not ripe for such a move, and detect a more general and increasing antipathy to the idea of handing over more power to Brussels.

Yet there are indications from Bonn and Paris that, whilst there may be practical difficulties about achieving monetary union as soon as they would have wished, they are nonetheless determined to maintain progress towards the sort of Union they wish to emerge. Chancellor Kohl is insistent that the pace of European integration should not be set by those who want to advance more cautiously, or not at all.

A commentator in *Le Monde* caught the common view in France that the two countries, France and Britain, start from different perspectives when they consider their place in Europe; 'For France, being at the heart of Europe remains a necessity. For Great Britain, it is just one option. Europe, seen from London, is not an end in itself, but a means of attaining specific objectives at particular times'. British ministers increasingly often do speak of a Europe in which they can pick and choose the parts they favour, a Europe 'à la carte' in which they seek allies with which they can achieve those things that matter. The difficulty is that when so many items on the agenda are unacceptable to London, then leaders in other capitals may hesitate before helping the country to fulfil its other aspirations.

> *The slowest ship in the convoy should not be allowed to determine its speed. If individual partners are not prepared or able to participate in certain steps towards integration, the others should not be denied the opportunity to move forward.*
> *Herr Kohl, February 1996.*
>
> *[In response] The other side of the coin is that the convoy ceases to exist if you do not accommodate all the ships within it...You have to find a structure which all the countries concerned are comfortable with.*
> *Malcolm Rifkind.*

The White Paper, March 1996

In advance of the opening of the IGC, the British Government produced a White Paper outlining its stance. In some respects it was pro-European, for it stated that; 'The United Kingdom's role as a leading member of the European Union is vital to our national interest'. It commended the EU as 'central to our economic prospects', and politically as 'the basis upon which we must consolidate democracy and prosperity across the whole of Europe'.

Yet it also insisted that the Union would 'only succeed if it respects the integrity of the independent nation states which comprise its membership; and if it is flexible enough to accommodate their political and cultural differences'.

The preparation of the negotiating stance for the IGC gave rise to debate about the impact of membership of the Community and latterly the Union on the country's fortunes. This is the opportunity to examine the issues involved more closely.

 Should Britain oppose any extension of majority voting?

The Balance Sheet of Membership

> *It was right to join, not just for the opportunities that the Community offers as a common market, not even for the economic strength of the Community collectively, but for the collective power of the European democracies to improve the general weight, politically and economically, of European opinion throughout the world. Nothing that has happened in the almost 20 years of our membership causes me to doubt the rightness of the original decision to join the Community.*
> *John Major, House of Commons, December 1991.*

Britain's membership of, and role in, the Community, was much contested in the early 60s, 70s, 80s and 90s. The issues have differed, but many of the same people who worked for entry originally continue to emphasise a European approach to the conduct of our affairs, and those who took a contrary view have seen their worst fears confirmed. However, along the road, there have been significant changes in the attitudes of some politicians and parties.

The Conservatives were originally more enthusiastic for membership and remained so until the late 1970s, whilst the Labour leadership was lukewarm, its supporters often hostile to the whole concept. In the Thatcher years, a coolness towards our European partners developed, and at the end of the decade Labour reversed the anti-EC stand it had taken in the early 1980s. In between the outspoken critics and fervent admirers in either party are many who feel that membership was, and still is, appropriate, there being no realistic alternative. However, they may be disappointed at the way things have turned out, and perhaps feel that the movement towards closer cooperation has gone too far, too fast.

Britain has now had more than two decades of membership, and the process of adaptation has influenced many aspects of our national life. It has not been an easy ride for governments or peoples. Just how beneficial the impact has been is not easy to assess. Spokespersons on either side of the argument are tempted to overstate their case and make exaggerated claims. Often, their verdicts are arrived at as much by instinct and preference, as by detailed knowledge, and because of this some conjure a scenario of dreadful catastrophe and others wax eloquently in their pursuit of utopian dreams.

The Case FOR Membership

For ardent pro-Europeans, the case has always been a **Political** one. British leaders recognised that, after centuries of fratricidal strife on the continent, others were making an attempt to resolve old conflicts, and lay the ghosts of the past. Such a reconciliation, particularly between the old rivals, France and Germany, was essential if Europe was to be strong and free. European statesmen saw a link between postwar economic reconstruction and political reconciliation. It was recognised that no one country could prosper on its own, and that an effort to achieve unity in Europe was a priority. In this way, Europe would carry weight in international relations and be a stabilising influence in the world. United, Europe could play a role in the improvement of international relations, and not be dwarfed by the Superpowers, the USSR and the USA, and emerging countries such as Japan and eventually China.

The development of The Six and now The Fifteen has made Europe a respected force in the world, so that other Powers and developing countries are prepared to deal with the Union rather than individual states. Its size and population give it great significance. If ever US commitment to the continent should weaken, it can survive on its own.

The question for Britain was whether it could afford to be side-lined from these developments. In former years, it might have dreamed of playing a world role, mediating in disputes of the day, but by the 1960s, such influence was waning; Britain was no longer in the front rank of European powers. Europe offered a new role, as the other elements of the 'three circles' counted for less.

Edward Heath was aware of the linkage of economic and political goals for the Community, and saw that by economic means the political objectives might be achieved. He believed that;

> *Our purpose in creating the new Europe is political. Let us never lose sight of that fact. It is to prevent Europe from being destroyed, either from within or without; to create the prosperity which will ensure support for democratic institutions; to provide the economic growth on which to base its security.*

For him, and for early supporters of entry, the case was essentially political. As Macmillan once put it, the issues were more significant than a petty squabble over the price of butter! In 1967, Harold Wilson had taken a similar view, arguing that; 'Europe is now faced with the opportunity of a great move forward in political unity, and we can - and indeed must - play our full part in it'.

Exactly how close that unity would become, and where it would lead, was unknown, but the dream of ever-closer-union has always been the vision of Euro-enthusiasts on the continent, and of the most committed supporters in Britain. In the face of such a vision, supporters were unconcerned about any loss of sovereignty in Britain, for as the White Paper put in, in 1971;'There is no question of Britain losing essential national sovereignty. What is proposed is a sharing and an enlargement of individual national sovereignties in the common interest'.

In such an organisation, Britain would have an opportunity to make its views heard, and its influence felt. Any loss of independence was more than balanced by the opportunity for greater influence over the course on events in Europe. Harold Lever MP, put the point well in a House of Commons debate; 'We should beware of clinging to a nominal sovereignty at a cost of losing a real and effective control over our destiny which we might have cooperatively if we pooled it'.

For enthusiasts today, the political arguments in favour of European unity are the overwhelming considerations. In the past two decades, the progress has not been as great as some would have hoped. Europe has not always spoken with one voice, and so they want to see it develop into something which is more than a forum where the Heads of Government meet and discuss ideas. To them, it is a community to which nations have handed over an amount of decision, so that decisions can be taken jointly, and to the benefit of all. At the very least, this implies close cooperation; for some, it is a reason for going ahead to build a real 'United States of Europe'.

The **Economic** case for joining the EC was that Britain wanted to benefit from the large market that The Six had created. It was felt that British manufacturers would be able to produce more cheaply because of economies of scale, and sell more of their goods in this dynamic and expanding free-trade area. The competition that British industrialists would be subjected to was thought to be bracing, encouraging efficient production. As a result of these new business opportunities, the nation's prosperity would be secured, and improved living standards would result. The White Paper prior to entry made the point that in the years after the formation of the Community up to 1969, the average income in The Six had risen by 75%, in Britain by 40%.

In the Referendum campaign, such arguments were re-emphasised, and part of the case for 'staying-in' was the disruption involved in pulling out. The 'Yes' campaigners stressed that;

- membership offered 'the best framework for success, the best protection for our standard of living'
- the USA and the Commonwealth wanted us to remain in
- outside there was a harsh, cold world in which Britain would find itself dangerously isolated with none of our friends offering to revive old partnerships.

Twenty years later, even some supporters may feel that some of the claims were over-optimistic. The increased opportunities for British industrialists have not generated the steady economic growth and prosperity anticipated, but most of British industry is today geared to Europe as the main outlet. Many companies have bases in Europe. GEC plants turn out products in a number of member countries, and others such as Rank Hovis Mc Dougall and Rank Xerox have put a lot of time and effort into building up sales in Europe.

By 1981, trade with the EC had produced a positive trade balance, though since then it has been less favourable. Exports to the rest of the world have gone up much less than those to the EU. Between 1972-94, the proportion of Britain's exports going to other members of the Community rose from 34-53% and that going to the Commonwealth fell sharply. For many years the overall terms of trade have been assisted by a substantial surplus in our oil trade, though in many goods Britain has fared better with Europe than with Japan and the United States.

Many British jobs depend on trade with the Union and would be threatend if we lost access to it. On the outside, British exporters would not only have to overcome the Common External Tariff in selling to the continent, but would have to comply with regulations and standards over which British Governments would have had no control. British industry is now economically integrated with the EU, and dependent upon it.

Apart from access to a vast market for industry, and for any British cititens wishing to work abroad, British citizens benefit from the funds established by the EU to help various groups of workers who have suffered from the impact of economic change. Such funds cover agriculture, social aid, and regional development. Britain has received well over £3,000m in grants from the Regional Fund, and the European Investment Bank has lent nearly £5,500m for schemes ranging from the Sullom Voe oil terminal to manufacturing projects in the Assisted Areas. Between 1994-99, the three areas benefiting from Objective One payments will between them obtain £2000m, and other regions of industrial decline or rural backwardness will also gain assistance.

Britain also benefits from inward investment. Its proximity to other EU markets, and relatively good labour relations, make it an attractive location. For many years, it has been the leading country for US manufacturing investment in Europe, and around 30% of Japanese investment in the EU comes here, in the form of Hitachi factories in South Wales, and Nissan and Toyota ones in England, among many other schemes. Outside the Union, Britain would be an unattractive base for such investment, as foreign companies would still have to overcome trade barriers in selling to the other member countries.

Whatever disadvantages membership may have brought, the situation would be worse if Britain was outside, for then the British would have no say over events which nonetheless would have an impact upon use. Within the Union, Britain has the chance to influence the course of events, and if other countries can be persuaded to align themselves with the British standpoint then majority opinion may move in a direction favourable to us.

The European Union is an increasingly important trading block and because it represents so many countries it has a louder voice in world affairs than would be the case if those countries spoke on their own behalf. By remaining within the Union, Britain has a voice which counts in the world.

The Case AGAINST Membership

Critics of entry were particularly anxious about the impact on food prices at home, and on Commonwealth suppliers of many basic commodities - eg, Caribbean sugar and New Zealand dairy products. Britain would lose its trading ties with markets such as New Zealand, and its freedom to buy where it could at the cheapest rates. They were unconvinced about the beneficial effects of exposure to the chill winds of competition, and claimed that Britain's relatively slow growth in the 1950s and 1960s had little to do with membership of the Community; there were strong economies both inside and outside The Six.

In 1975, the 'No' campaigners claimed that all of the promises made at the time of accession had proved illusory - the rise in our living standards, more investment, better productivity, faster industrial growth, more employment, a trade surplus with the EC members, had not come about. Since Britain joined, prices had risen because Britain could no longer buy goods in the cheapest markets in the world. The alternative they posed was for Britain to remain part of EFTA, and through that organisation to trade with the other EC members, without incurring the costs of membership.

Opponents of entry did not deny that the Community had been good for The Six, and had been instrumental in ending the dispute between France and Germany. They doubted the wisdom of Britain being part of the arrangement. They worried about the loss of Parliamentary Sovereignty, and lamented the inability of Britain to control its own destiny. Britain would lose much of its freedom of manoeuvre, for decisions would increasingly be taken in Brussels.

Some of them envisaged that the European Parliament would be strengthened and directly elected, and that the Commission would use its power to issue regulations binding upon the British people. Direct elections have come about, there has been a (slow) growth in the powers of the Parliament, and the Commission has issued a number of regulations which the British Government and some of the British people dislike. It has not been difficult for the popular press to whip up anti-Union feeling, by dwelling on some of its wilder (and often untrue or unimplemented) recommendations, such as those seeking to straighten cucumbers or to change the title of much of British ice-cream.

By the early 80s, a decade after entry, many felt that their fears had been confirmed. They were alarmed at Britain's unfair budgetary contributions, which meant that Britain was putting in much more to the Community than it got out. Agricultural spending via the CAP was foremost in their criticism, for it was felt that Britain was subsidising inefficient farming in France and to a lesser extent Germany. The result of the guaranteed prices that these farmers were given was the creation of the notorious beef and butter mountains which were often ridiculed and condemned.

Today, many erstwhile critics have accepted membership as inevitable though they continue to believe that Britain would have fared better outside, rather than inside the Union. As to the alternatives, some have favoured a loose trading alliance - EFTA, plus the USA and Canada - or Commonwealth ties, attitudes which long ago have ceased to be feasible. It was Enoch Powell, a former Tory minister and an advocate of the Parliamentary Sovereignty argument, who suggested that; 'The alternative to the Common Market is like the alternative to suicide - don't do it'. He and others believe that Britain could survive on its own. As the 'No' booklet in the referendum put it; 'Let's rule ourselves, while trading and remaining friendly with other nations'.

Of course, because Britain did not originally join the Community, the organisation was not devised and nor did it develop with specifically British interests in mind. Late-comers to the club could not expect that it would suddenly get the members to change everything for their benefit. Certainly, the industrial and trade benefits which optimists had spoken of did not quickly materialise, for Britain had the misfortune to join just as the 1973 oil crisis dropped Western Europe into a cycle of stagnation which lasted for several years. This accounts for some of the anguish now felt by many critics who look in vain for the suggested benefits which were to be gained from joining with The Six.

Of course, supporters of British membership now have the advantage that Britain is in the Union, and even if it were desirable, withdrawal would be hard to achieve. It would involve negotiating transitional arrangements, and would be a messy business. Britain would surrender any influence over the development of the EU, whilst in practice still finding itself subject to some of its decrees.

Sovereignty in the Modern World

A central criticism made against the EU is that it undermines national sovereignty. Critics would prefer to see power rest in the nation state, rather than in some international organisation. Those on the Left fear that a Labour Government might be prevented carrying out socialist policies because of the free market principles via which the Union operates. Those on the Right dislike the way in which Brussels seeks to 'interfere' in British policy on issues such as fishing and immigration, among many others.

What is Sovereignty? By sovereignty, we mean (according to the Oxford English Dictionary) 'supremacy in respect of power, domination or rank; absolute and independent authority'. Sovereignty is then about the exercise of power, and absolute sovereignty is no longer realistic.

Is Sovereignty Viable in the Present Day?

National sovereignty has been eroded over the postwar era, and British sovereignty was declining before the country became a member of the EU. In many areas of policy, there are constraints on our freedom of action, some deriving from treaty obligations and some from the realities of the modern world. Membership of GATT, the International Monetary Fund and the United Nations Organisation all limit absolute national sovereignty, so that the idea that any nation can act without regard to forces beyond the country is an illusion.

Sovereignty is not a timeless and unchanging concept, as one British MEP noted;

Sovereignty is the ability to do what we like when we like, and not be tied up with others...In practice, we've been trading bits of our sovereignty for bits of other people's sovereignty to make a stable world for ourselves.

He has recognised what pro-Europeans always claim. In the modern world, absolute sovereignty is unattainable. It may be worth surrendering a degree of nominal independence to achieve the possibility of exerting real influence. Outside the Union, Britain might have theretical freedom of action, but would be impotent to exercise any leverage.

Parliamentary Sovereignty

In the case of the EU, however, there is a legal transfer of sovereignty, for we have seen that European law overrides British law. This has been made clear in several cases, ranging from that of the Spanish trawlermen (see p160-161) to the issue of Sunday trading. In adjudicating on whether British law on shop opening hours on the Sabbath was at variance with the Treaty of Rome, Mr Justice Hoffman made it clear that the Treaty was the supreme law of this country. The real issue was whether British law was compatible with article 30.

The British Constitution has always stressed the doctrine of Parliamentary Sovereignty, whereby Parliament is the supreme law-making body. There is no limit to what it can legislate upon, and no other body can modify or question its decisions. The Courts interpret Acts, but do not pass judgement on their suitability.

In accepting a mass of existing European law on joining the Community, that principle was infringed for Parliament had never individually passed the laws concerned (It did so collectively, of course, by passing the European Communities Act). Since joining, regulations issued by the European Union are binding as they stand, and even with directives the principle - if not the detail - is laid down in Brussels.

This erosion of the power of Parliament is much disliked by those who oppose the Union. Tony Benn has argued that 'Parliament...can thus be pushed into the background as far as the laws are concerned. If by chance British legislation were to conflict with EEC legislation, the latter would be upheld by the European Court and enforced by the British Courts whatever Parliament said'.

Having giving its assent to British entry into the EC, the ultimate power which belongs to Parliament is that of withdrawal. It could always vote for Britain to leave the EU.

Most people have accepted that Britain is in for good, and the sceptics are involved in a damage-limitation exercise designed to ensure that it retains some freedom of manoeuvre in developing its economy, regulating its currency, and planning its social legislation, defence and foreign affairs.

Ultimately, Britain could withdraw, and this is the element of Parliament Sovereignty which remains unscathed. If one Parliament cannot bind its successors, then in the future a Government could always bring in legislation to take Britain out of the Union.

Why are the British lukewarm and the Irish generally keen on closer ties with Europe?

How true is it to say that 'Europe has been good for Britain, but Britain has been bad for Europe'?

'Only now are the full consequences of our European membership becoming apparent'. Discuss.

The Sun, 23.4.1996

TEACH YOURSELF

Attitudes of European Governments to Closer Co-operation in Europe, 1996

	Belgium	Denmark	France	Germany	Greece	Ireland
Single Currency	Yes	Yes strict insistence on convergence criteria	Yes	Yes - strict insistence on convergence criteria	Yes - little hope of joining this century	Yes
Common Foreign and Security Policy	Yes plus role in defence	Prefer Inter-governmental co-operation	Prefer Inter-governmental co-operation. Keen on EU defence role	Yes plus eventual role in defence	Yes	Yes, but prefer Inter-governmental co-operation
Other Policy Areas	Keen to extend EU intervention	Keen on social/ environmental issues	Traditionally keen on extending intervention.	Have often pressed for justice/ immigration initiatives. Costs a factor to bear in mind.	Keen to extend EU intervention	Cautious on social issues
More Majority Voting	Yes, for most issues	Yes, especially on social and environmental issues	Yes, in several areas	Yes, in several areas	Yes, but sensitive on some issues; e.g. frontiers	Yes, but sensitive on social issues
More Areas for the European Parliament	Yes, very keen	Not keen at all	Not very enthusiastic	Yes, very keen; Kohl personally committed	Yes	Yes, without enthusiasm
Federalism	Yes, very committed	Doubts; attached to sovereignty	Yes, but also emphasises national interest	Yes, very keen. View federalism as a de-centralising process	Yes, very committed	Yes, without any enthusiasm to move in this direction

NB The summary is based on the 12 members prior to the 1995 enlargement. The attitudes of the

Italy	Luxembourg	Netherlands	Portugal	Spain	UK
Yes - little hope of joining this century	Yes	Yes	Yes - unlikely to be in first batch	Yes	Parliament to decide at the time when the others go ahead
Yes, plus eventual defence role	Yes, with defence role	Yes, plus defence role as long as NATO agrees	Yes, but prefer Inter- governmental cooperation	Yes, with defence role	Prefer close co-operation, with clear national control Stresses NATO role in defence
Especially keen on social issues; support new areas of intervention	Keen on social policy and generally interventionist	Keen on EU role, but watchful on costs	Generally keen on intervention but watchful on costs	Keen, but very wary of costs to Spain	Case by case examination; need to be convinced
Yes, for everything	Yes, for most issues	Yes, for most issues	Yes, for most issues	Yes, but not on expensive policies, e.g. environment	Unenthusiastic about any extension
Yes, very keen	Not very enthusiastic - few MEPs	Yes, very keen	Not very enthusiastic	Not too keen	Not keen; prefer control via national parliaments
Yes, ardently committed	Yes	Yes, very committed	More doubtful about merits or likelihood	Yes, but attached to sense of national identity	Strongly opposed; view federalism as a centralising process

additional members have yet to clearly emerge on all of the issues.

Questions to Consider

1   Read the following passage, and then tackle the questions which
    follow;

    Everyone agrees that international cooperation is desirable - but
    when it comes to a loss of sovereignty, national concerns all too often
    prevail. A Europe with a single unified government is a most
    unlikely scenario, even for the inner core of EC member states.
    Much more probable is an extension of the present cooperative
    arrangements which have served the Community well since its
    beginnings (Europe 1993, Understanding Global Issues).

    i   Why might a loss of sovereignty matter more to some nations of
        the European Union than to others?

    ii When the 'inner core' speak of a 'more federal' Europe, what do
        you think they mean? Why does their image of a 'more federal'
        future sound more like a 'nightmare future' to many British
        politicians?

    iii How well have 'the present cooperative arrangements' served
        the Community/Union since its early days?

2   Read the extract below from *The Sun* (p 427), and then answer the
    questions which follow;

    i   How true is it to describe the European Union as an 'unelected
        body'?

    ii What evidence is there that the Union 'aims to devour our
        national identity'?

    ii Why do the French see national and European interests as
        compatible, whereas British politicians have often portrayed
        them as being in opposition to each other?

3   Choose any EU country which does not favour a more integrated
    Europe, and explain why its politicians and voters show a reluctance
    to embark on such a future course.

4 Choose one of the twelve members which then comprised the European Community, and explain the arguments which were used by a/ supporters and b/ opponents of the Maastricht Treaty.

5 Choose one original member of The Six and one country which has joined as a result of a subsequent enlargement. For the two countries, explain the gains which they were looking for at the time and assess the extent to which membership has provided these benefits.

6 Can Britain be fairly labelled as a 'Reluctant European'?

7 What have been the gains and disadvantages of British membership of the European Union?

8 'The British Eurosceptics are not really sceptics at all. They are seeking to derail the whole European enterprise'. Is this true, and if so are they succeeding in their assignment?

9 Could Britain survive outside of the European Union?

10 Account for the fact that France and Germany are committed to further integration, yet Britain is trying to slow down the pace of further advance.

11 'All countries within the Union are in it to further their own interests. Membership happens to suit some countries better than others'. Discuss.

Chapter Six:
Future

The

Intergovernmental Conference, 1996

Within the Maastricht Treaty, provision was made for further examination and revision of the three pillars of the agreement. The TEU was signed at a time of movement on the European scene, and it was not easy to foresee the direction of some of the changes which were taking place. The case for such a review has strengthened since 1991, for the Union has itself undergone change. It has now been enlarged to include three additional countries, and the promise of sympathetic consideration to applications for membership has been extended to the new democracies of Central and Eastern Europe, as well as to Cyprus and Malta. It is quite possible that within a decade from now, there could be a Union of well nearly thirty members.

In these circumstances, the leading figures within the EU all recognise the need for an overhaul of existing arrangements. However, there is far less agreement about the main issues up for discussion, and about the future direction which the Union might take.

In the Maastricht Treaty, the workings of several policies and institutions were outlined for further examination, among them;

- Subsidiarity
- Progress on the balanced development of the single market
- The Common Foreign and Security Policy
- The Protection of citizens' rights
- The Powers of the European Parliament
- The Competence of the Union, and whether it should extend to areas such as energy and tourism

Yet many others could be added to the list, and the Treaty recognised that it was permissible for almost any aspect of Union life to be reconsidered. The European Council has placed the issue of further enlargement on the agenda, and with it the implications for the size and appointment of European Commissioners, the extent of qualified voting and the ways in which institutional arrangements could be improved and machinery streamlined.

At the Essen Council in December 1994, it was agreed that a Reflection Group should be established to 'examine and elaborate ideas' on those provisions mentioned in the TEU, and on any other 'possible improvements in a spirit of democracy and openness'. It was to comprise the Foreign Secretaries of each country, in addition to the President of the Commission and two members of the European Parliament, each representing one of the two large blocs. It began its work in June 1995, and was to take evidence from the institutions of the Union on how the treaty was working in practice.

In the early submissions, there are certain features which recur with some frequency. There is agreement on the need to increase the democratic legitimacy of the Union, to bring it closer to European citizens. This also involves simplifying its procedures in order to make them more intelligible and widely understood. In the words of the President, Jacques Santer; 'The European citizen does not want to know all the ins and outs of everything, but he does want to know who is doing what, who to blame and who to press for this decision or that piece of legislation which concerns him'.

The key words in most of the early statements are effectiveness, coherence and democratic accountability. But in working towards these objectives, countries have their own criteria. They have different priorities, and different interpretations as to what would make the Union more effective, more coherent and more democratically accountable.

For some, the processes of handing power from sovereign states to Brussels and further integration must be halted. There may be a case in their eyes for transferring some areas of policy back to the competence of national governments. Further cooperation should be along strictly intergovernmental lines. Others, which form the majority, take a different view, and wish to see the lines laid down for a further deepening of the Union, with more majority voting, more powers for the European Parliament and speedier progress towards the achievement of a strong CFSP.

At the time of writing those willing to back significant reforms in EU decision-making form the larger group. Some of the same countries are also pressing for an end to the British rebate, and for an end to Britain's opt-out of the Social Chapter. Jacques Santer has let it be known that he believes that this represents a 'Europe à la carte', and he does not think that nations should be allowed to pick and choose the parts of the Union which they are willing to support. Many of these problems will be resolved only in the bargaining process, when concessions are offered in certain areas in order to see progress in ones that matter more to the majority of member states.

 What gains and concessions has Britain been forced to make in the IGC bargaining?

Enlargement

Article 237 of the Treaty of Rome makes it clear that the Union is open to applicant countries whose economic and political situation are such as to make accession possible. Subject to that qualification, 'Any European state may become a member'. In 1989 Jacques Delors aired the question in his mind; 'Is the time coming when we must start thinking about a 20 or even a 22-nation Community?'. Since he spoke there has already been the fourth enlargement, for once the Cold War was over Norway and traditionally neutral countries such as Austria, Finland and Sweden were willing to join - though in the case of Norway, its peoples again rejected the opportunity to do so, once negotiations had successfully been concluded.

Membership could rise to well over twenty states, in the next few years. This likely expansion derives from two main causes;

i   The attraction is the tariff-free single market, with its enormous potential for exporters. Some countries have been encouraged by the thrust of economic integration to seek membership, notably those on the periphery of Europe, Cyprus, Malta and Turkey.

ii The developments in Central and Eastern Europe, especially the break-up of the Soviet bloc, which have created several new democracies who want to join as soon as their level of economic development makes this possible.

Most observers agree that growth is likely to come, for at present nations of Europe are queueing up to join a grouping which they see as providing them with opportunities for greater prosperity and influence in the future. The EU has acted rather as a magnet, exerting a strong pull in Europe.

The EFTA Countries

Seven nations were in EFTA in the early 1990s, and of these three have subsequently joined the Union. For a long while a number of the EFTA states had considered its links with the EC to be unsatisfactory, although there was an agreement on the removal of duties on industrial goods after 1977 which made for an enlarged free trade area in Europe. But inevitably the EU was the senior partner in the relationship, for it contained the stronger economies. After the passage of the SEA, EFTA countries became increasingly aware that the rules for the creation of the single market had received no input from them.

The EC came up with a plan to extend the benefits of the single market to the other seven countries, a scheme which would prevent the necessity for any immediate widening of the Community. Agreement was reached on a proposal to allow The Twelve to join forces with EFTA members in a new European Economic Area (EEA), to create what was then the world's largest single market of 380m people in an area stretching from the Mediteranean to the Arctic. The link up was confined to the economic sector and involved the free movement of people, goods, capital and services. In other words, the SEA was to be extended to Austria, Finland, Iceland, Liechtenstein, Norway and Sweden (Switzerland rejected joining the EEA in a referendum in 1992).

The EEA began its operations in January 1994, and a year later three countries joined the Union as full members. By then, the passage of the Maastricht Treaty was enough to persuade The Twelve that the process of deepening the Community was already satisfactorily underway, and so they could again contemplate an expansion.

Central and Eastern European Countries

Most of the new democracies in Central and Eastern Europe do not look as though they will be ready to be allowed to join by the year 2000, although inside the Union their chances of survival in a stable form might be strengthened. It may be that some new form of satisfactory association will be devised to enable them to have some of the benefits of membership, without actually signing the Treaty of Rome.

Two countries from the region of the continent were initially accorded privileged associate status, Hungary and Poland. In 1995, they were joined by four more, Bulgaria, the Czech Republic, Romania and Slovakia. This was seen as a preparation for membership some time after the 1996 review, with negotiations perhaps beginning within a year or two of the signing of any new treaty. The agreements provided the six countries with new political links with the EU, including joint ministerial meetings on foreign and security policy, as well as economic, social and environmental cooperation. They introduce free trade with the EU for most goods, and assistance with economic and other reforms.

The applicant countries will be expected to bring their legal systems into line with those of the Union, and to make their regulations on subsidies and competition policy compatible with the Treaty of Rome. Full membership will depend on the consolidation of democracy and continued moves to a market economy. There has been some evidence of a backlash against free market liberalisation in Hungary, Poland and elsewhere, but of greater concern to Brussels are the as yet unresolved problems of national minorities between some of the new associate countries.

Other European nations, Estonia, Latvia, Lithuania and Slovenia are being encouraged to make 'Europe Agreements', and along with Albania and possibly Bosnia and Macedonia may well be promised eventual membership. Just as these European Agreements are less far-reaching than those with the EFTA countries, so those with other newly-independent states in the Balkans and the Baltic States are still more limited in scope. These offer trade and cooperation agreements which in due time may be upgraded to the status of European Agreements.

Some other new nations may only merit external links, such as Byelorus, Moldova, Russia and the Ukraine. Croatia and Serbia are currently excluded from consideration.

Membership for most of the countries discussed is unlikely in the very short-run, but is an aspiration to move towards after the establishment of ever-closer ties. Some are likely to be admitted much sooner, possibly by the end of the decade. Decisions on entry are likely to be during the 1996 Intergovernmental Conference, and a date for membership is likely to be laid down for some applicants at the same time.

Attitudes to, and Problems of, Enlargement

The Union has to reconcile two requirements. First, it must unhesitatingly and in accordance with article 237 confirm its openness to new applications. In addition, it must take care to strengthen its own structures sufficiently to maintain the impetus of its own integration. This forward movement must be safeguarded, even in an enlarged Union.

There are differing views within the EU about the admission of new countries, and it may well be that although negotiations with several of them begin in 1997-98 they will only be admitted as and when they are individually ready for the responsibilities of membership. Germany believes in enlargement, but would like to see the more economically advanced countries such as the Czech Republic and Slovenia come in first. France has been uneasy about the prospect of having first and second class applicants.

British Conservatives see this as 'their' issue, for they believe that the fall of Communism in Eastern Europe was a triumph for Thatcherite thinking and action, and that she played a key role in bringing it about. They like the idea of extending deregulated trading areas, and welcome the fact that the new democracies see free-market solutions as being British-driven. Above all, however, enlargement to the East might make it possible to slow the pace of integration in the West. Conservatives tend to view Europe in economic rather than in political terms, and enlargement makes a concentration on that area more likely.

France, particularly under Mitterrand, recognised that danger and feared that the strength of the inner core of the Community might be sapped by too wide an expansion which allowed in poorer eastern countries. Union policies such as the CAP are likely to be placed under heavy strain with the arrival of any new members, for whereas the accession of Austria, Finland and Sweden involved the membership of richer Powers who could contribute to the Union, others are likely to be more of a drain on funds.

Poland, the largest of the would-be members, is a good example of this dilemma. It has some positive things in its favour, such as a record of stable democratic institutions, a good record on the observation of human rights, a market economy and a willingness to adapt its laws to EU standards. It suffers from economic backwardness and low environmental standards, but more seriously its large farming sector could pose the greatest problems for the overstretched EU agricultural and development budget. As it struggles to cope with the transition in Eastern Europe, the Union will find itself in need of more funds. The scale of support necessary to put the new democracies on their feet is vast.

Mitterrand also recognised that in a broader Europe, French influence would decline, so that he placed the emphasis on deepening the existing integration of The Fifteen before moving on to the next burst of expansion. Like some other European leaders, he wanted to move onwards without the distraction inevitably caused by a flood of new members. Such arguments still carry weight among some members of the French Government. The British - and perhaps the Danes - apart, most countries do not see widening and deepening the Union as necessarily being alternatives.

Changes in Decision-making?

As there has been difficulty in agreeing on what powers the institutions of the Union should be allocated already, the problem is likely to be exacerbated in an enlarged grouping. Different procedures are certainly likely to be needed, for a Union of 20 or so nations is unlikely to operate efficiently or smoothly on the basis of unanimous decision-making. Enlargement could mean that the majority voting so disliked by the British becomes even more necessary if the EU is to take any decisions and ever move forward.

Some would argue that rapid enlargement makes it inevitable that the Union will have to develop into a more federal structure at some point in the future. Such an arrangement would provide a central body to take major decisions on a limited range of economic, political and security policies, whilst leaving other matters to be handled at the national level.

A Change of Character?

Without doubt, what was primarily a Western economic bloc is undergoing a change of character. The entry of East Germany, and the moves under discussion, have made it a European body, and the issue is how just how far-flung its boundaries will be. It now includes all of the most significant states of Western Europe, and there is the prospect of a substantial increase in the Centre and East of the continent. As it occurs, so the importance and predominance of the core countries is likely to diminish. The Franco-German axis may lose some of its influence, much to the pleasure of British negotiators, though Germany is likely to remain the foremost EU Power by virtue of its size and strength.

Just as the accession of Greece, Portugal and Spain had an impact on the character of the Community, by increasing the number of less prosperous and more agrarian economies, so too will the addition of further new members have a decisive effect for several of them are much less economically advanced than the West. In the same way that Mediterranean countries are noted for producing different fruits from those produced in the North, so too different products predominate in the economies of the new democracies.

The accession of Finland brought a new interest in the possible security problems created by its position adjacent to Russia. The widening of membership has obvious implications for defence and security policy, and countries such as Romania could well be invited to join bodies such as NATO. There may also be a greater emphasis on the problems of racial minorities.

Conclusion

The countries of Central and Eastern Europe still face considerable problems in overcoming their legacy of authoritarianism, economic mismanagement and environmental degradation. But they share a common European experience and culture, and wish to play their part in the institutions of Europe. Allowing them to do so is not just a matter of altruism. It will encourage them in their attempts at economic and political reform, and conducted at an appropriate pace will help to promote stability on the continent. It will also create a larger market for Union produce.

Not to assist them would mean the emergence on EU borders of an economically depressed and marginalised region, with shrinking markets and mass unemployment. This would do little for the prosperity or the security of the Union.

Current and Possible Applications for Membership; A Summary

Country	Comments on Likelihood of Admission
EFTA countries	
Iceland	Unlikely to apply. Preference for North Atlantic Free Trade Area. Difficulties with EU over fishing.
Liechtenstein	Unlikely to seek full membership
Norway	Rejected chance to join twice. May revive bid, if rest of Scandinavia appears to benefit from membership.
Central and East European countries	
Hungary, Poland	Associate status. First two to apply. Likely to be in next batch of entrants
Bulgaria, Czech Republic, Slovakia, Romania	Associate status, likely to join, and could be in next batch of negotiations with Hungary and Poland
Albania, Estonia, Latvia, Lithuania, Slovenia	Likely to be promised future membership
Bosnia	Could be offered future membership
Byelorus, Moldova, Russia, Ukraine	Unlikely to be offered more than external links
Croatia	Little chance of any invitation
Miscellaneous	
Cyprus	Applied in 1990. Problems over island's future, but in 1993 Commission let it be

known that partition not a permanent obstacle for Greek Cyprus. Likely in future.

Malta	Applied at same time as Cyprus. Links with Libya a problem, but Commission broadly sympathetic; early entry likely.
Turkey	Technically judged a European Power. Applied in 1987. Very keen, but problems over human rights record (treatment of Kurds), and occupation of Northern Cyprus. Opposition from Greece, EU as a whole not keen. Application on hold.

Only Morocco has ever been turned down as an applicant, on the grounds that it does not qualify as a European country.

'Enlargement to 25-30 states will destroy the original concept of the Founding Fathers of Europe'. Is this true?

What benefits and disadvantages are likely to follow the admission of Central and East European states to the EU?

The Past and Future of Europe

In the postwar period, many international bodies have been formed which enable the nations of the world to cooperate with each other, some on a global scale, some more regional in character. They have ranged from the United Nations and the General Agreement on Tariffs and Trade on the world scene, to Western gatherings such as the Group of Seven industrial states and the Western European Union.

Countries have joined up with one another in search of mutual benefit. Of those in Europe, the European Union has been the most significant. The very fact that so many new democracies in Eastern Europe are attracted to the idea of membership shows that they recognise that it is now an important player not just on the European stage but on the world scene as well.

It was not the first attempt at European cooperation, but it is the boldest in conception, the most developed and the most successful. In aim, method and achievement this one goes further than any other. It is far more than just a customs union. It has a number of distinguishing characteristics, including a very complete set of institutions and a wide range of policy responsibilities. But what makes it distinctive is the fact that members have been willing to hand over powers to some supranational authority, and be bound by its decisions and policies. Its aims were also grander, an ever closer union of European peoples.

In the search for new structures in Europe after World War Two, Monnet disliked the intergovernmentalism of the OEEC which he believed to be 'the opposite of the Community spirit'. He rejected 'mere cooperation', and urged the creation of 'new functional authorities that superseded the sovereignty of existing nation-states'. In his view, the sovereign nations of the past could no longer solve the problems of the day; they could not ensure their own progress or control their own future. From the beginning, British ministers doubted the wisdom or desirability of the integration for which he aimed, and disliked the spirit of supranationalism which pervaded the ECSC and the EEC.

Intergovernmentalism and Supranationalism in the EU Today

Within the Union, there are elements of intergovernmentalism and supranationalism. In many key areas from economic policy to defence, and from welfare to foreign affairs, key decisions are still taken by national governments, even if this is in some cases done after Euro-level consultation. Where decisions are taken by the EU, they are usually taken at European Council or Council of Ministers level, so that the leading representatives of each country can mount a sturdy defence of national interests. Many of these decisions are still taken on the basis of unanimity, and even where majority voting has been introduced there is always an initial search for agreement.

Yet there are important supranational characteristics as well. Decisions taken at European level have the force of law in member countries, and as we have seen European law is superior to domestic law. In Britain, this has serious implications for the doctrine of Parliamentary Sovereignty. Moreover, the Commission has the power to take decisions and particularly to issue regulations and directives which are binding on member countries. The growth of majority voting and the increasing powers of the European Parliament, though both have a long way to go, nonetheless suggest that the element of supranationalism is on the increase.

The process of integration has not always been easy, nor the path smooth. There have at times been difficulties between the member states, and the conflict between national interest and the interests of Europe as a whole has posed particular difficulties for some countries. Yet the direction of movement has always been towards greater integration, a term which the dictionary describes as 'the harmonious combination of elements into a single whole'.

Our earlier review (see p115-125) has indicated that intergovernmentalism and integration have been two forces at work in the evolution of the Community, and now the Union. At different times over the last forty years, one set of ideas has gained the ascendancy, as different thinkers and statesmen have pressed their particular viewpoint. The dispute is still at the heart of the controversy within the Union about the way it has developed and the future direction it should take.

The notion of intergovernmentalism has been remarkably resilient, and at different moments it has asserted itself strongly - whether in the failure of the EDC, the Luxembourg Compromise, the British fight over its budgetary contributions or the Thatcherite declaration in the Bruges speech. Yet despite these attempts to safeguard national interests, the Union has not only established itself it has moved more closely together. In the mid 1990s, it is at the point where fundamental decisions have to be taken about the future development.

A Federal Future?

One of the most contentious issues concerning the future of the Union is the extent to which it moves in a federal direction. Whereas Mr Heath is a willing federalist ('the sooner the better'), Lady Thatcher takes a different view. She fears that a creeping federal system is being achieved without it being fully appreciated, and urges the need to halt this 'conveyor-belt to federalism'. In the eyes of many Rightwing British politicians the word remains anathema, for they see ideas of federalism and national sovereignty as fundamentally incompatible.

Visions of the Future; Varying Scenarios
Federalism

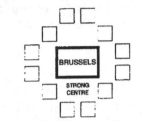

WEAK NATIONAL GOVERNMENTS

Federalism is a powerful but elusive concept, the more so as it tends to mean different things in Britain and on the continent. A federal structure is a form of government in which a constitution distributes powers between a central government and a series of states, giving substantial functions to each. Federations exist in Australia, Canada, Germany and the USA.

The trend in countries such as the United States over the past sixty years has been for more power to be taken at the centre, ie in Washington. This enables British politicians to portray federalism as involving increasingly centralised government. On the continent, federalism implies the opposite, decentralisation and subsidiarity. Subsidiarity enshrines the idea that power should only be exercised centrally if the central body can take action more effectively than the member states.

Confederalism

In a confederation, by a constitutional compact sovereign nations create a central government but limit its competence. The central government may make regulations for the constituent governments (ie, states) but it exists and operates only at their direction - rather in the way that under the Articles of Confederation, the thirteen Southern states operated during the American Civil War.

STRONG NATIONAL GOVERNMENTS

If Federalism, as popularly understood in Britain involves a strong centre (Brussels) and weak states, a confederal structure is the opposite, providing for strong, dominant national governments and a weaker centre. Such a pattern, applied to the EU, would allow for more emphasis to be placed on intergovernmentalism.

A Twin-Track Approach

Increasingly, the talk among writers on the European Union is of 'variable geometry', and twin or multi-track structures. This envisages that the countries of Europe will move ahead at different speeds, and that an inner core of the Union will be more tightly integrated whilst an outer tier or tiers will move more slowly.

Diagrams taken from POLITICS PAL, 1992

Most Europeans, including the Commission, wanted Maastricht to commit the EC to a federal European union. In itself, it is a harmless label, the word cited in the constitution of the European People's Party, the grouping with which the British Conservatives have developed closer ties. Yet in Britain, the word has horrifying connotations for many Conservatives, for whom stopping the drift in that direction has been an object of policy.

Britain gave federal constitutions to Australia and Canada, and has used the system elsewhere in the Commonwealth. Some experiments did not work well, as in the West Indies and Nigeria, whereas the first ones mentioned have been more successful. However, despite our willingness to use them elsewhere, federal solutions are clearly not seen as suitable for use by the Mother Country.

The Oxford Dictionary describes the meaning of 'federal' as 'an association of units that are largely independent' and 'a system of government in which several states unite under a central authority but remain independent in internal affairs'. As such, it is designed to allow the maximum devolution of decision-making possible consistent with the needs of a workable union. No-one was seeking to see the Australians governed mainly from Canberra, but to give the advantages of common action on major issues whilst fully satisfying and respecting local traditions.

The replacement term in the Maastricht Treaty is apparently more to the liking of the Government; it is the 'ever closer union' formula which is to be found in the Treaty of Rome. Yet this seems to have more far-reaching implications, for it implies a never-ending journey in which supporters seek ultimately to merge their identities. 'Federal' at least has an end in view, for it involves a division of functions between the centre and the individual member-states. It also allows for the notion of 'subsidiarity', the idea that decisions should be taken at a local level wherever this is feasible.

The point was well made in an editorial in 1991 of the *Agence Europe*. It noted that the phrasing of the Treaty of Rome

> *is far more menacing, to anyone concerned with preserving national sovereignty than a 'federal union'. An ever closer union 'must mean, if it means anything, that no matter how far we have gone in linking the member states to each other, we must strive to go further still. A federal union, by contrast, usually means one in which the respective spheres of competence of the Union and its component parts are defined in a manner intended to be permanent.*

The difficulty is that the word has assumed a significance out of all relation to what it really means. The media, especially the popular press, have often used it in the way that some Conservatives do, as if it implied the removal of power from the nation-state to some super-state. It is seen as denoting a move to centralisation and deeper integration so that MPs pounce on any proposal from the Commission suspecting that it brings the dreaded 'f' word ever nearer.

On the Continent, the term arouses no such anxieties, for it implies quite the opposite. To a German, the notion of subsidiarity (which assumed so much importance in John Major's thinking at the time of Maastricht) presupposes the idea of a federal European state. It is the very essence of federalism, with a division of power between the different layers of government, European, national and regional.

The word has become a slogan for all that those who fear the drift of events in the Union. In denying its use, they are not only rejecting the formal structure of a fully-fledged federal European state, but all the moves such as the single currency, the stronger European institutions and the increasing search for a common approach to many matters of policy. As Hugo Young noted in The Guardian, 'to be a 'fed' is merely to be on the pro-Union side of the argument. To be against the 'federal', is to propose oneself as a valiant upholder of the unchanging nation-state'.

Clearly, Maastricht and other recent developments have moved the Union in the direction of more common policies. The general flow of events is to allow the EU more power in fields as diverse as defence and foreign policy, monetary union and the environment, for the 'entire thrust is towards...consensual action on the basis of majority-voting'. In a general sense, therefore, federalism is already with us, but in the exact meaning of the term, the creation of a new system of government, it is a long way off. It is not a practical possibility at the present time.

A Multispeed Europe?

> *[A multi-speed Europe] built around a strengthened Franco-German axis could promote monetary union and a common foreign and security policy, as a way of combating regressive nationalism and stopping the EU from drifting apart.*
> German Christian Democrat spokesman, September 1994.

In the 1980s, it became fashionable for some commentators to speculate on the future of the Community. Most of them recognised Britain's reluctance to commit itself to closer integration, and the idea of The Twelve moving at different speeds was mooted. This would allow the integrationist states - a dedicated core - to move forwards at a faster rate, with other countries in the outer lane.

The talk was of a number of concentric circles, involving the core, then the remaining EC and EFTA countries, and then other nations, including the applicant ones and others which had various types of agreement with the Community. There was (in the days of President Gorbachev) also the vague concept of a Common European Home, to which all states which had signed the Helsinki Accord on civil rights might belong. If pursued, such an idea could have meant that all of Europe would be part of an outermost circle, stretching from the Atlantic to the Urals.

At the Edinburgh European Council, the idea of a Europe moving at different speeds was rejected by all of those present. Germany was keen to keep Britain on board, and to see Maastricht put into effect by all of the member states. Now, the idea has resurfaced, as a way of catering for the different approaches among The Fifteen. It is often referred to in connection with economic and monetary union. An inner circle could operate in a more federal manner and employ a single currency, whilst the outer track could perhaps use a common currency which could operate alongside their own national currencies.

The French Prime Minister put forward such an idea in late 1994, and his proposal was based on three tiers;

  i   A central core which was committed to economic, military and political union. This might have included the Benelux countries, France and Germany, and now might be widened to allow for any which wish or are able to join a single currency.

  ii A middle tier of other EU countries who are unable or do not wish to so commit themselves. Britain and Denmark are likely candidates for membership of this group.

  iii A final tier comprising all other countries which have economic or military links with the Union. This would now include the Central and East European nations, and others with whom there is any sort of agreement.

John Major was once dismissive of a 'multi-faceted, multi-speed, multi-layered' Europe, and saw a danger in there being 'an exclusive hard core either of countries or of policies'. He has more recently embraced the notion of 'variable geometry', by which he means that different EU states cooperate on varying aspects of common interest; 'Diversity is not a weakness to be suppressed, it is a strength to be harnessed'. The phrase in current use is 'flexible integration', a more diplomatically worded variant of the French suggestion.

Usually, terms such as 'variable geometry' have been used by those Germans and others who have favoured some kind of multi-speed Europe to describe their vision. For Britain the danger of any approach based on different rates of progress is that it will be in the slow lane on all key issues. The fear is that those nations which do not belong to the advance guard will be sidelined, and lose their ability to influence events in Europe. They would not be 'at the heart of Europe'.

There is nonetheless developing support for such an outcome. European statesmen realise that given the unwillingness of Britain to support the closer integration - along more federal lines - which the majority of the members would like to see, the scheme does offer a way forward which caters for all aspirations. If there is any chance of Europe managing the process of widening and deepening at the same time, it may be that an approach which enables different members to develop at different speeds is the only one that will cater for this. What is unlikely is that the British hope of preventing further deepening by supporting widening will work, for past history suggests that those committed to the latter have also been determined to maintain their commitment to the former.

The 'widening or deepening' debate is one which is set to continue, for the early pioneers were convinced of the importance of further European integration. Some critics of that vision, however, would argue that it has lost its relevance today. It may have been right for the time, but it is wrong for the world of the mid 1990s - the whole pattern of European politics has undergone such a profound change.

A Changing Europe

Some writers and politicians have argued that the entire existence of the European Community was based on the Cold War which began within a few years of the ending of the 'real war' in 1945. They suggest that a strongly united Western Europe was highly relevant in the face of possible Soviet aggression, but that circumstances have changed following the fall of the Berlin Wall and the collapse of the communist stranglehold in the East.

The case has been advanced by **Will Hutton** who sees the creation of the European Community as a postwar solution in a Cold War context; 'It was established to prevent another Franco-German war and its agricultural policy was designed to prevent mass starvation in Europe. The EU evolved within a dvided Europe constantly threatened with nuclear war, the rise of communism, the American military presence, and its own relative, global, post-imperial decline. Inevitably, it developed as a 'third way' project'.

There was more to the drive for closer cooperation than external threat from the USSR. Idealism and pragmatism both played an important part in those early days. Nonetheless, there is some truth in the picture, for it is true that the onset and development of the Cold War influenced the thinking of many Western politicians. It provided the justification for their wish to create a third bloc of comparable size to the two Superpowers, America and Russia. In this way, the West could better cope with the possibility of aggression, which might be especially necessary if the USA were ever to withdraw from the European arena, and countries such as France and then Britain found themselves a post-imperial role.

With the breakup of the Soviet empire and the transformation of its former satellites into new democracies, the perspective has changed. There is no longer a justication for a third way between two Superpowers, one of whom no longer exists. Few talk in the same way of the threat from the East, and if they do they might mean the different challenges posed by more recent world Powers such as China or Japan, or the new 'Asian tigers'.

When Western politicians speak of Europe it is no longer the limited club of six members but an association of fifteen nations of very different character from the North and South, as well as the West of the continent. There is no prospect of hunger, but rather the problems associated with a surplus of food produced under an agricultural policy designed for a bygone age.

In the era of the Cold War a preoccupation with deepening the bonds between all of the member states was understandable and perhaps inevitable. It is not so self-evidently justifiable in a very different Europe which is soon likely to embrace states of contrasting stages of development.

Martin Kettle has taken up this line of thought. In a penetrating article, he has discerned five 'big ideas' on which the present European Union is being constructed;

- Cooperation in foreign and security policy to allow Europe to play a coordinated role in world affairs
- Convergence on a federalist political model based upon solidarity
- Convergence on a deregulated free market governed by a stability-orientated monetary policy
- Convergence around a network of social benefit, largely to mitigate the effects of the tight money policy
- Enlargement to take in all nations, of whatever size, in central and eastern Europe

He points out that - other than Germany and the small Benelux states - none of The Fifteen are committed to all of these goals. Britain may be particularly lukewarm, but others lack enthusiasm for some of them. In such a situation, 'in an internally unequal Europe, a variable geometry solution is not so much an option as an inevitability, and that the push to the East is making it so'.

It is not just the ending of the Cold War which has been the catalyst for change in Europe. But that was an important factor in forcing the nations of the Union to think again about the European project in a new way so that they are collectively equipped to cope with a new agenda.

The EU has already produced substantial benefits, primarily in keeping the peace in Western Europe, consolidating democracy and contributing to general prosperity. The challenges for the future are to continue to do those things, but also to create a Union which can win the wholehearted consent of its diverse peoples, one which is free, strong and united in its determination to bring such benefits to all those who live within the continent.

Is the EU such a good idea following the ending of the Cold War?

? 'The British have won the 'widening V deepening' argument. Integration is obsolete in the 1990s'. Is this so?

TEACH YOURSELF

To Recap

The political situation in Europe is fluid since the ending of the Cold War. Already, the Union has responded to the break-up of Communist rule by admitting East Germany to membership, following German unification.

Other Central and Eastern countries have applied/wish to apply.

Three EFTA members, part of the European Economic Area, were the first priority. They were welcome as net contributors to the budget, who could make a useful contribution to the 'cohesion fund'.

European Union league table

Premier League
(on fast track to economic and monetary union)

Belgium,	Germany,
Denmark,	Luxembourg,
France,	Netherlands,

League Division One
(remaining EU members)

Britain,	Italy,
Greece,	Portugal,
Ireland,	Spain.

League Division Two
(signed up new members from January next)

Austria,	Norway,
Finland,	Sweden.

League Division Three
(countries promised eventual membership)

Czech Republic,	Poland,
Cyprus,	Slovakia,
Hungary,	Bulgaria,
Malta,	Romania

League Division Four
(countries likely to be promised eventual membership)

Albania,	Lithuania,
Estonia,	Slovenia,
Latvia,	Bosnia (probable)

Amateur League
(countries with only external links with EU)

Byelorus,	Ukraine,
Russia,	Moldova.

Do not ring us, we will ring you League

Croatia,	Serbia

The Guardian, 5.2.1994

The likelihood is a much larger Union in the future, with possibly well over twenty members within a decade.

To Widen or to Deepen?

The Benelux countries, France and Germany are keen advocates of deepening the existing Union bonds before greatly widening the EU. They want to see a more federal Community, bound by economic and monetary

461

union; a close-knit Europe, strong and prosperous, will be more able to help the poorer countries when they eventually join.

Britain and Denmark are much less keen on deepening the existing bonds, and favour a wider and looser Community. Many continentals feel that the British are in favour of widening, so that the deepening process is slowed down.

At the Birmingham summit in 1992, it was agreed that the Community should move forwards at the same speed. Since then, there has been more talk a 'two-speed' or 'twin-track' Europe, with members moving at different rates of progress. The inner core could move to a federal goal, and have a single currency, the others (including new members) would move more slowly and have a common currency, the Euro, and their own.

Questions to Consider

1 Examine the heading from the front page of *EP News* (26-30 September 1994), the magazine of the European Parliament, and then answer the questions which follow;

States warned not to block closer integration

NO TO EUROPE 'À LA CARTE'

i What do you think the headline-writer meant by referring to a 'Europe à la carte'?

ii Which country or countries are likely to favour such a vision of Europe? Give reasons for your choice.

   iii What are the differences between a 'twin-speed Europe' and a 'Europe à la carte'?

   iv Is it feasible to have a Europe in which the nations move forwards at different speeds?

2 What do you understand by the term 'subsidiarity'. Is subsidiarity a means of countering the development of federalism, or is it basic to a federal form of government?

3 In what ways has the ending of the Cold War had a significant impact on the development of the Union? Has the Union lost its raison d'être?

4 Do you believe that the development of the European Community/Union has finally resolved the problem of peace in Europe?

5 In what ways would you like to see the Union develop in the future?

6 Why are some politicians and members of the public unenthusiastic about moves towards an integrated Europe?

7 What might be done to give Europe a greater sense of a common identity?

8 What are the problems associated with an enlargement of the European Union? Does enlargement necessarily sap the strength of the inner core?

9 Is the creation of a United States of Europe an impossible dream?

10 a. What are the major difficulties associated with enlargement?
b. Should European Union membership be extended to the emergent states of Eastern Europe? (ULEAC)

11 A recent writer on world economic development wrote the following in his discussion of the European Union;

The need to compete against the Americans and Japanese in a global economy almost demands that the House of Europe be built. If it isn't, the individual countries of Europe will find themselves economically marginalised between two much bigger and more aggressive economies...Enough integration has now occurred to make it very difficult for anyone to withdraw...an internal dynamic has been set up whereby each step forward essentially forces the participants to take further steps forward.

i   How convincing do you find the case the writer makes for further integration in Europe? What other arguments might he have employed?

ii Why do you think that many people would find the idea of ever-closer-union not to their liking?

iii Do you think that the Maastricht Treaty represented another step in the 'internal dynamic'?

Acknowledgements

I am much indebted to the various people who kindly commented on the draft version of Introducing The European Union. Alan Davies (Chief Examiner for the syllabus) and Sarah Robinson (Subject Officer) both made interesting and helpful observations on behalf of ULEAC. Two leading members of the Hansard Society read the script most carefully. Michael St. John Parker offered several valuable insights and was very supportive of the enterprise. Professor John Pinder, a recognised authority on the EU, cast a critical eye over the text and highlighted any inaccuracies or ambiguities which troubled him - an indication of his meticulous approach in matters of scholarship. The observations of these and others have led to revisions in the final copy. However, I assume full responsibility for the facts given and judgements made, and have endeavoured to ensure that the script is as error-free as possible.

Permission was kindly given by a number of bodies to use material which they have provided. In some cases, this has been photocopied, in others extracts have been taken from the original. To those people who answered my often-very-specific enquiries, I offer especial thanks. The London offices of the European Commission of the European Commission, the European Parliament and the Conservative group of MEPs were particularly helpful in this regard. Useful material was received from the Party of European Socialists and several pressure groups, most notably the CBI, the Eurogroup for Animal Welfare, the Institute of Directors and the RSPCA.

465

A number of newspaper and magazine extracts have been incorporated. The Editors of *The Guardian* and *The Sun* have been most cooperative in granting permission to use their material, and (in the latter case) seeking out and providing original sources.

Wherever possible, I have endeavoured to acknowledge sources, and to anyone who has been quoted but not acknowledged I offer my apologies.

Lastly, but by no means least I would also like to record my thanks to members of the Design Studio, Sheffield Hallam University. Their expertise, patience and general helpfulness have all been available in generous measure.

Sources Quoted

The books and articles listed are those referred to in the text, and they are placed in the order in which they appear;

M. Holland, European integration; From Community to Union, Pinter 1994

P. Hennessy, Never Again; Britain 1945-51, Vintage, 1993

J. Monnet, Memoirs, Doubleday and Co., New York, 1978

M. Burgess, Federalism and European Union, Routledge, 1989

J-P Duroselle, General de Gaulle's Europe and Jean Monnet's Europe, in C. Cosgrove and K. Twitchett ed, The New International Actors; the UN and the EEC, Macmillan, 1970

F. Duchêne, More or Less than European? European Integration in Retrospect, in C. Crouch and D. Marquand ed, The Politics of 1992; beyond the Single European Market, the Political Quarterly, Blackwell

W. Nicoll and T. Salmon, Understanding the New European Community, Harvester Wheatsheaf, 1994

P Taylor, The Limits of European Integration, Croom Helm, 1983

N. Nugent, The Government and Politics of the European Union, Macmillan, 1994

D. Mitrany, The functional approach to World organisation, 1970

C. Pentland, International Theory and European Integration, the Free Press, New York, 1973

Ernst Haas, the uniting of Europe; political, economic and social forces, 1950-57, Stanford University Press, 1964

R Harrison, Neo-functionalism, in A. Groom and P. Taylor, Frameworks for international co-operation, Pinter, 1990

R. Keohane and S. Hoffman, Conclusions; Community Politics and Institutional Change, in W. Wallace ed, The Dynamics of European Integration, 1992. See also, The New European Community by the same authors, Westview Press, 1991

P. Fontaine, Europe - A Fresh Start; The Schuman Declaration, European Documentation, European Commission, 1990

Dr K. D. Borchardt, European Integration; The origins and growth of the European Union, European Commission, 1995

J. Pinder, The European Community, the rule of law and representative government, in Government and Opposition, 1991

L. Lindberg and S. Scheingold, Europe's Would-be Polity, Prentice-Hall, 1970

Philip Norton, National Parliaments and the European Union, article in Talking Politics, Spring 1995

A. Butt Philip, Pressure Groups in the European Community, Occasional Paper, University of Bath, 1985

R. Baggott, Pressure groups today, Manchester University Press, 1995

Wyn Grant, Pressure Group Politics and Democracy in Britain, Harvester Wheatsheaf, 1995

J. Curtice and M. Steed, in D. Butler and M. Westlake, British Politics and European Elections 1994, Macmillan (St Martin's Press), 1995

G. Smith, Implications of the 1994 Parliament Elections, article in Representation, Winter-Spring 1994-05

K. Milton, Interpreting Environmental Policy, Journal of Law and Society, vol 19, 1991

J. McCormick, Environmental Politics, in P. Donleavy et al, Developments in British Politics, Macmillan,1993

R. Ginsberg, Foreign Policy Actions of the European Community, Adamantine, 1989

F. Northedge, Descent From Power, British Foreign Policy 1945-73, Allen and Unwin, 1974

M. Kettle, The Tories, the Veto and the Laughing Greeks, article in The Guardian, 25.2.1995

W. Hutton, Winds over the West, article in The Guardian, 2.11.1995

M. Kettle, Europe Confused by Eastern Promise, article in The Guardian, 5.11.1994

Further Recommended Reading

Many of the books available for the student seeking to master the European Union are written at a very advanced level. In some cases, they are too obscure or theoretical to be of much value for the student looking for further references.

On Britain and Europe, I would refer the A Level candidate or undergraduate to two books. An introductory study of the subject is provided in **Reluctant Europeans; Britain and the European Community,** written by the author of this volume and available from the Politics Association Resource Centre (address at front). A more detailed survey is to be found in the recently-published **Britain in the European Union** today (written by Colin Pilkington, for the MUP) - a clear and comprehensive account.

On the European Union, Neill Nugent's **The Government and Politics of the European Union**, published in 1994 by Macmillan, is an authoritative and highly detailed work of reference. William Nicoll and Trevor Salmon's **Understanding The New European Community** (Harvester Wheatsheaf, 1994), is fairly comprehensive and more accessible. Martin Holland's **European Integration; From Community To Union** (Pinter, 1994) provides an interesting and thought-provoking account of progress towards closer cooperation in Europe. John Pinder's **European Community: The Building of a Union** (OUP, 1995) is a wide-ranging study, designed to appeal to all who pursue courses in European Studies, as well as to more general readers. Lord Cockfield's **The European Union: Creating the Single Market** (Chichester, 1994) is a lively and highly personal exploration of the area it covers.

Useful Articles for Further Reference

Contemporary Record

Britain and the EC, Stephen George, Spring 1989

EC Institutions, Juliet Lodge, February 1990

Britain and the EC; How Britain Has Adapted, Michael Clarke, February 1990

European Elections, 1979-89, Andrew Adonis, February 1990

Controversy. Has Britain Benefited from Membership of the EC? Stephen George and John Coleman, February 1990

Modern History Review

Perspectives. Britain and European Integration Since 1945, Stephen George, April 1992

Further Reading

Britain in Europe; European Perspectives, Andrew Crozier, April 1992

Themes; The Idea of European Union, Derek Heater, November 1994

Politics Review

The Conservative Party and Europe, Daniel Wincott, April 1992

Widening the EC, Clive Church, September 1992

Environmental Policy and the EC, Stephen Young, February 1993

Polemic. The Case Against EC Membership, Martin Holmes, February 1993

Pressure Groups and the EC, Sonia Mazey and Jeremy Richards, September 1993

Europe's Post-Maastricht Muddle, Philip Lynch, November 1993

Europe's Bill of Rights, Duncan Watts, April 1994

Social Studies Review

European Union and the Democratic Deficit, Juliet Lodge, January 1991

The European Community, Neil Collins, January 1991

Talking Politics

1992; The Economic and Political Effects of the Single European Act, Graham Stowell, Autumn 1991

Human Rights in Europe, Peter Cumper, Autumn 1991

The New Europe; What Role for the US? John Bendix, Summer 1992

Racist Trends in European Politics, S Hunt, Autumn 1993

Lobbying Europe, Duncan Watts, Winter 1993

European Union Electoral Systems, Alistair Jones, Summer 1994

Implementing Maastricht; the Limits of EU, Fergus Carr and Stephen Cope, Summer 1994

Lessons From the Maastricht Debates; The Referendum We Never Had, Anthony Batchelor, Summer 1994

The Glomar Exploration, the Common Fisheries Policy and the Factortame Case, John Dowdle, Summer 1994

The Impact of the European Union on the British Constitution, Pre-Maastricht, Philip Norton, Summer 1994

The Impact of the EU upon the UK Government and Politics, John Kingdom, Winter 1994

National Parliaments and the European Union, Philip Norton, Spring 1995

Understanding Subsidiarity as a Political Issue in the EC, Marc-Philippe Cooper, Spring 1991

Index of Main References

History

Personalities

Events, Organisations and Treaties

Institutions

Representation